A Northern Soul

A Northern Soul

The Autobiography

JIMMY NAIL

MICHAEL JOSEPH
an imprint of
PENGUIN BOOKS

MICHAEL JOSEPH

Published by the Penguin Group
Penguin Books Ltd, 80 Strand, London WC2R ORL, England
Penguin Group (USA) Inc., 375 Hudson Street, New York, New York 10014, USA
Penguin Books Australia Ltd, 250 Camberwell Road, Camberwell, Victoria 3124, Australia
Penguin Books Canada Ltd, 10 Alcorn Avenue, Toronto, Ontario, Canada M4V 3B2
Penguin Books India (P) Ltd, 11 Community Centre, Panchsheel Park, New Delhi – 110 017, India
Penguin Group (NZ), cnr Airborne and Rosedale Roads, Albany, Auckland 1310, New Zealand
Penguin Books (South Africa) (Pty) Ltd, 24 Sturdee Avenue, Rosebank 2196, South Africa

Penguin Books Ltd, Registered Offices: 80 Strand, London WC2R ORL, England

www.penguin.com

First published 2004
5

Copyright © Jimmy Nail, 2004

Grateful acknowledgement is made for permission to reproduce extracts from the following:
'Isn't it a Pity', lyrics by George Harrison © 1970 Harrisongs Ltd.
'Life's a Miracle', words and music by Paddy McAloon © 1995, reproduced by permission of
EMI Songs Ltd, London WC2H 0QY.

Photographic credits:

63, 70, 87, 91: © BBC; 76: photo by David Bailey © David Bailey; 78: © BBC/Red Rooster/
Big Boy Productions for BBC TV; 81, 83: photos by David Appleby © Disney Pictures

All other photos are the author's own.
Every effort has been made to trace or contact all copyright holders of the illustrations.
The publishers will be pleased to make good any omissions or rectify any mistakes brought to their attention at the
earliest opportunity.

The moral right of the author has been asserted

Set in 13.5/16 pt Monotype Garamond
Typeset by Rowland Phototypesetting Ltd, Bury St Edmunds, Suffolk
Printed in Great Britain by Clays Ltd, St Ives plc

A CIP catalogue record for this book is available from the British Library

ISBN 0-718-14653-0

This book is dedicated to the memory of my mother, Laura

Acknowledgements

I began writing this foreword ensconced in the luxurious surroundings of the Conrad Hilton Hotel in Bangkok, Thailand. We were about to begin what was likely to be the final chapter of the *Auf Wiedersehen, Pet* adventure. A few days later I travelled to Chiang Mai in the north, there to begin my elephant-riding orientation. Twenty-two years ago I was on the back lot at Elstree Studios doing a crash-course in bricklaying. It's a measure of how far things have come.

We were hard at it in the jungle on the evening of Saturday, 17 July when word reached us that Pat Roach – our beloved 'Bomber' – had passed away. We'd all hoped and prayed that the big man would be able to make it for our last adventure. He'd beaten the odds so many times. Sadly it was not to be. Pat was an extraordinary man and his death has left a terrible void. It feels as though our body has lost a limb. We carry on, however: Pat would've been upset if we'd done otherwise. So, of the original *Auf Wiedersehen, Pet* seven, there are now five of us. As the band grows smaller, the bond grows stronger.

I've done my best to make sure all details are correct, but if your name happens to have been spelled incorrectly, my apologies.

Although the words within this book are my own, its production has been a true team effort. I wish to express my sincere thanks to all those who have helped me over the eighteen months I've been working on it, and in particular the following people: to Paul Stevens and the entire staff of ICM London, who've looked after me these past twenty years. To my editor, Rowland White at Penguin Books, who bravely led me through the often difficult stages of this process and for whom I have nothing but admiration and respect. Not many people would've taken it on, and I'm glad to be able to write we're still on speaking terms! To Hazel Orme, who patiently guided me through the book's numerous grammatical and structural errors until it got to the shape it's in today.

As regards photographs, I've made every effort to give credit where it's due, and my thanks go to those credited for allowing me to use stills that are not my own. I must make special mention of the lovely George Wiggins, who took some wonderful shots of me, no easy thing to pull off. The one featuring the late Tommy Cooper, Miriam and myself is a favourite. Cheers, George.

Thanks are also due to the following people: to Ian La Frenais, who got me started and has always encouraged me to keep writing. To Duncan Heath for the very best advice and guidance, along with a lot of fun. To all my friends in Newcastle, who have kept their counsel over the years when it would have been easy for them to make a bob or two. To Olivia Harrison, for sending me a photograph I didn't even know existed until it landed on my doormat one morning.

I am indebted to Roger Bamford, who took a monumental gamble twenty-two years ago when he offered me the part of Oz and the opportunity of a lifetime. We salute you, Baron B – absolutely!

I wish to say thank you to my sons, Tom and Fred, for their understanding. It can't be easy having a well-known parent and it's my hope that what's written here might one day give them both an idea of why certain things were as they were. The biggest thank-you goes to their mother, my soul-mate, Miriam. Through you I have come to know the meaning of love.

I

I entered this world on Tuesday, 16 March 1954, at 5 Gleneagles Close on the newly built Fairways Estate in the east end of Newcastle upon Tyne: big, strong and healthy, the first and, as it turned out, only son of Jimmy and Laura Bradford, brother to Valerie, then nine, and Shelagh, seven. It was a home birth, more common in those days when hospitals were primarily for the sick. Everyone was well pleased: my dad had longed for a son and my mam was relieved at having provided him with one. However, my arrival meant they'd have to leave their little two-bedroom flat and move to somewhere bigger. Also, there was the matter of my name. My mother wanted Michael but my dad wanted another James in the family. Cue heated debate. My mam thought she'd prevailed until she was well enough to go out, when she found my dad had, unbeknown to her, already been to the register office and put me down as James. So there's me not even a day old and already causing problems. I guess there must have been a radio playing somewhere in the house because, from the very beginning, I was music nuts.

Locally that year, the mighty Newcastle United – and they truly were mighty back then – were taking a break from winning the FA Cup, having lifted the trophy the previous two seasons. They'd win it again in 1955. So I can say they've won the FA Cup in my lifetime, which is a crumb of comfort as all there's been to speak of since then was an against-all-the-odds triumph in the Inter-Cities Fairs (now UEFA) Cup way back in 1969. I recently watched a repeat of

I

the final on Sky Sports and the footage was black-and-white. Nationally, on the day my mam was trying to get rid of me while simultaneously trying to make me appear, Lord Montagu of Beaulieu was making headlines for all the wrong reasons: he was appearing in the dock to answer charges relating to questionable acts with off-duty airmen. Who'd have predicted our paths would cross one day? I met the good lord almost fifty years later while I was playing a concert in his back garden. On the day, I thought it best not to mention our somewhat tenuous connection.

Eighty miles to the west of London and the High Court, in Oxford, Roger Bannister managed a mile in under four minutes that year, the first man to do so, in a time that's still impressive today; he was wearing T-shirt, shorts and spikes, but was without the benefit of Kevlar running shoes or a wind-assisted lunch-box. When I'm fit I run a mile in around ten minutes. At a push I could do one in under eight, but it would be painful and I'd be gasping at the finish.

McDonald's fast-food restaurant chain was founded in 1954, a birthday I'd prefer not to have shared but we have no say in these things – so, hey-ho. The end of post-war rationing corresponded with the beginning of the Suez crisis. Not realizing Suez was a region and, never having seen it written down, I assumed it was 'sewers' and to do with drainage. It certainly turned into a big stink as far as the British were concerned. Aden was the other place that figured large in the news of the day: I remember seeing in the newspapers photos of British troops in khaki battledress being shot at by unseen people referred to as terrorists. It's nothing new.

Across the Atlantic, in Memphis, Tennessee, a young man by the name of Elvis Aaron Presley was shaking his hips and releasing his first single: the raucous, rip-roaring 'That's Alright, Mama' marvellously muddied the waters that separated/segregated 'black' and 'white' music, scared the pants off a nation's parents and allowed Elvis to take the first explosive step on a career journey that would turn the world's musical landscape upside down.

About a hundred miles up the freeway, in Washington DC, Senator Eugene McCarthy was giving anyone not swathed in the American flag a right old roasting. Were he still alive today, there's no doubt he'd be a happy man right now.

Fairways was a post-war estate built by the local council on what had until then been a golf course. The street names were culled from famous courses – Gleneagles Close, Carnoustie Crescent. The old clubhouse became the local Conservative Club; no change there, then. Just how the members must have felt at seeing their beautifully manicured lawns and putting greens dug up to accommodate council houses can only be imagined, but dug up they were and families like ours were given wonderful new homes.

My parents were both from Walker, a socially deprived district on the Tyne's north bank and about a mile west of its mouth. The community had grown rapidly as a result of and in tandem with maritime employment opportunities on the river. As the twentieth century dawned, a local invention was about to revolutionize the way the world moved around, just as another had some two hundred years earlier. Back then Stephenson's steam locomotives had changed the world; now it was the turn of the turbine. This revolutionary advance in propulsion power was already well on the way to changing how world shipping, and in particular naval vessels, were powered. In the space of a few hectic years these miracles of heavy engineering made the old piston-driven steam engines obsolete, and they were designed and built on Tyneside. The legacy of George Stephenson was carried forward by another engineering genius, Charles Parsons, the man who first put the turbines into the ships. All this, along with an already established reputation for building the world's finest vessels, made the north-east of England an economic powerhouse. Work was plentiful.

My father, born James Bradford on 26 March 1914, came from a large family of Irish descent: five brothers, Davy, Danny, Benny, Jimmy and John, and a sister, Katie. They lived in Pottery Bank, right on the river and one of the roughest places in the city. My paternal grandparents were long-dead when I was born and, by all accounts, things were hard. According to my dad, it wasn't unusual for the boys to have to share a pair of shoes, given to them by the Police Boot Fund; sometimes you walked to school barefoot. My dad was forced by circumstance to endure a hard early life and it turned him into a hard man. The deprivation and suffering were undisputed and very real. He was finished with school and into the shipyards at the grand old age of fourteen.

He was also something of a sportsman. For young working-class men in the 1920s sport offered one of the few escape routes from the life they'd been born into. First it was boxing, which saw him fighting as a teenager in amateur contests and doing well locally, but a trip to Manchester, where he came up against an opponent who could box, rather than just fight, and got completely hammered, put paid to that as a career option. He then turned his hand, or rather his foot, to soccer.

He played first for Hartlepool United, then, some time in the 1930s, he went to Huddersfield Town, in those days a successful club. According to my mam, he was injured almost immediately and spent the rest of his time there, a single season, trying unsuccessfully to regain his fitness. At some point on his travels he ended up in digs with Hughie Gallagher, a footballing legend who met an untimely end.

According to my dad, Gallagher had argued with his son and, in a fit of temper, had hit the lad. Inconsolable, he'd gone out, waited for a train to come along and put his head on the line.

My mam was born Laura Johnson on 14 February 1915, Valentine's Day. The third of four children and sister to three boys, two older, Billy and Jack, and one younger, Edward, the baby of the brood. The Johnsons were from St Anthony's, also in the Walker district but fancying itself back then as slightly more genteel. As with my dad, my mam's parents had died long before I was born. Her mother had died in tragic circumstances: while heavily pregnant she'd been trying to turn a mattress when she began haemorrhaging. Laura was at primary school when a kid burst into the classroom and told her, 'You've got to come home, your mam's dead.' Her unborn baby was also lost. Not long after, Laura's father died of a broken heart, according to my mam, and from then on the four orphaned kids were brought up by their aunties, Sarah and Isabelle Topping. Sarah was married to George and I knew them as Aunts Sarah and Belle and Uncle George. Taking on four young kids would be quite an endeavour today, never mind back then, but it was what people did and not uncommon; there was no sophisticated social services set-up to offer help and guidance. The only other option would have been the poorhouse.

Much to my disappointment I hardly ever got to visit my dad's brothers and sister. In fact, so rarely did I meet up with them that I can still remember my one and only visit to Aunt Katie's Victorian terraced upstairs flat in Walker. A big woman with silver grey hair tied up in a bun and wearing big white billowing skirts, she was a daunting figure to a five-year-old, as she stood at the top of her outside back stairs puffing away on an untipped cigarette while her substantial behind rested against a wooden railing. Although this would have been the late 1950s it was like a scene from *Oliver Twist*.

I got to see slightly more of my uncles on my mam's side. Billy, a railway worker late of the merchant marine and the Middle East, was the eldest. I remember Uncle Billy as a right misery with a long grey beard. He'd occasionally come to visit, arriving on his moped in a full-length greatcoat and peaked crash-helmet, looking old-fashioned and uncool. He seemed older than God. He had quite a dry sense of humour, though. Jack, the teacher, who ended up as head of a grammar school in Hemel Hempstead, was big, loud and surly. I only remember meeting him once, on a trip to his home in the south. Edward was an engineer at Spadeadam. His son, my cousin Neil, has one of the family's most treasured possessions, a winner's medal from the 1924 FA Cup final, won by my mam's uncle, George Mooney, while playing for Newcastle United. I have to admit to being envious of Neil: were that medal in my possession I'd have it on permanent display at St James' Park.

According to my mam, my dad was quite the romantic in those early days, which is hard for me to imagine. He would often come round to where she lived and serenade her, accompanying himself on a squeeze-box accordion. That must have been a sight to see, as they're bloody hard things to play. God knows what kind of gyp he got from the neighbours. In describing this happy, fun-loving, carefree young man to me, my mam was telling me all about a person I'd never met. The reason for that was that this earlier, jollier version of my dad went off to fight in the Second World War along with the rest of his generation and never returned. His wartime experiences had changed him, and many other young men.

My dad wasn't one for long conversations, but on one of

the rare occasions when he did talk to me about the war, the old man described a scene so sad, so heartbreakingly awful, that it brought tears to his eyes, which blokes like him tried to avoid at all costs. Since the outbreak of war in 1939 he'd been an able seaman in the Royal Navy and was at one point serving aboard HMS *Saxifrage*, a flower-class cruiser sent out to help safeguard the merchant-marine convoys on their regular runs taking much-needed supplies north to Murmansk to help the Russians. His description of the people who were waiting in Murmansk to greet them, desperate, freezing, starving, scrabbling on the dockside for scraps of food, hugging and thanking the British sailors for their efforts, was moving enough, but it was recalling the Royal Navy's operational procedures when a merchant vessel had been hit that so upset him.

These merchant ships, laden to the gunwales with their precious cargoes, were slow and therefore vulnerable to attack by the ever-present German U-boats. Sitting ducks. Royal Navy anti-submarine vessels carrying their deadly depth-charges patrolled constantly, but they couldn't be everywhere, and when one of these merchant vessels found itself on the wrong end of a tinfish it invariably went down quickly; those crewmen lucky enough to survive the initial attack ended up in the freezing sea. In such situations the priority was to make sure that as much of the convoy as possible made it to Murmansk, so a Royal Navy vessel was despatched to make a single sweep of the area where the merchant ship had sunk. Rope webbing was thrown over the side, and as the ship sailed at reduced speed through the icy water, anyone who could summon up the strength would grab on to the webbing and either clamber or be hauled up to the comparative safety of the deck. But they were only allowed to make one sweep: every moment they were away

7

from the main convoy left it more vulnerable to further attack. So, my dad and the rest of his shipmates, most of them young lads like him in their teens and twenties, would do their best, shouting encouragement at the poor souls and urging them to grab on to the webbing. But not all those in the water could manage it: their frozen fingers couldn't grip or they'd fall back into the water before they could reach safety. The memory of looking into the eyes of men only yards away, knowing they'd be dead in minutes, then sailing away into the darkness as their cries for help gradually faded to nothing, brought only a shake of his head.

During those early years my dad occasionally talked about the time he'd spent in America during the war while seconded to the US Navy for some eighteen months. He'd laugh as he recalled the on-deck sloppiness of the American sailors, with their caps askew and their tunics unbuttoned, their informal manner when engaged in conversation with an officer. If they'd behaved like that aboard a Royal Navy ship, he said, they'd have been frogmarched to the brig and been up on a charge. He spoke of being billeted just outside New York with some women called the Andrews Sisters, who were, according to him, entertainers and quite famous at the time. As I was mesmerized by Elvis and Co. at the time, the name meant nothing to me.

He told me of an occasion when he and his mate were eating in a New York restaurant and Bob Hope, seeing their Royal Navy uniforms, had come over to their table to wish them well. Later on, when they'd finished their meal, they requested the bill, only to be told that Mr Hope had instructed the management to give the two Limeys anything they wanted and put it on his tab. Same thing had happened to them in a bar owned by the ex-boxer 'Two-Ton' Tony Gilento.

My dad spoke of evenings on the Andrews Sisters' porch in upstate New York while they sang their close-harmony songs for him and his mate. He told of sailing down to the Florida Keys, of Key Largo and Key West, and he said it was the most wonderful place he'd ever been to, that the water was such a clear blue you could see right through it. I took all this to be the yarn-spinning of an old man of the sea. I mean, why on earth would the Royal Navy have seconded my dad to the US Navy for eighteen months? After all, he was just an able seaman first class, not a submarine captain. Once or twice he'd mentioned something called Combined Operations he'd been involved with, but he was a sailor, not a spy. All the same, to a kid they were great yarns.

In most respects my dad was an old-fashioned guy, a man very much of his time, not inclined towards deep, meaningful conversation with a five-year-old. That's understandable, after a working day that required him to leave the house at six thirty a.m. and return most nights at around ten after putting in a heavy manual shift, but I wish it had been different. It wasn't, though, and other than the occasional chinwag with the old man, most of my parental contact during those early years was with my mam.

As a result of physical injuries, predominantly leg wounds, that he sustained while serving in the Navy, my dad spent months in a convalescent hospital, his footballing days over. On being demobbed he was fitted with callipers that had metal rods running vertically to the outside and inside of the leg and thick leather collars around the knee, thigh and ankle to enable him to walk. They lived inside the wardrobe in my parents' bedroom long after my dad had stopped using them and they puzzled me for most of my early years. I'd often sneak in there just to open the wardrobe door and stare at them leaning in the back corner, imagining them to be some sort of robot skeleton, or bazookas maybe. If I asked my mam about them, which I did from time to time, she'd tell me, 'They're your dad's. From the war.'

The war changed my dad from a happy-go-lucky young man with his eyes fixed firmly on the future into a hard-drinking introvert; bitter, cynical, haunted by the past. Although his upbringing and social circumstances had him firmly marked down as a Labour Party man, he never aligned himself to any one political party, believing them all to be a wash-out in terms of their supposed worth to the working man. From what I've seen, he wasn't far wrong. In the days before therapy, psychoanalysis and the recognition of post-traumatic stress disorder and its psychological effects on servicemen and women, many a confused soul sought refuge in the drink. My dad was one and, it has to be said, the drink didn't suit him. He was never violent in the house, at least not physically – maybe because he knew from first-hand experience how much damage fists could do. I cannot recall an instance of him raising his hands to me or anyone else in the family. No, the damage my dad inflicted was the kind that goes unnoticed by the human eye: it came from his mouth. On the odd occasions I was around to hear and not tucked up in bed, he said things to my mam that were cruel, nasty and spiteful.

By the time I came along things weren't going well between my mam and dad. This, coupled with the gap between my birth and that of my nearest sister (some nine years), leads me to believe I must have been a mistake, the result of a temporary lull in the domestic warfare, a 'brown-ale baby'. As a result of my birth my mam became dangerously anaemic and suffered severe post-natal depression, with anxiety attacks and claustrophobia. As with my dad's problems, it went unrecognized and untreated, and my mam ended up spending a lot of her time a bus-ride away with her aunts Sarah and Belle, away from her husband and family. I was too young to take on board what was happening.

My overriding memory of visiting aunts and relatives is of having to sit in gloomy parlours with dark wood cabinets containing hand-painted china tea-sets to be used only on special occasions, and heavy lace curtains up at the windows. We listened to the big Bush valve radio with its massive circular tuning dial and place-names like Belgrade and Stockholm written in tiny dark-red letters. A television was beyond the wherewithal of the Bradfords and the Johnsons. Sundays were the worst, having to sit there while your mates were all out playing footie or climbing trees, having adventures. I'd be made to sit there as thick dry slices of fruit cake were pushed towards me, and I wasn't allowed to move until I'd eaten it all, by which time I usually couldn't move anyway. On a Sunday afternoon it was the BBC's Light Programme or the Home Service – there were no commercial radio stations – with programmes like the wonderful *Round The Horne*, with Kenneth Horne, or the slightly less-than-wonderful *The Clitheroe Kid*, starring the shrill-voiced Jimmy Clitheroe. It was harmless and daft. Shrill-voiced he might have been, but Jimmy Clitheroe was one of the first people I heard on the radio with a regional accent. It wasn't unlike my own, and everyone laughed at it.

Never-ending afternoon would eventually drift into interminable early evening and *The Black and White Minstrel Show* or *Sing Something Simple*. These were the radio forerunners of the 1960s television shows featuring white guys with their faces blacked up, looking like cartoon Negroes. George Mitchell was their leader. For a young kid itching to be out causing mischief with his pals it was stifling, yet those enforced listening sessions instilled in me a love of radio comedy and an awareness of the beauty and potency of words and melodies that has stayed with me ever since.

Ah, melody. It came by way of the radio, hymns sung at school and Hollywood film musicals I sometimes got to see at picture houses such as the Scala, the Essoldo, the Stoll or Black's Regal. I could sing every one of those film and radio songs all the way through, even the ones I didn't like. I could whistle them, too, as my dad had taught me how to do it with the aid of an entire box of matches. At his signal I'd purse my lips and blow out the lighted match. In no time there was a note, then another, and I was off, whistling melodies day and night. Whistling Rufus, my mam used to call me.

Other than the flicks and the odd 78 r.p.m. record my sisters occasionally bought, the BBC, via radio, was the sole provider of all the latest hit melodies and our entertainment. The BBC was well respected in our house, a national institution. I loved it. We didn't have a clue as to how the radio worked, but we knew that when you switched it on, magical sounds came out of it.

When I was a kid a lot of my pals smoked, but not me. I have never in my life smoked a cigarette, partly because I had to listen to my dad cough his guts up every morning before he could get up. He suffered from emphysema, a respiratory disease. I thought it was the fault of the tabs, as cigarettes were then known. Another reason I abstained dates back to when I was six or seven. On one of those dreaded Sunday visits to Walker I was talking with Uncle George. A lovely big gentle man who would then have been around sixty, George had a speech impediment, one of those little things that could be rectified these days in a matter of hours but which was then left untreated. It was difficult to understand what he said, which was never much at the best of times as he was embarrassed by his speech. He smoked a pipe, which fascinated me. The television series *Maigret* was big at the time, and the eponymous hero smoked a pipe, so I'd constantly badger Uncle George for a try of his. The answer was always no, but one day he relented. He filled it up with shag tobacco, set it ablaze and handed it to me with the instruction to take a great big suck and breathe it all in. This I did with the zeal of the inquisitive child.

A moment later I turned blue, then a sickly yellow, and was violently sick on the carpet. There was hell to pay: Uncle George got a right ear-bashing from aunts Sarah and Belle – didn't he know I was only a bairn, what was he trying to do and all that. But Uncle George knew what he was doing, and I owe him a big thank-you for helping to ensure that I was never tempted to stick one of those filthy things in my mouth and set it on fire.

If the street I lived in was my playground then its two bits of grass were my Wembley. For as long as I can remember I've been football daft, with Newcastle United being the focal point and recipient of my devoted support. I'm so glad I was born and raised in an area where love of the beautiful game is almost mandatory. Also, with Newcastle, it's one toon, one team. As someone who's lived more than half his life in London I feel it's different in the south: London has half a dozen top clubs and many more in the lower divisions, so support is more spread out. Londoners know their football and love their teams, no doubt about that, but we Geordies, I think, have a greater love of the game itself. When the team does well up there in God's country, the whole city perks up, gets a lift; it's noticeable wherever you go, especially on those Saturday evenings straight after a home game. Conversely, when the toon take a pummelling in the Premier League, which thankfully happens a bit less regularly, these days, or loses a big cup-tie, the whole city feels the pain of communal loss. But that love for football is always there: if an opposition player comes to St James' Park and turns in an outstanding performance, he'll most likely be applauded off the pitch. As with the people, so with the team: hard but fair.

I must admit to one brief spell when my allegiances lay elsewhere, not with another club, never that, but with a single player, the greatest footballer I've ever seen. I was about ten when a young lad called George Best began getting noticed with Manchester United and, like most young lads through-out the land, I was George-Best potty. Because of his looks, long hair and lifestyle, he was treated like a pop star, and was often referred to by the media as the fifth Beatle. If George was due to do his thing with Manchester United, the gate at St James' Park would swell by thousands. People, women especially, who might not otherwise go to a football match would make the effort to see Bestie and they were usually rewarded with displays, or at least glimpses, of sheer genius. Speed, balance, poise, vision, bravery, stamina, two good feet and he could head the ball as well: George truly had it all. There are plenty of people who feel he never fully realized his true potential. Maybe, but anyone who ever saw one of his spellbinding dribbles as he set off towards goal will tell you it doesn't get any better. On that pitch and with a ball at his feet, George Best was way beyond the normal parameters of human ability. He was in a place few of us ever get to go. I used to dream of being able to do just one or two of the many things he could do.

One year Father Christmas brought me a George Best Manchester United replica kit, such as it was in those days. I was so knocked out by it I wouldn't take it off for almost a week. I played outside in it, I even slept in it. Everyone around me was football daft, my pals, the big lads, my dad, the grown-ups. And England hadn't won the World Cup yet. Football was a credo, a way of life in Newcastle, and it still is today. The team carries the name of the town. Both have been big influences on my life.

Twelve houses made up Penfold Close, two sets of semis on either side and a four-house link-terrace at the top. At number one were the 'later' Allens, who arrived after us, Stan and Steve and their parents. They moved in when I was about ten. I can't remember who was there before them. Next door at number three were the Robinsons, with kids Elaine, Valerie and Norman. Elaine wore short skirts. Mrs Robinson seemed a bit stuck-up, which always struck me as strange, her living where she did. The Erskines were at number five: Madeleine was much older than me, sexy but way out of reach, and younger Robert was a bit of a bully. They moved, and the Nansens arrived. In later years Matty Nansen became a drinking pal of my dad's.

The Marshalls lived at number seven, kids Keith, Brenda, Trevor, Phillip, Judith, Johnny, Stephen and Andrew. Mr Marshall was a real card, with a sense of humour as dry as a bone. Trevor was my age and we became big buddies, the best of mates. Hated each other one minute, loved each other the next. In the middle of a round of 'Knights in Armour' one day, using bits of old fencing as broadswords, I belted Trevor over the head, not knowing there was a four-inch nail in the sharp end of my sword. Trevor ran off into his house, screaming blue murder.

A few weeks later he got his revenge while he was digging the back garden. I was standing near him, watching, and he whacked the spade down on my toes, cutting clean through my plimsoll and all but severing my big toe. It hurt. I screamed and hopped home sharpish. That necessitated six weeks of visits to Walkergate Hospital, where nurses had to keep removing my big toenail with a pair of tweezers. I guess we were even.

The Grahams were at number nine, their son David and his sister, much older than me. Tall people, proper grown-ups. Mr and Mrs Graham must have been at least a hundred. David had great pushbikes – he had a Flying Scot, dead cool, but with mudguards! Nobody had mudguards except the old people. The Gummets lived at number eleven with their kids, Peter and Susan. Peter was a year older than me so we hung out a lot together. Susan was younger and plump. Mr Gummet expected Peter to follow him into the Army, where he'd been a career soldier. Peter had a go in the TA and said it was great, but told me years later that he'd hated every minute of it.

The Yeats family occupied number two, with kids Ian and Lorna. Ian was a pal. Dad Harry was a great bloke, wise, funny, and always had time to talk to us kids. He worked at De la Rue Bros, printers on the Teams Valley trading estate. They printed money, banknotes. It was a job for life, so they said. Ian would follow when he was old enough, so they said. The McCarthys were at number four, mam, dad, Wilfred, Cyril, Mickey, twins Leo and Peter, Mary and Susan. Mr McCarthy was in poor health and couldn't work so they were always struggling. Great bloke, though, short and plump with a bit of Edward G. Robinson about him. Always ready with a smile. When I was older the McCarthys moved out and the Lusks moved in. Geoff was my age and he was a nice kid. I quite fancied his mam.

At number six were the Witheys and their daughters, Sylvia and Edna, both older than me. Mr Withey had a face like a tombstone with a friendly smile. Edna Withey was a dish. Dead trendy, with big hair and mini-skirts. And kinky boots, like Cathy Gale's on *The Avengers*. Unattainable. A horny hormonal young 'un could dream, though, and very often did.

The 'original' Allens lived at number eight, Albert, Tilly and kids Anne, Tess, Gordon, Joan, Rose, Vincent, Paul, Bernadette and Christine, strict Roman Catholics. All in a three-bedroom house. Mrs Allen went out to work every day. There was us at number ten, and the Rogers family next door at number twelve. Elder brother Ivan, and twins Pat(ricia) and Peter. All older than me. Mr Rogers worked for the railways in Ireland; we never saw him. Mrs Rogers was very bad with her nerves. She used to bang on the window with her knuckles when we played football in the street. If the ball ever went into her front garden, it called for unspeakable bravery on the part of whoever had kicked it last to leap over the hedge and retrieve it. Ivan was a printer. Peter went into the post office as a telegraph boy; you got a uniform and an underpowered motorbike. Ivan once got Peter some cards printed up that said, *Have Gun: Will Travel*, taken from the western series of that name that was running on television at the time, starring Richard Boone. That was cool. Underneath, in smaller letters, it said 'Wire Palladin'. I didn't understand, and thought Wire must've been Palladin's Christian name. I remember there was a lot of stuff like that I didn't understand, names, places, etc. Words I'd hear but never saw written down. I began to be inquisitive about words, about their meaning, their sound, their spelling, their origin. I began to ask questions.

The Hewitts lived just round the corner at the bottom of the street, with kids Peter, Les, David and Angela. David was the same age as me and Trevor and dead brave, so we three buddied up. That was our little gang, me, Dave and Trevor, the three of us. Old Jock Hewitt had been on

17

submarines in the war, and the word was it had sent him a bit doo-lally. He used to drink whisky, then raise holy hell in the house and sometimes out in the street. Next door was the Cairns family. Their oldest lad, John, was known as Sputnik. I never found out why, it was a mystery, but we took it to be derogatory. Could he run! He had a fantastic turn of speed, especially on the wing. Like a whippet, he was, lightning quick. There was no way of stopping him other than with a foul. Mickey, his younger brother, was called Mick the Greek, again for reasons unknown. I don't think there was any Greek connection – perhaps it had more to do with his swarthy skin colour than anything else. Not far along, at number 100 Fairways Avenue were the Baldwin brothers, Harry and Brian, regarded by all my pals' mothers as trouble. They were a little older than I was so they ignored me. Their mam made and sold toffee cakes for a penny. We'd call with our coppers and she'd take the cakes off a little shelf by the door and hand them over. We'd lick and lick until they were all gone. They tasted delicious.

Harry Baldwin used to hang out with Johnny Fail, who lived across the road from him at the bottom of the big field. Johnny was the first person I knew to have long hair. I'm sure he wasn't aware of my existence. He was one of the big lads and never acknowledged us lot. Early evening, around six thirty, we youngsters would stop kicking a ball and look on in admiring silence as Johnny Fail walked past us, with his hair touching the collar of his shirt, on his way into town. Phew!

Me and Trevor and Dave would meet in the street to plot and plan our escapades: crossy-gardens, knockie-nine-doors, Montekitty, a game whose rules I could never grasp. Apple-raiding, bogie-building. Down to the 'cowfield' with our jam-jars to collect frogspawn to take home and watch until it turned into tadpoles. The wheat in the cowfield grew high in the summer and we'd sneak around playing Japs and commandos and making a right old mess. We'd sometimes try to eat the wheat but it was horrible. How could that have anything to do with nice sugary breakfast cereals?

Shows like *Ready Steady Go!* and *Juke Box Jury* were on the telly every week, bringing us the very latest in fantastic pop sounds. I'd stand there, transfixed, as bands like Manfred Mann blasted out tracks like '5–4–3–2–1' with wailing harmonica. As soon as the programme was over I'd be out in the street to meet Ian and Trevor and Dave and talking, discussing, comparing. Ian didn't like Manfred Mann's new one. What? How could you not? It was like a train coming through the living room! And what about that new one by the Kinks? They had cool shirts with frills and the singer had a gap in his front teeth. So it would go as we talked and played air guitar until the sun went down and long after. We'd dream of being in pop groups and becoming millionaires, with American convertibles and Chelsea boots, just like the Animals who were from down the road in Walker.

Although there were roads and plenty of places to park, there were hardly any cars, anywhere, as few people could afford one, so you could play outside as much as you liked without worrying your mam. This meant whole days spent kicking a ball, usually a tennis ball, around the grass and against the kerb for rebounds. Sometimes someone would appear with a real, big ball and then we'd all go round the corner to the field and have a big game. Jumpers for goalposts and mind out for the dogshit. No one ever wanted to play in goal. I still reckon you have to have a screw loose to want to be a goal-keeper.

Mr Robinson, the window-cleaner who lived at number three, had a big motorbike with a sidecar for his ladders –

sometimes he gave the kids a ride. Mr Marshall, a manager at Pickfords Heavy Haulage, had a company car, a Morris shooting-brake. Later the street began to fill up with vehicles as more families could afford them. Not us, though. I pestered my dad for years, feeling that without one we were second-class citizens, but he would have none of it. He used to tell me that if a man drank, he shouldn't drive a car. That was it. No discussion. So we never had one. My sisters both bought cars, but that wasn't the same: I wanted to go on family drives to the country for picnics, like the smiling people in the adverts. Instead, for us it was the bus, full of smelly strangers. It turned me into a bad traveller.

I don't remember us as being particularly poor or short of anything: we just seemed the same as those around us, no better or worse off, but one of my strongest childhood memories is of walking across the big field towards the shops at the Four Lane Ends, with my mam carrying two bags filled with empty pop bottles. In those days they were made of thick glass with a big black screw stopper and you got threepence, about a penny in today's money, when you returned one to wherever you'd bought it. To me those walks to the shops were an adventure, an opportunity to hang on to my mam's coat and play, but they must have been difficult for her. Not only was she unwell with anaemia and what was known mysteriously as 'women's trouble', she had her pride. It was expected of a wife that she would get by on whatever housekeeping her husband gave her, never mind if he didn't give her enough, which was often the case in our house. If we passed a neighbour on the way to the shops, the clank of those bottles in the bags left no one in any doubt as to where we were headed, and why.

2

To be sung to the melody of 'My Darling Clementine':

> Benton Park School, Benton Park School, is a load of misery.
> If it wasn't for the teachers, all the schoolkids would be free.
> Build a bonfire, build a bonfire, put the teachers on the top,
> Put the prefects in the middle and burn the fucking lot!

Little wonder things went wrong from early on.

As my daily routine had until then consisted almost entirely of climbing trees, eating the locally made Tudor crisps and playing football with my pals, I was none too keen on interrupting it to attend the local primary school, Benton Park. I'd heard rumours: lessons, uniforms, teachers. It was no place to have fun. It did have a football pitch, though, and Trevor and Dave would be starting at the same time. So I gave it a go, and didn't like it one little bit. In fact, so much did I not like it that on one occasion when my mam was literally dragging me towards the school gates, I moved my weight forwards, throwing her off balance. My mam disappeared over a wall.

Benton Park Primary was where I first encountered Ray Black, institutional discipline in the form of rules, and girls. Ray lived up near the Four Lane Ends, where the big shops were, with his mother, three brothers, Eddie, Joe and David, and three sisters, Norma, Muriel and Moira. Ray's dad had been a sea captain but he was dead. Ray was the only lad I knew who didn't have a dad. I thought that was awful and mightily unfair. Racing bikes were all the rage and Ray had a good one, a Merlin, mustard-coloured lightweight frame, ten-speed Campagnolo gears, the works. I was dead envious. Even as a boy Ray was a man of few words, never used ten when half a dozen would do. He was great, a proper pal, a hard-case no one messed with. He knew all about conkers and frogspawn and racing bikes. We remain the best of friends.

I had a problem with discipline from the word 'go' – or, more accurately, 'GO!' I've still not got the hang of taking orders impolitely issued. Girls were just plain weird; none of them liked football or climbing fences, and they seemed to spend an awful lot of time in the toilet. I found girls a puzzle from day one, yet despite everything I was inexplicably drawn to these strange non-boys.

My first teachers were the unfortunately named Mr Willey, and Mrs Thompson. Mr Willey loved to tell us of his own love for the north-eastern dialect; his favourite words were 'claggy clarts', which, loosely translated, means a sticky, muddy mess. He introduced us kids to Owen Brannigan, the great bass-baritone singer. Brannigan was a Bedlington lad who'd achieved international recognition in opera; Benjamin Britten was impressed enough to write a part in *Billy Budd* especially for him. To most folk up north, however, Owen Brannigan was known for his recorded interpretations of local traditional songs. Mr Willey, a big man himself, was a huge fan of Brannigan and would sing us songs such as 'Caa' Hackie', all about a cow that wouldn't wade through water – never mind that there was a rock 'n' roll revolution going on outside in the streets. Wonderful stuff it was, of real value and importance, though I thought it tripe at the time. Some of Brannigan's recordings are still available from Windows' music store in Newcastle, and a single listen to something like 'Canny Tyneside' is all you need to understand what all the fuss was about. For me Brannigan was a Geordie Paul Robeson.

Mrs Thompson was older than Mr Willey: tiny, blonde, plump with a sexy asthmatic wheeze and always jolly, she looked to me like a kind of Easter egg. Always there for a reassuring cuddle, she was very kind – so kind in fact that she spoiled me: I had soon assumed all teachers were the same. Ha!

Mrs Martin was my last teacher at Benton Park, and she was horrible. With her tweed suits, glaring eyes, whining voice and gold-capped teeth, she resembled a well-dressed witch. On one occasion, having told me to stop talking in class, she hauled me into the stock cupboard, tied my wrists together, put a piece of masking tape over my mouth, switched off the light then left, locking the door behind her. The only thing I could see were the luminous numbers on a clock sitting high up on a shelf; it tick-ticked away, making the time pass even slower. I was ten years old.

The headmistress at Benton Park was Miss Green, a spindle-thin woman, bone-dry, plain of feature and dress, and without the slightest hint of a personality. As kids she and my mam had been at Heaton High School for Girls together. My mam had won an assisted place, through a scheme that helped bright kids from poorer families. She was convinced this was why Miss Green bore me a grudge.

The girls in my class with whom I tried to make friends were Olwen 'Olly' Thompson, Linda Heads and Lynn Morpeth. Where are you now, girls? Linda had an older sister called Sandra, whom I fancied, but she wore fashionable clothes, went into town at night and was out of my league. Also, their mam, Mrs Heads, disapproved of me, sensible woman, so there was no joy there. They lived in a private house, as we called all non-council houses, just along from the school. There was another girl, Janice Burdon – we all gave her a terrible time. I can't remember why, maybe she was just poorer than the rest of us. Whatever the reason, Janice was on the receiving end of some awful, cruel stuff.

When I was about ten I found myself spending a great deal of time hanging around outside the home of Judith Sanderson. She was a beautiful girl a year or two younger than me with a beaming smile, long dark hair she wore in a pony-tail, long legs to match and soft unblemished skin. Unusually, her skin was darker than most of the other kids because her mam was Indian. At that time there was no Asian community in Newcastle to speak of, interracial marriages were unheard of, and to me it was nothing more than a novelty – rather exotic, having an Indian mam. Years later, Judith told me of the almost-daily racist slurs and insults her mother endured. Perhaps Mrs Sanderson, like Mrs Heads, wasn't keen on the prospect of having her daughter mauled by sweaty little mitts. Our brief friendship was discouraged and eventually fizzled out.

My days at Benton Park Primary were marked by what seemed like some pretty extreme stuff. I once decided I'd had enough of everything so I'd run away. Ray Black and I made our way to Paddy Freeman's park and played there all day until we got bored and returned home. In those days it was safe enough to do such things but I was still in for a roasting when I got home. On another occasion I organized a lunch protest when our meals didn't arrive on time. Fists clenched, we all started banging the handles of our knives and forks on the tables and chanting, 'WE WANT WER DINNER! WE WANT WER DINNER!' Although I was displaying obvious leadership qualities, I got a smack for that one.

The aim of every nipper on the Fairways estate was to get into the gang. The big lads were in charge: they organized apple raids and crossy-gardens and you had to pass various tests before you were allowed in. The one that scared the hell out of me was having to learn, and then recite, the devil's prayer: 'Damn, damn, bugger-hell, shit, shite, amen.' Every night I'd cower under my heavy Navy-issue blanket, whispering bits of the blasphemous verse, expecting a thunderbolt to come down from heaven and hit me on the head. Then there was the ordeal of having to recite it in front of all the other kids. That was really tempting fate, but thankfully the much-feared thunderbolt never materialized.

One of the best times of the year was 5 November, Bonfire Night. Good old Guy Fawkes, we got up to all sorts in his name. Rockets fired through letterboxes, bangers tied to cats' tails, air bombs aimed at garages. All the things you feel really bad about once you get older and have a bit more common sense. How no one ever got badly injured I'll never know. The building of the bonfire became almost a civil engineering project, planned months in advance and guarded day and night during construction. The whole estate would use the evening of 5 November as an opportunity to get rid of any old furniture. During the weeks beforehand I would run home from school, wolf down my dinner and then be out knocking on doors to see if anyone had anything for the bonfire.

The centrepiece was always a pole of some sort, which reached high into the air. Stacked around it was all the stuff we'd collected. Watching it grow bigger by the day and the week was so exciting. We also had to guard against rival gangs coming to torch it early. That was a favourite, and complex plans were laid to avoid such a disaster. Someone would always be at the site, day and night. It meant having to sleep there on occasion – I shudder when I recall what we used to do. We'd make a kind of den right inside the bonfire, an Aladdin's cave decked out with old settees and carpets, and sleep in there. Thank God nobody ever came along and set fire to it when we were inside.

The search for a suitable centre pole began early on and the big lads were choosy about what they'd use. One year they felled a working telegraph pole on Coach Lane. Thankfully there weren't many cars around back then, or police, for that matter. I watched it fall, incredulous, and then all we little 'uns carried it shoulder-high, like munchkins, marching through the estate and on to the big field.

Try as I might to make it the opposite, there was no getting away from it: school was getting in the way of my having fun. As the years passed, rules loomed large in my little life. I never had a problem with doing as I was told, as long as an order, instruction or command was delivered with courtesy. If not, that was when the problems started. It was all too often a case of 'Do as you're told, boy!' Put like that, I never could. My biggest problem was that I couldn't keep my mouth shut. I wanted to answer every question and would call out the answers instead of putting up my hand. This led to my being first ignored, then told off and eventually punished. I couldn't see the justice in that. I began to feel victimized and also to harbour a grudge against the teachers, the grown-ups, the people in charge. The worst thing about it was that I was usually correct with the answers, which made my sense of injustice all the greater. If only I'd kept my gob shut, put my hand up and waited like everyone else! Too eager to impress, I guess.

At the age of eleven, every kid in the country had to sit the eleven-plus examination, which decided your next scholastic port of call and pretty much the course of your life. From Benton Park the top tier of boys went off to Heaton Grammar School, there to study the more academic, artistic and scientific subjects with a view to tertiary education; the middle tier went on to Manor Park Technical School, with slightly less emphasis on academic study and more on engineering, wood- and metal-working crafts; the rest were off to Chillingham Road Secondary Modern, to be prepared for a life of manual labour. These kids could look forward to apprenticeships in the construction industry: bricklaying, plastering, jobs that were then regarded as okay if you were capable of nothing better.

I was dead-set on making it to Heaton Grammar. My sister Val had been part of the first wave of young working-class people to benefit from greater educational opportunities in the 1960s and had gone on to study English at Leeds University, eventually becoming vice-president of the students' union. The whole family was rightly very proud. Trevor Marshall's older brother, Keith, had made it to Heaton Grammar, and I was impressed.

I had this idea that I'd emulate my sister, make the family proud of me, become an English teacher at Heaton Grammar, there to roam around its stone corridors in a threadbare tweed jacket with a pair of glasses, a leather briefcase and a book in my hand. James the academic. So I tried really hard in the eleven-plus, gave it my best shot. When they read out the results, in front of all the class, I was crestfallen to learn I'd only secured a place at Manor Park, the technical school.

The teacher who read out the results was a rather unpleasant middle-aged man called Mr Turnbull. He looked at me and said, 'Manor Park, although I don't know how you managed that!' I felt ashamed, felt I'd let the family down. I also felt thick. The results couldn't lie, could they? Although going to Manor Park meant I'd actually passed the eleven-plus, this was my first taste of being marked down as a failure. I didn't like it. Worse still, my best pal Ray was on his way to Chillingham Road. On the plus side, though, Trevor Marshall and Dave Hewitt were both headed for Manor Park, and it was literally at the end of our estate, no more than a few minutes' walk, so it wasn't all bad.

Many years later I returned to Benton Park to watch my niece, Kathryn, perform in the annual school nativity play with the rest of the nippers. My mam was there, too, and at some point she bumped into her old schoolfriend Miss Green, who'd become Mrs Hayes and had long-since retired. 'My, hasn't your Jimmy done well for himself?' My mam agreed I had. 'Who'd have ever thought it? What a surprise.' Not to me, replied my mam, he was always a bright lad. In fact, my mam recalled how surprised she'd been, we'd all been, at my not making it to Heaton Grammar School all those years ago. 'He did pass, actually,' said Mrs Hayes, 'but we decided to award him a slightly lower mark as we didn't want Benton Park to gain a reputation for sending disruptive pupils up to the grammar school.' My mam didn't tell me any of this until years later for fear of what my reaction might be, and I have to admit I was profoundly upset and angry about it for a long time, but that anger passed and gave way to disappointment. For me the saddest part is that, through incredible good fortune, my life eventually turned out all right. I beat the odds. I won. But how many other kids' lives were blighted, and at what eventual cost to both themselves and the state? And all because people like Mrs Hayes regarded their own perceived good name as being of more importance than the interests of their pupils. Things are different now, I hope.

Back in the class, Mr Turnbull put the tin hat on a miserable day by taking me to one side and telling me that he knew a lot of the older boys at Manor Park School and he'd ensure that when I got there my life would be hell. Those were his words. I remember them clearly: no one had ever said anything like that to me before. Why he should have wanted to do this I don't know. He had a daughter I used to hang around with, but we were only little. Certainly too little for any of *that*. Whatever, his sadistic promise meant that, although we were smack-bang in the middle of the most creative cultural times there'd ever been, with top tunes being released every week, the summer of 1965 was an anxious one for me. I marked the days off in my little diary. It was a sad, disappointing end to a precious part of my childhood and a brutal indication of what was to follow.

September 1965. Manor Park: the big school. Full uniform, blue blazer with a badge on the breast pocket. Boys only. Phoney coat-of-arms, phoney Latin motto underneath, swords, shields, the whole nine yards. A technical school, a fifties innovation to the education system, aimed at bridging the gap between the clever kids and the dunces.

In the early 1960s various scandals engulfed the Tory party and rocked it to its foundations, the most notorious being the Christine Keeler/John Profumo affair. As a result, a Labour government under Harold Wilson had swept to power in 1964 on an 'out with the old, in with the new' ticket. Labour had been in the political wilderness for more than a decade. Their election victory was followed by a period of massive social change, the likes of which this country had not seen since the immediate post-war years of the 1940s when the welfare state was introduced. This time round, though, the working classes were empowered as never before: sustained expansion, most notably in areas of education and housing, was matched only, and ominously, by spending. The hangover wouldn't be felt until the dark days of the 1970s, but the 1960s were a swinging groovy party that everyone seemed happy to buy into. In terms of the country's long-term good, it had its downsides – in municipal architecture for a start – but at the time it was incredibly exciting, especially if you were a teenager.

The nation needed engineering trainees, civil, mechanical and electrical, and schools such as Manor Park were meant to be feeder farms, set up solely to supply the shipyards, building sites and mines with much-needed raw material. The headmaster, Mr Laidlaw – or Check, as he was known to us kids – was short and wore a flowing gown that made him look a bit like a baldy bat. With his wizened little face and flat square Slavic head he looked quite scary in an academic way.

From day one it was a different proposition from the relative idyll of Benton Park. Any similarity ended with the names. Manor Park said discipline, loud and clear. Some of the boys were like men: they had stubble, sideburns and 'taches. Some of the teachers were animals. And from day one I didn't fit in.

It started badly. My own fault, mind. On leaving Benton Park Primary I was still wearing my beloved short trousers with the neat presses in them and continued to do so right through the summer, running around the housing estate, kicking a football or climbing trees. Murder on the knees, it was, but long trousers would have been like wearing two skinny sleeping-bags. When the time came to think about a uniform for the big school I was in no doubt: I'd be wearing short trousers. Did I not want her to get me a pair of those long ones like the other lads were getting? asked my mam. Nah! They looked ridiculous, those long trousers. And Trevor and Dave were going to be wearing their shorts. So that was that. Until day one.

First day at the big school is always traumatic. Major nerves. All that noise, all those unfamiliar faces, people milling around, hundreds of kids, dozens of teachers, and I didn't know any of them. Just Trevor and Dave, and I couldn't see either of them. And what about the big lads Mr Turnbull had briefed to make sure my life was hell? Where were they hiding? From outside the gates the place looked like a zoo. Never mind, take a breath and in you go. It must have been about a minute before some wag shouted out something about 'Look at the little pouf in his little short trousers!' Then the laughing started.

When you're a kid, laughter in such circumstances can be excruciatingly painful and it cut into me like a knife. I stood out like a sore thumb. I was different from the rest and I didn't want to be, not on day one, not like this. I looked around for help, for kindred short-trousered spirits, and finally spotted Trevor and Dave – in long trousers. In no time at all I was rolling around on the playground Tarmac in my brand-new school uniform scrapping with the wag responsible for the slur. That scene must have repeated itself half a dozen times that first morning.

When I got home at lunch-time my mam was waiting at the front door for me, dying to know how my first morning at the big school had been. She was shocked to see the state of her little lad and, more particularly, of his brand-new school uniform. It was in tatters. I insisted she go down to J. T. Parrish's department store in Byker and get me some long trousers, begged her, told her my life was on the line. This she did and by the second day of that term I had long trousers. They felt like sackcloth, weighed a ton and itched like hell but they were the same length as everyone else's. Bearing in mind we had little money and clothes had to be bought with coupons – a clandestine and expensive credit

31

system run by local department stores – it was good of my mam to make it work. In all my life she never once let me down, never disappointed me. I only wish I could say the same of myself.

In terms of my time at Manor Park, those trousers were a taste of things to come. Some of the teachers were violent back then and thought nothing of dishing out the kind of beatings that today would merit a long jail sentence. On one occasion a teacher gave me such a hiding I was reduced to tears. I'd closed my eyes in class and our German teacher, Mrs McLennan, one of the few women at the school, had decided I was asleep and told me to report to a senior colleague. Of all the things I might have been guilty of, sleeping in class was not one. I couldn't have gone to sleep: my mind was too active. I was terror-stricken and begged her not to send me out, knowing what I'd be in for. I pleaded with her, but she wouldn't have it, so up I went to the next floor where the teacher was giving a lessson to 3T, a class with some of my pals in it. I knocked on the door. Through the little glass panel I could see him as he prowled around the room. After a moment he waved me in.

He was a muscular man, not bulked up as a weightlifter might be but broad-shouldered, slim-waisted and fit. Rumour had it he'd been a goalkeeper before becoming a teacher. He wandered up and down the aisles, not saying a word, as the class sat in silent, abject terror. After an age he said to me, 'Why are you here, boy?'

I told him Mrs McLennan had sent me up and then tried to explain what had happened.

He raised his hand for me to stop, so I did. 'Were you sleeping, boy?' he asked.

'No, sir,' I said.

He made his way towards me by first walking up an aisle, slowly, then down another, even more slowly, dragging it out. Then, all of a sudden, BANG, his open palm smacked into my face. I'd never had a smack as hard as that in my life. My eyes watered. I could feel the skin going all warm and red. On top of that I was humiliated: some of my mates were watching this. No one laughed, though. It was too dangerous.

That was just the start of it. He took a handful of my hair, yanked my head backwards and asked me again: 'Were you asleep, boy?'

'No, sir,' I repeated.

Wrong answer. He dragged me to the door and opened it with the hand that was still clutching my hair, then it was out into the corridor and we were heading for the stairwell. He banged my head against a door panel with such force that the glass broke. Luckily for me, there was Georgian Wired Polished glass in the doors, a type of clear safety glass, with wire strengtheners running through it, so it didn't shatter into shards. But it was also very thick so it hurt. Downstairs we stopped outside my classroom and he continued questioning me while he smacked me square in the face.

After about six blows I gave up and admitted to something I hadn't done. I lied, which I suppose I should have done earlier. But I had been telling the truth. That's what you get for being honest. I was then made to go back into Mrs McLennan's classroom and apologize to her. I think she got a bit of a shock when she saw the state I was in.

Part of me wanted to tell my dad about it so he'd come to the school and punch seven bells out of the teacher. I'm certain he would have if he'd ever found out about it. But another stronger part of me wanted no embarrassment, no fuss. Peer pressure. I couldn't have my dad fighting my school battles. I determined to deal with it myself.

It would be ridiculous to suggest all this grief at school was one-way traffic, that I was innocent of every bad thing that ever happened in that place, the victim of mistaken identity, and that the teachers were all guilty of conspiracy, victimization, persecution, assault and battery. I accept I must have been a handful and there were some bad moments, stuff I really shouldn't have been doing. I once caught 'Jakey' Duckinfield, another of our German teachers (what is it with me and the Germans?), smack in the face with a snowball as he crossed the yard on his way into the school buildings, knocking his glasses clean off his head. What made it worse was that, trying to go one better than everybody else as usual, I'd put a stone in the snowball. As soon as it connected I regretted it and felt terrible – though not as terrible as Jakey Duck no doubt. I remember thinking, That's not the way we should be seeing our teachers, scrabbling around on the ground in the snow. I'd made him look a fool in front of the whole school and I was ashamed of myself. When I saw him get to his feet and look around, I melted into the crowd, a real coward. Very poor show. Sorry, sir.

Drawing on my extensive bonfire experience I organized a book-burning, inspired by the pictures on television of protesting students in Paris. Kids brought their textbooks on to the playing field, made a big pile and we torched them. It was a blazing success until the teachers arrived and put it out. Unfortunately, some of my textbooks, with my name and class details written inside, were retrieved from the smouldering embers and I got a right belting.

Staying with the pyro theme, I set the school on fire one day, with the aid of a magnifying-glass and some sunshine. We'd often try to alleviate the tedium of morning assembly by burning holes in the big curtains in the assembly hall. One day I succeeded and we left them to smoulder. Soon after we'd all left the assembly hall, the fire brigade arrived. The next morning Mr Laidlaw was purple with rage. He wanted any boy who was sitting in the vicinity of yesterday's blaze to remain behind. It didn't take them long to rumble the culprits, and we got a fierce lashing with Mr Laidlaw's leather belt. We half-dozen culprits had to sit outside his office for a long while, sweating and fretting. Then at last we were called in, one at a time. I was near the back of the line and watched as my mates emerged, tearful and sore, rubbing their palms. Then it was my turn. Into the inner office and out with my hand. It didn't half hurt.

So, I was no angel. But two things are beyond question: first, they started all the violent stuff, and second, my behaviour was never bad enough to justify those appalling physical punishments. I was not alone in being on the receiving end, thank goodness. Lots of my pals were beaten just as badly, sometimes on the flimsiest pretext, which made me feel a little better. Eating a sweet in class, God forbid, often resulted in a smack on the side of the head, the worst possible place to land someone a blow in terms of potential damage, and a ringing noise in one ear. Goodness knows how many eardrums were perforated. I remember Dave Hewitt being hit so hard across the face the whole class was shocked. Different teachers had their own preferred way of dishing out punishment. Mr Niblo, the art teacher, would clip your arse with the edge of his stiff leather belt. That stung. Mr Found, the metalwork teacher, was fond of twisting any bits of hair you might have cultivated down the sides of your head and in front of your ears. Round and round his finger, until you were on tiptoe, humiliated and in great pain.

One of the reasons it all went so horribly wrong for me

was that I didn't understand the rules by which the big school worked. The kind of iron discipline they adhered to was alien to me. I'd not had it banged into me at home or in primary school like most of the other kids. When I was asked a question or was wrongly accused, instead of grovelling or lying, which would have been the sensible thing to do, I'd tell the truth, argue my case and, worst of all, question those in authority. It was a case of 'Children should be seen and not heard', as near-neighbour Mrs Mather was fond of repeating to my mother. Any kind of misbehaviour was tantamount to mutiny and fists would flail. This only compounded all the feelings of injustice and persecution I was beginning to harbour towards anyone in a position of authority. Hitting me was the wrong thing to do, the wrong way to go.

My experiences have led me to believe that it is counter-productive for any adult to strike a child. I've had rows in the street with people over it. Once you've done it, carried out the threat and whacked a kid, then where do you go? Do you hit them ever harder? It's wrong.

For the first three years of learning at Manor Park the kids were split into five classes: S, T, U, V and W. On my arrival I found I'd been marked down for class One U, which after a year became Two U and finally Three U. Then, for some unfathomable reason, it became Four T1 and Four T2. I ended up in Four T1.

As far as I can recall, everyone seemed to get on fairly well, but as with all large groupings of kids, you have your factions and favourites, and some of my classmates became closer pals than others over the four tumultuous years I spent at Manor Park. Ken Smith, Hacker Howe, Tommy Johnson, Mickey Gordon, or Toffo as we knew him, after Gordon's Toffees, Mickey Young and I had some right old times, daft stuff, but memorably enjoyable.

In our first year we all went off on a school trip to Obervesel, near Heidelberg in Germany, ostensibly to experience a different national culture, broaden our horizons and offer us the opportunity to try out our newly acquired linguistic skills on the unsuspecting natives. I remember it was a major number in our house trying to get the money together for the trip but somehow my mam managed it. It was so exciting, going away like that for a week or so with all your pals. A lot of things stick in my mind about that trip: looking out of the windows of the converted castle we were staying in and seeing foxes running around the multi-tiered vineyards outside; chasing Hacker Howe down the corridor while he stuffed into his mouth what was left of a big bar of chocolate he'd refused to share, just moments before he crashed into a bright white wall and spat the goo all over the place; slices of cream-covered cake in the Heidelberg cafés, so big and thick and rich they had the greedy little Geordie gluttons reeling.

My prevailing memory, though, is of setting David Phillips's hand on fire, time and again, with lighter fuel. Most of the kids I was with were already addicted to cigarettes, but the lighters at home were big, expensive metal things you could have used to cook a meal. Everyone used penny books of matches. No one owned a lighter. They were uncool, something your dad might use. On the continent it was different. The lighters were colourful and cheap, so we all bought one, or more than one, whether we smoked or not. How cool was that? So, we'd gather by the sink, douse Dave Phillips's hand with the lighter fuel, light it, then stand back and marvel at the scene taking place before our rapidly watering eyes. After a moment's waving and flailing, and to great cheers, he'd stick his blazing mitt under the cold tap. It worked particularly well in the dark.

Although I was not an unintelligent kid, I found some subjects unfathomable. Physics and chemistry were beyond my grasp. It could be argued that the fault lay with the teachers and their inability to impart the fundamentals of their chosen subject, but I doubt it. Some kids did well with certain subjects while others didn't. Either I wasn't ready for that type of theoretical knowledge or I was too lazy to apply myself. Probably a bit of both. These days I can recognize the numerical link between physics and mathematics and I find it interesting in a non-involving way. I've even grasped the basics of quantum physics, which I'm rather chuffed about. Back then, forget it – I did. All of it. I was too busy thinking about music, girls, football and ten-pin bowling.

And what was happening in the world of pop culture during the latter part of the 1960s made it hard to concentrate on anything, never mind logarithms, concentric circles and litmus paper. There were simply too many top tunes out there, all the Motown classics, the perfect accompaniment for a broken teenage heart, all the blues-rock bands like Fleetwood Mac and Free, which struck a chord with rampant young men, and let's not forget the Beatles, my favourite of them all. Like most of my pals I was music daft. I couldn't recite a verse of a poem to save my life but I could have told you the entire lyric of any song that had charted in the last ten years, no sweat. Of course, that was regarded as of no use whatsoever, a complete waste of time and energy.

In the spring of 1969 I went along to the pictures one afternoon and got a vicarious taste of freedom and rebellion courtesy of Peter Fonda, Dennis Hopper and Jack Nicholson. The movie *Easy Rider* was a real landmark in independent filmmaking, packed with incredible images, performances, dialogue and music, and destined to earn many millions of dollars. From the very first track, Steppenwolf's 'The

Pusher', with preceding rasps from the exhaust pipes on those chrome-plated, chopped-down, iconic Harley Davidsons, the soundtrack was amazing. I decided I had to have a motorbike. I started off on a scooter, a Lambretta 200 GT, then changed to a tired old Triumph Tiger 110. Riding around the north-east of England in the pouring rain was not quite *Easy Rider*, but the dream was there and we lived it in our heads. I never had a licence, or insurance. Never bothered with any of that.

3

There was something else. In June 1967 my sister Shelagh died, just days before her twenty-first birthday. Shelagh was a nurse and she'd been deeply affected by the death of an elderly patient she'd been looking after. Her doctor had put her on a course of anti-depressants. She was taking these pills with a drink in an early birthday celebration, and the result was terrible and tragic. She was a lovely girl, full of fun and always smiling. I wish I'd known her better, that I had more memories of times with her, good or bad, but she was grown-up and I was just the kid brother. It was a hammer-blow that left the whole family reeling. My mam never properly recovered.

It was a Saturday morning and I clearly recall the little police panda car pulling into our street. A visit from the police was rare. We kids all waited to see which door they would head for. I was surprised and puzzled when they made for mine. They knocked on the door and a moment later my mother appeared. The policemen must have told her straight away, because she started screaming and became hysterical, grabbing clumps of her hair and pulling at it. That day she went grey. I saw it with my own eyes.

The neighbours came running out to see what all the noise was about. I was frightened – I wanted to go to my mother but it was just as well I didn't make it to the front door, I guess. Mrs Marshall took me into her house and held me in her arms. As I sobbed into her bosom a wonderful feeling of safety and all-enveloping warmth came over me. I didn't understand what was happening. I was thirteen and I'd never been held so closely by any woman, not even my mam. It was very pleasant – but it was only happening because my sister had died.

It's easy, with the benefit of hindsight, to make a link between the tragedy of Shelagh's death and my going off the rails, but it wasn't so obvious then. There were no counsellors, therapists or child psychologists around to help a kid identify and deal with the traumatic effects of bereavement and grief. I'm not suggesting this was the sole reason for the deterioration in my behaviour over the next ten or so years but I think it must have had a bearing on it. The family, which was a shaky unit anyway, pretty much disintegrated in the wake of Shelagh's death. Family, friends and neighbours did what they could. My pal Ray came down to see me on his Merlin and told me he understood how I was feeling because he'd lost his father at an even younger age, which really helped – it made me feel like I wasn't the only kid going through it.

My mam was shattered by the loss of one of her children, and was never again the happy, smiling mam I'd known and grown up with. An inquest into Shelagh's death recorded a verdict of misadventure, and the Catholic Church refused to conduct either the funeral service or the burial. Everything changed. For Mam organized religion went out of the window, and didn't return until she was nearing the end of her life. Unlike me, both Val and Shelagh had been educated at Catholic schools at my dad's insistence, and my mam had gone along with it – anything for an easy life, I guess – but after Shelagh died she forbade the priests to come anywhere near the house. That was fine by me: I found their frowns and sweeping black gowns spooky. My mam would go to her aunts' and cry away the evenings. My dad sought solace in the bottom of a glass. Val had to struggle with the loss not only of a sister but of a friend, ally and confidante. Only two years separated her and Shelagh, and they had been very close. Val was helped through those dark days by her husband, Mac, who shared our loss and looked after Val selflessly, just as he has throughout their time together. I didn't know what to do, where to turn: it seemed like everyone around me was preoccupied with their own grief. I ended up turning inside myself and, to all intents and purposes, turning off.

After Shelagh died, my mam, dad and I continued to live in the little house in Penfold Close, but it seemed a colder place, even on the occasional warm day. This was when my childhood innocence died. There was no way to avoid the pain, or to shut it out of my life and my heart. Worse still, I had to watch as my mam struggled on, heartbroken and depleted. I so wanted to make her feel better, but I couldn't.

At this point music played a big part in my life. I could get lost in it. Words and melodies helped me through the really low times when I had nowhere else to turn. I remember listening to the Beach Boys' 'God Only Knows' a lot and wondering whether there could actually be a God up there after what had just happened to us. I'm afraid the jury's still out on that one. I'd always loved the Beach Boys, ever since those fun-fun-fun beach-inspired tracks with their sublime harmonies that seemed to be bursting with sunshine. Brian Wilson wiggled his toes in a box of sand under the piano as he wrote those tracks and it shows. The term 'genius' is much overused these days, but I do believe that, for a time back then, Brian Wilson was plugged into something to which no one else was privy. His compositional skill, choice of instrumentation and structure, with gorgeous tumbling harmonies everywhere, are real works of modern art. The truly ground-breaking *Pet Sounds* gets all the glory but listen to any Beach Boys record, particularly *Surf's Up*, and marvel at that bass playing those counterpoint passes. Groovy. After the tragic summer of 1967 the Beach Boys became even more important and precious to me.

The whole world was changing and Swinging London was in full swing, but my school years from 1967 to 1969 were unhappy ones and I was pleased to see the back of them. It wasn't that I didn't like learning or lessons – I loved some of it: English, history, languages, geography, art and sport were all enjoyable but I was unable to find any focus and knuckle down. No music lessons. At that time too! All those wonderful sounds, and we were made to ignore them. Get caught whistling a melody that was less than a hundred years old and you were in trouble. At school the teachers tried to pretend the cultural revolution of the 1960s wasn't happening but they couldn't stop it. England was a creative fulcrum, and a musical tidal wave swept away everything in its path, willing or not.

I was one of the willing legion of young folk. Like everyone else my age I dreamed of joining a band, bringing fame and glory to the family and the region, and music was the only way I figured I might ever do that. But the music was already changing, becoming more experimental, introspective: as a hurt individual that suited me fine.

I began to miss games lessons because I didn't like getting changed in front of all the other kids and the teachers, so that was the end of my football. I'd not been allowed to play much footie since I'd failed to turn up for a trial with Newcastle United. No big deal – they gave half the kids in Newcastle a similar trial. I wasn't anything special in terms of ability, but I was tall, so I might have made a half-decent centre-half. But I had no self-confidence. Come the morning of the trial, a bitter Saturday in winter with the north wind whipping in off the sea, I dragged my little arse out of bed and tried to look out of the window. It was snowing heavily. I had to breathe on the window-pane to see out, and what I saw convinced me I should go straight back to bed. Which I did. On the Monday, when I went into school, Mr Thompson collared me. Why hadn't I turned up for my trial, he wanted to know. I said there had been a blizzard blowing. He told me that was no excuse and that any boy who couldn't be bothered to turn up for a trial with Newcastle United couldn't really want to play football and didn't deserve to play football ever again. As of that day I was dropped from the school team and never allowed to play another game.

As the year wore on, it was time for my interview with the careers officer, an individual despatched from the local education department, supposedly to advise and guide young people towards a fruitful and rewarding future. The reality was a middle-aged man behind a desk, uninterested in his job and the kids before him. I stood in the snaking queue and after an age I got to have my five minutes. It went thus:

Without looking up: 'What do you want to do, then?'

'I'd quite like to be an English teacher.'

Looks over his glasses and gives a little laugh. 'An English teacher? Listen, son, for the likes of you there are three basic choices: the shipyard, the pit or the building sites. The sooner you get used to that the better.'

So that was it, my future. All mapped out with nowhere to go. I came out of that meeting angry and upset. Was that all my future merited, a measly five minutes? Had that man not been watching television and listening to his radio? It didn't have to be that way, *their* way, the old way. Things had changed. There was a whole world of opportunities. Maybe a degree was beyond me but there were other routes. I didn't tell anyone about it but I decided that if that was all society had to offer then fuck society, and fuck all those who belonged and behaved and toed the line. Fuck them all. I would do it my way, for better or worse.

So that was me and schooling finished, thank goodness. I'd had more than enough, and I'm sure that as far as the teachers were concerned the feeling was mutual. Grown-ups, and teachers in particular, were fond of telling you that your schooldays were the best of your life. If that was the case, I argued, what was there to look forward to? That usually merited a clip round the ear.

Relief, then, at this mostly muddlesome, often violent period of my life coming to an end. No more beatings at the hands of grown-ups. From now on things would be different: the next time anyone laid a hand on me I'd fight back. There was a lot of rage inside me – I was almost waiting for the first opportunity to present itself. But along with the relief I felt frustration, rooted in disappointment that I had not done myself or the family justice. My sister Val had beaten all the odds by going to university, my sister Shelagh had died young, and now there was me. What was I? A failure. My mam must have been so disappointed in me but she never once let on. There was never any criticism, only support, encouragement and love. I didn't deserve it. But I did feel certain I was capable of more than I'd managed at Manor Park. Whose fault was it? Mine? Theirs? A bit of both, I guess. Anyway, it was time to move on and I never once looked back.

That's not absolutely correct. One of my happier memories is of landing Mr Found a slap across his chops. It was September 1969, a few months after I'd left school and I was working split shifts with my buddy Tommy McCulloch at the petrol station, which meant that when I was on the late shift I was free until two o'clock. I could hang out over the lunch break with my mates who'd stayed on at Manor Park, then pedal off to work on my pushbike. I was sitting in the school bike sheds talking to some pals when Mr Found bowled up and told me to leave. I told him to fuck off. Everyone looked so shocked. Then my pals laughed. Mr Found started scowling, then lost it completely. He came towards me, seething, so I landed him a slap, which brought a cheer from all my pals, along with more laughter. That was a moment of liberation for me. The teachers didn't fancy it so much on level terms. I pedalled out of the gates and off to work, the hero, and very happy, too.

Every single day, Tommy McCulloch and I talked and planned and dreamed of having a band, of gigging, of doing it: making music. We lived for it and spent all our time, when we weren't pumping petrol, either listening to it or talking about it. Tommy was already no slouch on the traps — he'd bought a drum kit on the never-never, much to the annoyance of his mother and the neighbours. Unfortunately he'd developed a habit of equating tempo with power, so if a song needed to be played a little faster he would automatically hit the drums harder, and if the song needed to be played slowly it would also get to be played quietly. We spent all our free time indoors, practising and rehearsing, preparing for when the big moment presented itself.

The jump from boy to man was abrupt and seismic. In six weeks I'd gone from the problems of the playground to the reality of working for a living, earning a wage, and suddenly my life was transformed in a most wonderful way: I'd spent years having adults tell me I was good for nothing, but the pay packet I now received every week was confirmation that I was good for something. After years of being forced by adults to do things against my will, I was working with people who let you get on with things. Granted, it wasn't exactly neurosurgery, just pumping gas and changing oil, but I was beginning to realize not all adults thought the same way, and some were even a good laugh. For the first time in my life I was being treated as a responsible person, given some respect; along with that came self-esteem.

It was autumn going into Christmas, and bitterly cold. The garage was run by a big fat man with a beard called Andy Lane. He was hardly ever there, and the workshops were run by a guy called Don Taylor. There were two apprentice motor mechanics, Mickey Ford and Mod Bentley. A lively pensioner, Jimmy Nelles, made up the cast. It was a right hoot, a laugh a minute. Tom and I made a lot of money by draining the dregs from all the discarded oil cans into a gallon can and selling it as new. We even had a name for the stuff, DucVeeDol, made up from the names of the most popular oils of the day. I say we made a lot of money but it was pennies in comparison to the wages of today, of course. Back then, though, it felt as if I'd won the football pools. A pair of Levi's was less than three pounds, remember. I used to be paid about a fiver a week but I'd always make two or three times that from tips and the oil scam. I kept a big tower of loose change on top of the gas fire at home, with instructions to my mam to help herself any time she wanted to. Of course she never did. Neither did my dad, for that matter. It was always there, same place, same height, same wobbly tapering shape, half-crowns at the bottom and tanners at the top, never disturbed. I wouldn't be surprised if she dusted round it.

Money was fab: it meant freedom and independence. It meant Levi's, Ben Sherman's and ox-blood brogues, clothes your friends admired, new clothes, bought for cash instead of the cast-offs and Parrish's Wranglers they mocked you for. It meant brown ale and dry cider. It opened the door to girls. I could buy drinks to impress then. And something more: knowing I'd earned it myself gave me a good feeling when I spent it. The beer seemed to taste that much better. Nothing tasted better than the first pint of the day, earned by my own honest graft, my own sweat and effort. I was fifteen and no longer poncing off my parents. I began to understand how working for a living builds your self-esteem and helps you define your value to and place within society, however lowly the work might be. It was a good feeling and I'm thankful it's never gone away.

I've tried to explain this to pals who make their living on the wrong side of the law but they won't have it. It's not because, as some would have you believe, some people are just born bad: that's bollocks, in my humble opinion. Most of my pals were driven by insecurity and fear, specifically the fear of being judged unfavourably by others, and, worst of all, the fear of failing, and being seen to fail. Because humiliation would automatically follow.

There was a single-minded determination among my friends to avoid being assessed, tested, judged. 'Here comes the job interview, what will I do?' I've been there: anxiety, palpitations, racing pulse, nausea and fear sit like bile in the pit of your stomach. It's real and sometimes unbearable. Turning to crime in order to avoid having to punch the clock banishes any possibility of being judged – unless you count the law courts. They are an unavoidable staging-post for many, who end up being judged in a way they often loudly denounce but tacitly accept. It's a lifestyle that breeds contempt towards the man in the street, the tax-payer, the ordinary Joe who knuckles down and plays the game by society's rules. I have no time for those who choose such a lifestyle, but it's rooted in the same fear of failure that's driven me all my life.

The local pub where I spent most of my teen time was the Sun Inn. George, the manager, was a tall, thin, fussy man with slicked-down dyed black hair and a pencil moustache. He turned a blind eye to our under-age drinking as long as things didn't get out of hand, which, of course, they did all the time. There was always some fool standing on top of a nice slippery Formica table-top singing and shouting. Then someone would get bored with the impromptu floorshow, give the entertainer a shove, he'd take a tumble and a punch-up would ensue. All the familiar faces hung out there, all my pals, and new ones, too. Lads from Longbenton I'd not met before. The crowd I'd grown up with relocated from the streets to the pubs.

Although our house was no more than a hundred yards from my pal Tom McCulloch's, the county boundary line ran between the two, separating our estate from his; we were on the Newcastle side, he the Northumberland. He'd attended the Thomas Addison School, where a young Peter Beardsley was a few years behind him. I'd sometimes go down the bank into Longbenton with Tom and hang out with his mates. Most were in work, so we all had a few bob to spend on drink and clobber. There were no drugs around – or not to my knowledge. The Longbenton lads were an unusual crowd, mob-handed yet fiercely individual, tough, loud and often eccentric in their choice of dress, their manner and language, all struggling to find their identity, their place in the world, just like me. Gambling was a big thing with a lot of those lads. I'm glad to say it's never interested me. Betting talk, five-threes and short heads, was and still is a mystery to me, and I struggle to place my annual futile flutter on the Grand National. I'd often see lads putting the entire contents of their wage packet on a dog at Brough Park, only to tear up the betting slip after the race had been run and the chosen mutt had failed to do the business. Dejected and prickly, they would spend the next seven days cadging pennies from pals who'd either been a little luckier or a little more sensible than themselves. Beer was always there to ease the pain, make things feel better and punctuate those frequent gaps in the conversation. Someone would always stand you a pint.

We all had our favourite bands. As it was the early 1970s, there was plenty to choose from. I was listening to a lot of chart stuff at the time, radio-play singles, until I met Chad Shepherd. A mate of Tom's from Thomas Addison, Chad was a walking pop-music encyclopaedia, a one-man music-knowledge bank. His tastes have mellowed over the years, but what he didn't know about the music of that time wasn't worth knowing, ditto what he didn't like. He'd often be singing obscure things I'd never heard of – Frank Zappa's *Willy The Pimp* was one such gem. I bought the album on the strength of Chad's singing it and was mesmerized. Where on earth did Chad hear those cuts? At the Rex Hotel in Whitley Bay, where a disc jockey would travel up once a week from Liverpool just to play them. Free was another band whose work Chad seemed to know back to front. Out I went and bought *Tons Of Sobs*. On getting the album home and listening to it on my catalogue stereo system, I discovered, among a host of delights, the vocal talents of Paul Rogers and the incomparable bass-playing of the man who became my all-time favourite, Andy Frazer.

After a glorious, wild and lucrative six months on the petrol pumps with my pal Tommy, I saw it would make sense to have a trade under my belt and applied for a job as an apprentice at C. A. Parsons, Engineers. In the early part of the twentieth century Charles Parsons had designed and built the very first turbine installed within a Royal Navy vessel, the aptly named *Turbinia*. The fledgling company quickly established itself as a world leader in turbine-powered propulsion and was employing ten thousand people when I started work there in 1970. The turbines themselves were an awesome sight, with their high-carbon steel blades splaying out several metres, glinting in the sunlight and reaching up towards the high roofs of the huge cathedral-like sheds that housed them. Like big industrial catherine wheels, they were. The casings and housings were structures in which you could easily have hidden a fleet of double-decker buses. The place was an institution locally, nationally and internationally, known to one and all; it embodied everything the North East stood for in the eyes of the world.

They gave me a job as an apprentice welder and I hated it from day one.

Around this time, coming up to my sixteenth birthday, I performed my first ever gig – sort of. For years I'd been throttling a broom handle in the bedroom while Tommy banged biscuit tins with knitting-needles, and we'd convinced ourselves we were the next whoever, but the thought of making the quantum leap on to a live stage, singing into a real microphone in front of a crowd of people I didn't know, was terrifying. Yet one day when I was asked by Chris Saint, the son of our family doctor, if I was up for singing with his band at a gig they'd lined up at a youth club in Gosforth, I said yes straight away. I had to, really. I couldn't keep telling all my pals I was going to join a band and conquer the world, then bottle it when the first opportunity arose. I knew all of the songs they were planning to play: 'The Hunter', 'Johnny B. Good', 'Hi-Ho, Silver Lining', that type of thing.

On the night I took the stage and we were off, no time to worry. I struck a pose, closed my eyes and sang the songs as best I could, risking only an occasional peep at the sparse crowd. Much to my relief, there was no adverse reaction. There was hardly a reaction at all, but that was fine by me. All I cared about that night was eliciting no adverse response. I made it through and wasn't put off trying again.

Punching the clock, arriving on time: I could never bring myself to do it. I don't know why. I was the same throughout my schooling. Maybe I just loathed people telling me what I had to do, and conforming. Maybe it was stubbornness. I know I'm not like that today and, thankfully, I'm beyond having to clock in. Mind you, I still have to report to wherever it is I'm filming at a time of someone else's choosing, but it doesn't bug me the way it used to. The film business has shown me the importance of punctuality. Back in my teens, I didn't see it and couldn't bring myself to obey that ticking master. I was always late, two minutes, three minutes, five minutes, but never early. I was always there, too: I was never off for a day or two like a lot of the other blokes.

I'd been offered a welding apprenticeship, a much-coveted gig and one that would guarantee me, as a qualified trades-man, a job for life. Welding was not something I'd wanted to do and I found the prospect of messing around with heavy plant and thick sheet-metal daunting and off-putting, but as I didn't know what I did want to do I thought I'd better take the offer. In fact, nothing else was on offer and I had to earn and make some kind of plan for the future. Dreams were one thing, but reality was more pressing. Time-served welders were in demand all over the world, which at the time struck me as glamorous. Working abroad would be like touring with a band, I convinced myself. I so wanted to go *somewhere*, and having a trade behind me would enable me to do that. I had an urge to move on, move out, escape my surroundings and do certain things differently from my parents and their generation. The way the Animals had.

It was just as important not to do certain things my parents had done. I wasn't alone in this, or so I thought. Lots of my pals talked about joining bands, heading down to London, making loads of money and even travelling the world. Harry Baldwin and Johnny Fail had been to London with a band and had a go. Most of it was just talk, of course, usually dismissed with cruel cynicism by the older men. We regarded them as spineless old bastards who'd never dared to have a go at living their now long-dead dreams. Most of the older men didn't want you even to try – that was more than some of them could bear.

One old guy, Jock, was the exception: he was always critical of the moaners and cynics. He could see them for what they mostly were: envious, and bitter about their own lot. He'd explain to me how the whole system was geared to the working man's disadvantage. I don't know what his politics were as he never spoke about party allegiances, but he was always encouraging me to get out there and get away: there was a better life to be had elsewhere. He was convinced I was too bright for a life spent in the factory. Maybe my reluctance to toe the line had something to do with it, but he kept on about how, if I didn't make a move, I'd become one of those old cynics. The prospect of that scenario scared me into activity.

For the first few years of my time at Parsons I worked in a place called the Bart shop, a long, narrow, single-storey building split down its length by a dividing wall. We had one half of the building and the fitters and turners the other. I have no idea why the place was given that name but it must have had some kind of engineering relevance. Our half was an experimental set-up where the welding and metallurgical work was concerned with NDT (non-destructive testing) relating to fault-finding within the finished welds and seams.

The turbines, once operational, had to be able to withstand thousands of pounds in pressure so we would test new welding rods, fluxes, heat procedures and so on.

The man in charge was Terry Allen, a likeable young guy, who was much kinder to me than he had any cause to be. He was ably assisted in his labours by an assortment of white-collar oddballs, among them Dave the Scot who liked a drink or ten, Tony from Staines, who rather than bring himself to say 'shit' would laboriously pronounce 'S H one T', and John Batey, another lovely local guy who told me possibly the worst joke I've heard in my life. There were two blue-collar guys in there: welders John Bell, ex-Navy, old school, grumpy, much older than me, and Rob Brown, a quietly spoken lad with a mop of curly hair and a couple of years on me.

I'd not had any experience of working with blokes in managerial positions like Scots Dave, who often came in extremely hung-over. These guys liked to have a laugh at work, talk about music and stuff I could relate to. They were older than I was, but there wasn't the generation gap. By and large they liked the same music as I did. They made the workplace fun. I was right at the bottom of the food chain, of course, and always in trouble over my time-keeping, but it was interesting work, thought-provoking and challenging, with day-release for an engineering qualification on Wednesdays that took me over the Tyne to Hebburn Technical College, near to where my dad worked at Reyrolle's. I really enjoyed the work, especially the investigative side: maybe the future television cop was showing signs of stirring.

Parsons confused me: it represented both security and entrapment. There was a job for life, should you want it. Understandably, an awful lot of lads did. But that long-term life-plan was not what I was looking for and it scared me. I was tempted to follow a long tradition of notable escapees. Local legend had it that Animals vocalist Eric Burdon had worked a lathe at Parsons, and Brian Johnson after him. Brian scored a couple of bona-fide hits with his band, Geordie, and he was gone. He reached even loftier peaks a decade later with AC/DC. No more punching the clock for him. In terms of making it, that was good enough for me.

My time-keeping continued to be atrocious. I hated getting out of bed so much that I developed a system to fool my mam, who was always up well before me due to her constant chronic back pain. She'd shout up the stairs to me and I'd swear I was up. Then she'd shout that she couldn't hear me walking around, and I would lean out over the edge of the bed and thump my fist on the floor to replicate the sound of walking. 'There, I'm up,' I'd lie.

'No, you're not,' she'd reply. 'You're thumping the floor with your hand!'

So it would go every weekday morning. It would have been so much easier just to get up.

Getting the bus to work at six forty-five every morning was never fun, and it was almost unbearable if there were no seats downstairs: that meant going upstairs into the smoke-filled haze of the top deck where the workmen, and women employed as cleaners, sat puffing away on their first fags of the day. The air was so polluted you could hardly see the back of the bus from the top of the stairs at the front end. The combination of stale sweat, cigarette smoke and cheap hair lacquer made me feel sick.

My days at Parsons were spent welding pipes and eating in the subsidized canteen, where the guys met up for a bite and a natter. A lot of them would make the dash to the nearest boozer, the Turbinia, but it was too much of a rush for me so I never did. I couldn't see the point of giving myself indigestion for the sake of a couple of pints and, besides, I never felt like doing anything in the afternoon once I'd had a drink.

I had to catch the bus in the mornings but I'd often walk the couple of miles home in the evenings, happy, singing to myself, up the Benfield Road, which became Coach Lane, then left after passing the Northern Counties College where I'd broken my elbow a few years earlier, on to Fairways estate and home. I remember walking into the front room one day when I was about seventeen to find we'd finally landed a colour television courtesy of Radio Rentals. The programme being broadcast as I walked in was *The Land of the Giants*, and had American space travellers togged out in red costumes wandering around overgrown gardens in lush green under-growth. I stood there for ages, staring at the multi-coloured kaleidoscope in the corner. I couldn't believe my eyes. It felt like we'd just caught up with all that had happened in the 1960s. Better late than never.

After a couple of fairly leisurely years in the Bart shop I transferred to the auxiliary shop, where the turbines were assembled. I was now on the shop floor and, this being the 1970s, had to join the union. As a research and development area, the Bart shop was beyond its reach. Off I went to see big Ted Gallagher, the Boilermakers' shop-steward, whose son, Mickey, was a good pal. I'd come to know him through another school pal, Lewis Wilkinson. I thought my friendship with Mickey would cut some ice with big Ted but I was mistaken.

Ted was a fearsome bugger, six feet plus and square-shouldered. He took his union duties very seriously. I had to do the same – and union membership was essential. The unions were very powerful and you did as you were told. A union ticket meant the difference between being able to work and not. Never mind if an employer offered you a job: if the members of a trade union didn't want you in, you weren't allowed in. After a while I got my ticket and slept a little easier.

By day, apprentice welder; by night, full-on paid-up music nut. Other than the one night a week I stayed in to watch *The Old Grey Whistle Test* on BBC2, with 'Whispering' Bob Harris introducing some of the best bands and music to be heard, I'd be in from work by four thirty and out again by six thirty every evening looking for music, adventure and fun. During my apprenticeship, unlike in my petrol-pumping days when my pockets seemed always to be full of change, I didn't have much dosh, but a quid still went an awful long way: you could buy eight pints of beer with enough change for the late bus home. That journey was an adventure in itself, with punch-ups galore and people jumping out of the upstairs exit door at the rear just to save the walk down the stairs.

A gallon of beer for a quid! That's a cheap headache by anyone's standards. With the drink came confidence. With the confidence came social interaction. The city centre became my playground, its pubs my watering-holes. The cast of characters ranged from openly gay barmen at the Chancellor's Head pub in the Bigg Market, which must have taken some bottle, to Homburg-wearing spivs in the Grapes Vaults, and thousands of colourful individuals in between.

The boozers were always jam-packed, with music blaring out of the jukeboxes. The atmosphere was highly charged and fights would often break out, but they'd be over in minutes. My social train was beginning to roll and something was needed to oil the wheels. Over the next few years I went from drinking moderate amounts, three or four beers a night, to extremes. Thank goodness I never developed a taste for spirits or I would have been in real trouble. Some of my pals developed serious health problems because of the amount of drink they put away but they were in the minority back then.

The 1970s had seen pop become rock and groups become bands. It was a more strident, aggressive genre, which suited this angry young man down to the ground, although there were many notable exceptions. A lot of people tend to credit bands like the Rolling Stones, the Who and Led Zeppelin for toughening up and supercharging pop music, causing it to metamorphose into what's now called rock. They were all rock 'n' roll revolutionaries, but if you listen to the Beatles' *circa* 1964 rendition of the Tamla Motown cut 'Money (That's What I Want)' – credited, coincidentally, to a Mr Bradford – you'll hear big chords whacked out and hanging in the air, courtesy of George Harrison, long before Keith Richards, Jimmy Page and Pete Townshend took up the cudgels.

4

Tommy McCulloch, Ray Black and I went anywhere and everywhere to see live bands both good and bad, but the number one venue for full-on rock 'n' roll, the metal Mecca, was the Mayfair ballroom. A thirties-era city-centre dancehall, this two-storey wallpapered palace played host to every band that made a mark in the 1970s and quite a few that didn't. This was a time when great bands were out there playing live; the music was mostly thrilling, occasionally transcendent, always entertaining, and on consecutive Friday nights for almost a decade I was lucky enough to catch, in no particular order, David Bowie, wearing shorts so short his bollocks were visible; Mark Bolan, sitting on a rug on the stage with an acoustic Tyrannosaurus Rex; Queen, with a very young Freddie Mercury cavorting around in an ermine-trimmed cloak and a bejewelled crown, supporting the James Gang featuring Joe Walsh on guitar; the Irish blues-rocker Rory Gallagher; the mighty Led Zeppelin; from America, Spirit, a three-piece featuring guitarist Randy California and bald drummer Ed Cassidy; the Sensational – and they were – Alex Harvey Band, featuring a pierrot-painted Zal Cleminson on guitar; Arthur Brown's Time Machine (he was completely crazy, got stuck in a plastic test-tube, set his hair alight) with Andy Summers on guitar; the Baker-Gurvitz Army, with Cream's Ginger Baker on drums and the Guns' Adrian Gurvitz, who split the arse of his tight white loons almost immediately he came onstage, on guitar; Jeff Beck, one of the truly outstanding electric guitarists of the era; Black

Oak Arkansas, with their bare-chested singer Jim Dandy; the Red Indian rockers Redbone; Deep Purple, with Ian Gilmore on vocals and the barmy Ritchie Blackmore on guitar; Jon Hiseman's Colosseum; Quintessence, and their semi-hit single, 'Gungami', on the back of which they toured for years; Blodwyn Pig; the Savoy Brown Blues Band; AC/DC, who were always the best night out, had the biggest riffs and were so loud they rattled your fillings; wonder guitarist Nils Lofgren; his boss, the great Neil Young, a true rocker; Free, one of the best of them all, with Paul Rogers on vocals, Paul Kossoff on guitar, Simon Kirke on traps and Andy Frazer on bass; Bad Company, with Rogers and Kirk; Back Street Crawler, with Kossoff; Terry Reid's River; from Ireland, Skid Row, featuring a very young Gary Moore; Thin Lizzy, with Phil Lynott on bass guitar, what a really lovely man he was; heavy rockers Hawkwind, with their Silver Machine; Climax Blues Band, beautifully losing their sense of direction; Vinegar Joe, featuring Elkie Brookes and the late Robert Palmer; twin-guitar riffers Wishbone Ash; Nazareth, with gravel-voiced Dan McCafferty up front; Family, with raging Roger Chapman on lead vocals and step-ladders, a set of which he threw into the crowd one night in a fit of temper because the riggers weren't finished in time – I was right at the front and they bounced off my napper; American rockers Cheap Trick; Patto, with Mike Patto on vocals and the amazing Ollie Halsall on guitar; Head, Hands & Feet with guitarist Albert Lee; and Alvin Lee's Ten Years After. It was a roll-call of great rockers and a cornucopia of eclectic electric styles and vocal hybrids. It was like the Woodstock festival landing on Tyneside every week. Occasionally the local Odeon would play host to some visiting big-shots like the Who or Pink Floyd. The Who turning all their stage-lights on the audience at the finale, 'See Me, Feel Me', was one of the great tingly moments.

Then there were all the local bands: Raw Spirit; Blondie, with Keith Fisher on drums, who became Yellow; Sneeze, with their cover of Spirit's 'I Got A Line On You, Babe' and Rod Foggan on vocals – he sounded great and really looked the part; Brass Alley, later Long Vehicle, with Dave Ditchburn on vocals; the wonderful Junco Partners, R&B-meisters, veterans of the Club à Go-Go; and the Sect, with lead guitarist Deck Rootham, the daddy of 'em all and a real hero to Tommy and me.

Those were the people who shaped my thinking at this time. The way I dressed, the places I hung out, the people I hung out with came from the music. Loons were the order of the day and I had a pair – skin-tight, bright red satin. I was built like a stick-insect before all the drink put pounds on me so I could get into them, but getting out of them or taking a leak was a right carry-on. Out we'd go on the drink and at closing time we'd head to the Mayfair for the main band kicking off around eleven. We'd often sneak in the back way, through the fire doors, but I came a cropper one night when I got caught and the bouncers dished out a severe whacking; one smashed my jaw with the brass-balled end of a walking cane. The blow was so hard I saw stars and came to on the deck a little later. Trevor was with me, and when the police arrived for their nightly look-see he tried to explain what had happened, but they just assumed I was drunk and started slapping my face to bring me round. That hurt. I was arrested for being drunk and disorderly, the one-size-fits-all charge of the day, and later fined.

The other thing about going round the back of the Mayfair was it gave you a chance to see the trucks. Huge artics from Edwin Shirley Trucking or Trans Am Trucking would be backed up against the lift doors. To me they symbolized the power and glory of rock 'n' roll, those great automotive beasts, in the employ of rockers and rollers and booked to take the tools of their trade, amps, guitars and drums, around the country and beyond to facilitate the nightly creation of electric rock music. How we dreamed of being out on the road with our own trucks. The idea seemed impossibly ambitious, but people like us were doing it, and there they were, up on stage, just a few feet away from us. Later on I'd come to realize how far those few feet actually were, and how unlike us, in terms of musical talent, those guys were, but the important thing was that they inspired us, and many like us, to get a guitar and have a go.

I bought my first electric guitar when I was sixteen, a walnut-finish Gibson SG, for £170 on the drip from Dixon's Music in the city centre. Did the classic: brought it home and tried to plug it into the wall-socket. I didn't realize you needed a load of other gear to make a noise. I couldn't afford an amp or combo so I rigged it through my stereo system. It overloaded the speakers something awful but it sounded great to me and I spent many a happy hour attempting to play along with my favourite albums. *Led Zeppelin II* was a good 'un for that, T. Rex's *Electric Warrior* another.

For my first taste of mega-rocking, who better than Black Sabbath to introduce me to the world of ultra-loud music? Their breakthrough single 'Paranoid' was just out and Ozzy Osbourne and his merry men were breaking big everywhere. They were also forging a brand-new genre: heavy metal. People who know Ozzy only through his recent reality-television incarnation probably have no idea how immensely influential he has been.

Off we went, Tom and I, to the Mayfair, got there nice and early and waited right at the front for the Sabs to appear. The Mayfair had a revolving stage with a flat wall running the width of the turning circle, a relic from the era of the dancebands with their tiers of players. Tom and I were waiting patiently when the stage began to rotate and Ozzy and the Sabs were revealed. Big cheers. So far, so good. After a moment Ozzy counted them in with the traditional 'One, two, three, four . . .' and they began their set with the loudest noise I'd ever heard in my life. It's difficult to describe the volume levels the Sabs were working with then. The only sound that comes vaguely close to it is the noise a 747 makes right at the point of maximum reverse thrust just after it lands. I was standing right up against the banks of WEM speakers and bass bins and the racket made me feel unwell. We thought we knew all about decibel levels, what with the local bands we were used to, but this was on another level – it was beyond beyond. I've never heard anything so loud before or since, thank God.

There were also quite a lot of fights, Friday night scraps – 'Who the fuck are you looking at, pal?' and the like – almost always fuelled by drink and usually over nowt. People got their teeth kicked in, their eyes blackened, or their noses broken. My mate Denny Harwood famously lost the end of his nose in a punch-up. He took it out of the guy's gob and carried it off to hospital where they sewed it back on. That was an exception, though. Most of the time it was confined to fisticuffs.

What we got up to seems tame by the sad standards of today. Bitten-off noses apart, there was never any wounding for wounding's sake: knives were considered cowardly, and guns were unheard of. If you were really unlucky you might end up with a glass in your face, as happened to my pal Tommy. I was at home one evening when there was a knock on the door. I opened it to see him standing there, the left side of his face wide open and pouring blood. He'd been in a punch-up at the Newton Park pub and in the heat of battle one of his pals had accidentally whacked a beer glass into his face. I called an ambulance and he was taken off to hospital to have it darned, but he was left with a terrible scar. In that same fight big Peter Knox took a flying dive at some poor unfortunate, missed them, landed on a table and flattened it.

An even more terrifying experience involving Tommy occurred on a trip to the Lake District. We'd taken off with some pals for a nice wet weekend but Tommy was sporting a fully wired broken jaw, the result of a fight we'd all been involved in some weeks before. It was both gruesome and impressive to behold, a latticework of thin metal strands running between his teeth and gums. He'd been told by the doctors he'd have to wear the wires for six weeks or so. Food had to be mulched and consumed through a straw. On no account must he drink alcohol. If he were to vomit he'd choke, simple as that. Not even a fool would risk going on the bevvy in those circumstances, would they?

There we were, in a lovely old hotel bar by the shore of Lake Windermere enjoying a beer in front of a big open fire. By this time Tommy had managed to work open the wires a little so he could put a straw or a sodden bit of sandwich through the gap in his teeth, but he couldn't resist a pint, or two. Suddenly he went all quiet. 'I'ng gonga ge hick!' he spluttered. 'You'g got to get theve wirev off!' He started to retch, so I ran to the reception desk, no more than a glorified counter, told the man we had an emergency on our hands and did he have any pliers? He shook his head, bemused. 'There's these,' he said, and held up a pair of mole-grips, a type of adjustable pliers with vice-like square-ended jaws.

I grabbed them from him and ran back to the bar where Tommy was choking. I held his head back, stuck the mole-grips into his mouth, fastened on to one of the metal clasps and heaved as hard as I could. Tommy yelled as the wire gave way. I ripped out another, then another, until they were all done. By now there was blood everywhere but we'd averted a catastrophe. Tommy never went back to the hospital to get his jaw rewired, and he never was sick.

I broke some bones in my face when I dived at someone and missed them one night. I collided with a concrete post, breaking my nose and shattering my cheekbones. I was so anaesthetized by alcohol I wasn't intending to go to hospital to get my mush mended until Tommy had a look at the state of it and told me I really needed to go. That gives you an indication of the amount of drink I used to get through. The doctor on duty held up the X-rays of my face. My cheekbones were in bits. It was a little scary. I asked what they could do and was told the bones had to knit back together in their own time. They offered to reset my nose but it would have meant breaking it again, so I passed on that. The doctor warned me that once the bruising disappeared my injuries would be very painful. I laughed like a tough guy.

A few days later the bruising had passed, and I was climbing the walls with the worst pain I have ever suffered, so bad I had to call the emergency doctor, who prescribed Distalgesic, a pain-killer, which was useless. I could have done with morphine but they never dished it out in those days. There was one alternative, though, a medicine not only readily available but proven to work – hadn't it worked when I'd given myself the injury? The drink got me through those days and weeks when nothing else was on offer and I was glad of it.

The worst injury I ever received, though, came when I was hit over the head with an axe – just a small one. One minute I was sitting on top of a guy punching his head – don't ask me why, I can't remember – and the next thing I was coming to in the middle of the main road just in time to see a double-decker bus bearing down on me. I got up and made the pavement, where a pal asked me what all the mess was down the back of my treasured Levi's buckskin jacket. I took it off and saw a trail of congealed blood. Mystified, I put my hand to my head and found to my horror that it was wide open. I walked up to the Royal Victoria Infirmary where the doctor told me the wound would need a lot of stitches. He pulled out some scissors to cut the hair from around the wound, but I stopped him: I wasn't willing to let him cut my hair, which was long and curly. They told me, 'No haircut, no stitches.'

I said, 'Fair enough,' and left, but the wound was bleeding so badly I had to go back and let them chop off my locks.

Such was the amount of alcohol I'd consumed that the next morning, a Saturday, I woke up having forgotten what had happened the night before. I raised myself up to get out of bed and – 'Uuah!' I screamed. The pillow was stuck to the back of my head. I flailed around, panic-stricken, and it flailed with me. My mam walked in, alarmed by the shouting, saw my head with the pillow stuck to it, and screamed. What an almighty racket. Gradually I got my bearings, remembered what had happened and managed to calm her. 'It's all right,' I told her, 'it's just where I got hit with an axe last night.' Cue more screams.

That passage might read like a scene out of a horror movie but it was a one-off. Regular punch-ups never struck me as anything out of the ordinary, but it has been pointed out to me that this is not the norm for most people – but that was how it was back then, young men letting off steam, and still is now, to some extent. Indeed, if anything it's got worse, with indiscriminate violent attacks replacing fights, and no one giving a shit about the elderly or the vulnerable or even about life itself. There's no respect for anyone or anything, and that saddens me.

In the Sun Inn I met a young lad who became a lifelong friend. I was in the back lounge one evening when a group came in and made for the bar. They were all tall, slim and blond, wore sealskin boots and spoke in a foreign, yet vaguely familiar tongue. It was immediately apparent they were not from Longbenton. They were trying to make George, the manager, aware of what they wanted and getting nowhere fast so I went over and asked if they needed any help. The one who had the best command of English told me they wanted beer. I reassured them that they'd come to the right place. What kind of beer? I asked. They conferred for a moment. What would I recommend? asked the spokesman. I suggested Newcastle Brown Ale. They all nodded. I ordered a round for them. George, all suspicious and beady, served it up. So, bevvies ordered, who was going to pay? Their spokesman asked me how much it was. I tried to explain it was 2/6d (12.5p) per bottle, but they seemed to be struggling with the maths. George was hovering, waiting to be paid. Their spokesman held out some notes and asked me to take what I needed. I explained I only needed a pound. They questioned this. The spokesman held up a pound note and pointed to the beers. 'For one of these, you get eight of these?' I nodded. Much excitement. It turned out they were Norwegians, from Bergen, on a two-week educational break. What an education they received over the next two weeks!

The spokesman's name was Sweinung Osebakken, which was quite a gobful for a lad like me – not used to words and names made up of more than two syllables. At seventeen, Sweinung was a year younger than me. On the face of it we didn't have much in common, but once we started talking about music and I learned he was the singer in a band, that was it: we were off. We and the Bergeners spent the next two weeks on the bevvy in Newcastle, cementing already strong

Anglo-Norwegian ties and having some right old laughs along the way. Norway has always been known as a great seafaring nation and lots of the visiting lads were bound for careers in either marine engineering or the North Sea oilfields and their itinerary reflected this. A surreal moment occurred as they were being given a guided tour around C. A. Parsons. Unaware of their presence, I was working away in the cavernous auxiliary shop. I lifted my welding mask and heard a lot of shouting and whooping coming from across the shop floor. Then, I saw all my new Norwegian mates giving me the thumbs-up, waving and shouting my name, much to the puzzlement of the Parsons management representatives.

At the end of their visit, Sweinung invited any of us who fancied it over to visit him in Bergen. I went the next year with Ray Black, via the Newcastle–Bergen ferry service, and we had the most wonderful time. What a breathtakingly beautiful place it is, with its fresh clean air, its deep lakes and majestic snow-capped mountains. Without exception, the Norwegian people were warm and welcoming, way beyond friendly, a direct consequence of Britain's assisting them in their fight against German occupation during the Second World War. They were immensely grateful for our help, and said so many times. We had a great time, with trips into the mountains, fishing in the fjords, canoeing on crystal-clear mountain lakes, skiing, water-skiing, walking and, very occasionally, a pint of beer. The reason it happened so rarely was the cost: a pint of lager set you back about four pounds, which was thirty-two times the price of a bottle of brown ale. Mind you, they weren't averse to getting round the problem with home-brewed hooch. A lot of people used to brew it in their baths. It was akin to swallowing fire.

Those two weeks had quite an impact on my life. Through the most unlikely introductions, we'd met a bunch of lads from a foreign land who turned out to be very much like ourselves. Our own small circle was widened, our experiences enhanced and our confidence boosted. We had met some foreigners and after two weeks of daft carry-on we had all come away the better for it. No one had been hurt, no one had gone missing. So began an unlikely love affair between me, Norway and its warm-hearted people, which continues to this day.

It was in 1971 that I got my first real taste of the entertainment business. One evening, as I stood at the bar of my other local, the Newton Park Hotel, I noticed a guy sitting in the corner. Nothing unusual in that, but he was no regular: short and thick-set, overweight, black hair, balding, tanned, polo-necked, covered in very heavy gelt and minding a large ledger. Believe me, this type of person didn't tend to use the Newton Park Hotel. If I'd had to make a guess as to his occupation I'd have said he was a Hollywood producer, and I would've been dead right. I asked the bar-flies who the guy in the corner was and was told by one that he was a film producer. Intrigued, I asked what the fuck he was doing in our pub. Was he lost? No, he was hiring. Extras. For his film. Putting folks' names in that ledger of his. I made my way over to him and volunteered. To my amazement I was accepted and told to report to an address in the city centre. My pay would be twenty pounds plus meals for a night's work. I would have done it for free.

I spent a week of nights hanging around in the cold and wet, and loved every second of it. The idea that you could get a full meal in the middle of the night struck me as wonderful. Back then I was always starving. The scene I was involved with took an age to shoot and I wondered why. After hours of farting around with lights and props and people, the star arrived, in a Rolls-Royce. Sheltered beneath an umbrella held for him by a minion, he walked through the scene with the director, a serious-looking little man sporting a flat cap and a beard. Michael Caine was a much bigger, beefier bugger than I'd thought he was. Not that I'd ever imagined meeting him, not in a million years, and not that I did, but I got really close to him that night, close enough to be impressed by the way he did his thing. He'd stand behind the cameras, staring ahead of himself into nothing, waiting under an umbrella for that moment when someone hollered, 'Action!' and everything changed: the real world stopped for a moment and pretendies began. Suddenly, all mean-eyed and square-jawed, he'd stride purposefully past me and my mate, Sid Butcher, and into the Oxford Galleries dancehall. God help whoever he was after. On no account were we to look at either him or the camera.

So, we did our scene, Sid, Michael and me. Again and again and again. I remember thinking, between takes, God, what a fuss, people picking little specks of fluff and dust off the star's jacket lapels. Why didn't he just do that himself? Lazy bastard. The director's name was Mike Hodges. Alan McKeown, Michael Caine's hairdresser, was sitting in the back of the Rolls-Royce. Later he and I worked on another production where I had a bit more to do.

Get Carter, the first movie to be shot entirely on location in Newcastle, came out not long after and went on to become a landmark British movie, the very finest of its genre, some film buffs say. A cold blue slice of tough *film-noir*, it's stood the test of time and depicts a long-gone industrial Tyneside. Unsurprisingly, I wasn't invited to the London première. I went along to see it at the pictures when it went on release in Newcastle. Suddenly, after about an hour into the film, there I was, tucked in behind Sid and opposite Michael. Then I was gone, and Michael had moved on. Talk about blink and you'll miss me! No matter, I could tell people, girls in particular, I was now in films. But so was half of Newcastle. Nobody gave a shit. I experienced my first taste of performance-related disappointment, but soon got over it. Along with everyone else who had worked as an extra on the movie, I filed the experience as one of those magical things that happen once in a while and forgot about it.

All in all, and punch-ups apart, the early 1970s were marvellous times. It was great for anyone like me who loved live music and dreamed of emulating the people up there on the stage. As you can only discover amplification and its power once I doubt anything like it will ever come round again.

I qualified as a welder, with a City and Guilds certificate to prove it, but left just before the statutory four years were up. I was fed up with it and wanted to do something else. One Sunday afternoon when I'd just returned from a second trip to Norway, I called in to the Sun Inn for a pint. I bumped into Chad Shepherd and we got to talking, catching up. When I asked him what he was up to, he told me he was off to London in a few hours' time to work down there. How about me, what was I doing? Nothing much, I said. I was at a loose end and skint. When Chad asked me if I wanted to go with him and his buddy, Tony Fleck, I thought, Why not? I went home and grabbed the bag I hadn't had time to unpack, gave my mam a hug, and I was off.

Chad's gig was plumbing. He'd landed a job on a site in South London and I got fixed up as a hod-carrier. That, dear reader, was the hardest of hard work, back-breaking. Nowadays cranes drop the pallets, each containing a thousand bricks, on to the scaffolds for the bricklayers to get stuck into, but back then it was a dozen at a time in a hod. That I could cope with, but there was a pressing problem I had to sort out. I had come back from Norway wearing clogs, which were the only shoes I had with me. Climbing a ladder in clogs with a hod on my shoulder was a recipe for disaster and I fell off a good many times. At the lunch break I blagged a sub from the site agent and got myself some boots.

For a while, we lived in Bayswater, West London, in a little terraced hotel just off Queensway where we shared a room with a single bed and a sink in it. I used to lay the wardrobe flat and kip in it until a maid came in one day and opened the wardrobe door. Gave her such a fright we were asked to leave. Bayswater was great: there were loads of pubs and plenty to do. There were girls, lots of them, but they came and went and nothing serious developed. We were always out pubbing and watching bands. Music-wise it was heaven: we were spoilt for choice.

There were all the big gigs happening, of course, but the real energy was coming out of the pubs and bars. We used to see one of the first pre-punk bands, the UK Subs, at least once a week. They had a regular gig in a pub basement near our hotel. They were electric, so exciting, and the place was always jammed. After all the fatuous pomp-rock of the early 1970s, when many musicians disappeared up their own oeuvres, nihilistic songs like '(I Wanna) Live In A Car' were a breath of fresh air. The Subs blew away the cobwebs, they didn't give a fuck, and neither did I. More than once and uninvited I jumped up and joined them on the stage, bawling into the microphone. The flame burned deep inside me and sooner or later it would have to be allowed either to burn bright or blow out.

After our eviction from bijou Bayswater we moved across the river to Mervan Road, Brixton, known to us all as the Geordie Embassy, an upstairs apartment occupied by Jimmy

Kit-Kat and Scotch Charlie. It was so named because anyone and everyone from our neck of the woods who was in town seemed to end up sleeping and often living there. Whenever there was a football match in London that involved Newcastle United you couldn't see the carpet for bodies. It was pointless planning anything on days like these and we didn't bother trying: we just went with the flow and the flowing beer. Brixton was a great place to live, and inevitably, there were punch-ups. It could get pretty hairy.

Chad never got involved with all the football-based rucking; he was just too sensible for that. My mate Ray Black was the same. And it got beyond mad sometimes. Once we drove a passenger train out of a station to escape some irate Arsenal fans, Brian Blackburn playing Casey Jones. Another time I jumped on to a fairground ride in Battersea to get away from some guys. Thinking I was safe, I gave them two fingers, only to find them waiting for me when the big-dipper ride came full circle. And I remember a scrap kicking off in the infamous Blind Beggar pub in London's East End, and people getting their heads thumped with pool balls.

Chad and I often used a boozer called the Prince of Wales, right on the main junction in Brixton, just up from the tube station and opposite the old town hall. There were some heavy-duty people in there and quite a few carried guns. We became friendly with a big Irish lad called Brendan and after that never got any grief from anyone. I did, however, have a nasty experience coming out of the tube late one night. As I hit the street a couple of blokes came at me, one of them wielding a crow-bar. The bottom edge of a crow-bar is very sharp indeed and this bloke was intent on sticking me. I got away without mishap, but I never found out what it was about.

Chelsea was another place Chad and I loved to have a

beer and a bite, and the King's Road on a Saturday afternoon was always lively, even before the punk explosion of 1976. Our favourite place was a restaurant called the Crockpot where we'd feast on beef Stroganoff and drink ourselves silly. We had plenty of work and plenty of cash. We were out every night of the week making merry. We'd sometimes hire a car and drive up to Newcastle for the weekend. Going home with some money in your pocket felt good: you could buy your round in the pub, pay your way, and look after your mam. You could hold your head up.

This was the pattern of my life for those few years, from 1974 to 1976, up and down from Newcastle to London, plenty of money, no ties, lots of fun, and very happy I was.

It's funny how you can't see certain things until you're outside or beyond them, at which point they become glaringly obvious. So it was in 1976, when I was twenty-two, a grown-up and a big kid at the same time. Immature is probably the best word for how I was. Selfish, too. I didn't give a shit about anything, including my own safety, and many a time risked my life trying to pull off some silly stunt to entertain my pals. Swinging Errol Flynn-style on a chandelier in an hotel one afternoon almost got me killed. But I'd been dodging the bullets, metaphorically speaking, for quite a while, thinking I was a clever shite, when in fact I was heading down a one-way street, sinking deeper and deeper into a morass of punch-ups and drink. Then the bomb dropped.

It was springtime when I was arrested in Sheffield for fighting. I was charged, found guilty and sentenced to four months in prison. Over the following summer, the hottest for more than a century, I spent twenty-three hours of every day locked in a tiny cell, witnessing and experiencing brutality, violence and hatred, served up and dished out by inmates and guards. I also met kindness and encouragement. Although I didn't know it at the time, those experiences did me good and have stayed with me for the rest of my life. The whole thing scared the shit out of me, that's for sure. Character-building, some might call it, and it was certainly that.

5

It was a Saturday night during the spring of 1976 and I'd been to a football match earlier in the day somewhere further south with a bunch of mates. We'd travelled down by rented van, about fifteen of us. On our way back we'd decided to spend the evening on the drink in Sheffield city centre before heading home up the M1. I can't remember a lot about that night, partly because of the amount I'd drunk, partly because it wasn't a particularly memorable night. We had a pub-crawl and a couple of punch-ups and that was that. One fight was pretty horrific with people getting thrown head-first into walls and such, but it had nothing to do with what supposedly happened later on.

I was arrested late on Saturday night, along with a couple of other lads from our travelling party, and charged with assaulting a guy in the street. I can't recall what I was supposed to have done to him and the police records on the case, hand-written back in those days, I'm told have been either lost or destroyed – but I hadn't done what I was later charged with: I hadn't chinned that guy. I maintain that to this day. I was taken in the back of a police van to a local nick and photo'd, fingerprinted and charged.

Having your fingerprints taken is one of the most degrading things imaginable; your hand is forced down on to a long thin inky pad then over on to the charge-sheet, again and again, until each digit is done. The policeman has to hold your hand in his. That wasn't nice, that contact with a member of the filth, as they were known to us lads. You can't get the indelible ink off your fingers, they don't allow you to wash it off, and it's all so bloody grubby. It's everywhere by the time they're done – up your arms, on your face, your dick, your clothes. It makes you feel like a criminal whether you are one or not.

At that point I did not consider myself to be a criminal, rather someone mistakenly arrested. As I'd never been in trouble for violence before I wasn't too worried. I figured the worst that could happen, if I were found guilty, which wasn't very likely, was I'd land a suspended sentence. But I wasn't guilty and I told them so. While I was waiting in a corridor of the police station to be locked up, a lift door opened and two uniformed policemen carried a plain-clothes officer out. His face was caved in, pulped, the way it might be if a person had been thrown head-first into a wall. It was a shocking, horrible sight. His carriers were promising they'd find the bastards responsible and when they did they'd not leave the nick alive. I believed them and counted my blessings. Things could've been a lot worse.

After a few hours of tile-counting in the cells I was released on to the street and expected to make my own way home. I can't remember how I got back to Newcastle – I must have caught an early-morning train, I guess – but I'd sobered up long before. Getting arrested tended to have that effect.

I had been charged with assault with intent to occasion actual bodily harm. At the time of my arrest I had informed the police officers that I was innocent and intended to deny the charge, so I was eventually summoned to appear at Sheffield Crown Court. I wasn't working at the time so I was granted legal aid. The barrister I was allocated by the court was an affable young man called Nathanson. He wore the wig and I was most impressed by the tradition and protocol. I told him what had happened and he said it would all be all right. If the jury found against me, which was highly unlikely in his learned opinion, it would be a slap on the wrist. Confirmation of what I'd thought. I felt fine about it all. At no time did I have the slightest inkling of what was about to happen.

I'd not told my parents anything about this in the woefully misguided assumption that either it would all blow over or I'd get off. They didn't need to know. If I'd told my mam it would have worried her sick – and unnecessarily: I was about to walk away from it a free man. I got there for the hearing on a Tuesday and, much to my surprise and dismay, was quickly found guilty, even though the lad I'd supposedly chinned said he thought it was me but he couldn't be sure. My features were distinctive even then: there wasn't another face like mine out there. Of course I'd failed to grasp the hopelessness of my plight. The plaintiff was a local lad. I was a marauding outsider, a hooligan, a dole-wallah, scum. Fair enough, I was sixteen stone at the time and must have looked scary to the ladies and gentlemen of the jury.

As I was innocent I showed no remorse. Surly, burly Jim, what a bloody pillock. If I'd had half a brain I would have admitted it, been contrite and thrown myself on the mercy of the court, but that wouldn't have been right – not the done thing when you're a big stupid tough guy who believes himself innocent. Also, it would have required quite an act of me, and I couldn't have pulled it off to save my life. I was far too shy – it may surprise you to learn that away from the job I'm a very shy person. Then another big shock to the system: the judge ordered me remanded in custody and sent to Armley jail in Leeds until the following Friday, when I'd be brought before him for sentencing. I couldn't believe it as I was led away down the stairs inside the dock. Only a couple of hours earlier I'd been sitting on the train having a beer. It felt like a bad dream.

Being put into prison is a demeaning process, deliberately so, I'm sure. You are stripped, both literally and metaphorically, and come out the other end as a number, with a bundle of clothes countless others have eaten, slept and come in. I spent the couple of days in Armley's grim surroundings feeling sorry for myself until I met a funny guy who had been handed a long custodial sentence for stealing milk off a doorstep, at least that was how he told it. He was on his way to Parkhurst on the Isle of Wight. The trial judge had called him an habitual offender and said a long jail term was the only suitable sentence. This guy made a persuasive point: you're not supposed to pay for the same crime twice in this country, yet when he was sentenced he received a longer stretch than he would have if he had been a first-time offender – his previous was taken into account. A moot point. An injustice? Maybe. But, wait a minute, what was I doing there? This was jail. I couldn't take it in. Those few days passed very slowly, but at last I was on my way back to Sheffield for sentencing. I wondered if my pals had been remanded. Never mind, it would all be over soon and I'd go home. Everyone I spoke to, from the milk-thief in the cell to the prison officers, said the same: the judge had given me a couple of days inside as a taster and would send me packing with a grave warning as to what would befall me if I broke the law again. After two nights on a wooden pillow I was ready to listen.

I was led up from the holding cells into the dock, feeling dirty, tired and embarrassed. At least it would all be done with in a couple of hours and I'd be on the train having a beer. I looked around the courtroom and was stunned to see my mam and dad sitting at the back looking concerned. My first thought was, How unusual. I'd never seen them out together before as a couple. How on earth had they found out about this?

If a judge starts his summing up with all the bad stuff you've done in your life, it's pretty certain he'll then move on to talk about your good side and you're looking at walking away with a stiff talking-to. If, on the other hand, he starts off with all the good stuff, you're invariably in trouble. And wouldn't you just know where this one started? After listening patiently to probationary reports about me, and after my brief, Mr Nathanson, had explained to the court that I had an offer of work in Saudi Arabia as a welding technician for an oil company called Aramco, which was true – although I'd lied about my age to get the gig and would probably have been rumbled long before I got there – his lordship gave his judgement. I'm sure he'd already made up his mind. It was indeed a pity to see such a bright and intelligent young man, from a good home and with honest working parents, in front of him on this most serious of charges, but the court simply could not have people running around the streets of Sheffield like Attila the Hun attacking innocent people. His voice had become a blur – it was like audio treacle. I couldn't hear him properly. Did he just say I had to go back to prison? For four months? I must be dreaming. It can't be happening.

No such luck. I was led back down the stairs and to the holding cells by the prison guards. They shook their heads. They were surprised, they told me. Not half as surprised as I was. I was in shock. I asked Mr Nathanson if he planned to appeal. He looked surprised and said, 'Appeal? I thought it went rather well.' I found out later that mine had been his first case.

I didn't think that day could get any worse, but I was wrong. My parents were allowed to speak to me briefly through a thick sheet of perforated Perspex before I was carted off to jail. I felt so bad about them being there I would rather not have spoken to them but in the circumstances I couldn't refuse. I had to sit there, in handcuffs, and watch as my beloved mother, then my father wept because of what I'd done. The sight of my dad crying threw me. You'd expect it of a mother at a time like that, but my dad was such a tough, hard man who never showed emotion and I couldn't imagine anything moving him to tears. Yet there he was, sitting in front of me in his crumpled old coat, sixty-two years old, weeping silently.

I was so ashamed of myself – I still am. Despite all they'd done for me, despite a safe home and all their loving kindness, I'd made it to the bottom of the barrel. They had supported me as best they could, always arguing my corner, but I'd proved them wrong and everyone else right. It was, without doubt, the lowest point in my life. But it was an important day in so much as I made a vow to myself: I would do anything and everything to ensure that I never again brought that kind of suffering upon my family.

I was told I'd have to spend the first couple of weeks in Armley from where I'd be transferred to Durham. Home Office rules state that a prisoner should be housed in the jail nearest to his home to make visiting easier for his family. At least that was something to look forward to. I can't remember anything about my time in Armley other than that I was there for a week before I was transferred – not to Durham but to Strangeways in Manchester. Trips to and from the different nicks on the prison buses were surreal. I felt like an extra in a prison movie, handcuffed to another con I didn't know. As far as the world outside was concerned, that's what I was now: a con.

Through the prison-van windows Strangeways looked daunting, grey and brutal, with a huge brick chimney rising hundreds of feet into the sky. It made me think of Nazi concentration camps as depicted on old newsreels.

Reception involved stripping off and having my clothes taken away. Someone looked up the crack of my arse to see if I was smuggling anything in, then it was a nit-check, a visit to a store where they gave me a prison uniform and that was it: I was inside. They didn't have any shoes that fitted me properly so I was given a pair that were far too big, cheap black slip-ons. That really upset me. It was one thing having to wear prison-issue clothing: having been boiled to near destruction it was anonymous. But those shoes stank of someone else. Who'd been wearing them before me? A rapist? A murderer? A child-killer? I've never been able to put on a pair of costume shoes. Instead I carry a large stock of my own footwear. It's a pain in the arse, but there you are. The odd time I've done period stuff I've simply taken off the hired footwear. Nobody's noticed.

Another Home Office rule was that short-term prisoners weren't supposed to be banged up with long-termers because it caused friction: it was too much of a wind-up for the long-termers to watch as cons serving short sentences came and went. In my case this rule went out of the window. Deliberately, I believe. I was put into a cell with a local Mancunian lad. He had a broad back, red hair and wild eyes, and paced the floor of the cell all day, every day. On my arrival he asked me what I was in for. I told him for fighting. He wanted to know the charge. Assault, I replied, but this was still not detailed enough for him. Was it ABH or GBH? I couldn't remember, but felt that wouldn't be an appropriate answer. I guessed GBH would cut more ice with him so I plumped for that. He nodded approvingly. I'd guessed right.

My respite, however, was short-lived. He wanted to know how long a stretch I was doing. Sitting on the edge of my bunk, head in hands, feeling hard-done-by and well sorry for myself, I told him the bad news. Four months, I said, and looked up, hoping for sympathy and understanding. Instead my cell-mate scowled.

'Four months? Four fucking months!' he snarled. His eyes seemed to be bulging.

'Why?' I asked. 'H-h-how long are you in for?'

'Six fucking years', he growled.

I fought to keep my eyebrows down. 'What for, if I might ask?'

He explained he'd been in the city centre with his wife having a drink and some guy had kept staring at her. He'd asked him to stop but the guy had continued to stare, so he'd gone out to his van, got his axe out of the back, re-entered the boozer and set about parting the guy's hair. I sat there in stunned silence, not knowing what to say. I decided it was best to say nothing.

I was introduced to prison routine and slang. I figured it would be sensible to keep my mouth shut, do exactly as I was told and learn fast. I queued for my meals three times a day. Open up in the mornings to slop out. Bang-up in the evenings. Lights out. Slopping out was by far the worst part. There were no toilets in the cells as there are today, just a bucket, so if you needed to crap you were supposed to use the bucket and empty it first thing the next morning. Most cons caught short in this manner would crap on to a newspaper, then throw it out of the cell window. Sometimes there'd be a low, dull thud, other times a squelchy splat. Certain cons would be assigned the truly wretched task of collecting up those gruesome projectiles every morning. I dread to think what they'd done to land such a gig. Trying to hit a guard with a shit-parcel was a regular pastime and a major talking-point. It did happen occasionally, a con would get lucky, a guard much less so, and there was talk of long-term psychological damage: prison officers seemed always to be on the look-out for a way to retire early on full pension.

Almost every day at the same time, just before lunch, my cell-mate followed a strange routine. He would grip the bars outside the tiny window and haul himself up so that his face was level with the bars. There he would remain, his heavily muscled arms shuddering with the effort of it, until he could sustain it no longer. Then he would fall to the floor, moaning and rubbing his aching biceps. For a long time I wondered what this was about but he never offered an explanation and I didn't have the bottle to ask him. But one day curiosity got the better of me.

What he showed me made me want to cry. When you looked out of the window you could see the prison's long perimeter wall receding from where we were. It was nearest, and therefore highest, to our bottom left, and as it ran back and up, towards our top right, it appeared lower, although this was an optical illusion. At its furthest point, however, you could see over the wall and on to a bit of the adjacent pavement. At an agreed time every day his wife would stand there with their little daughter and he could see them for as long as he hung on to the bars.

It made me think of Sarah, Val's little girl, who was about two, the only baby in the family. I worried about Sarah while I was locked up. There were some terrible types in there, sex offenders, child molesters, and although they were segregated for their own safety, just being near them made me worry about how safe Sarah was on the outside. In my letters home I wrote about the need for vigilance where she was concerned.

Sex offenders came in for awful treatment at the hands of the inmates and with the tacit approval of the warders. I once witnessed a man's head held under a scalding tap by some inmates as the warders looked on. He was screaming while everyone else laughed. It was gruesome and it was wrong. I've no time for sex offenders and their like, but no matter how bad their crime, it's not right for the mob to take the law into their own hands.

The governor of the day was a Bible-basher, apparently, and considered pin-ups to be against the will of God, so you could lose your remission for having a picture of a bird on the wall of your cell. He also had a thing about food: he felt the prison should be self-sustaining wherever possible so we baked our own bread. It was awful: each slice looked like a small beige roof-tile with a texture to match. It had the absorbent capability of Formica. It was of no use for mopping up your dinner gravy, but as there never was any gravy this wasn't a problem. Most of the guys gobbled it down, but not me. I'd been spoilt by all those lovely dinners, pastries and pies my mam made for me.

Another Home Office rule stipulated that inmates weren't to be given the same meal twice in succession. I went down to breakfast one morning, joined the queue and held out my pressed metal tray. A dollop of piping-hot slurry was deposited in one of the indentations, causing the tray to slew to one side. I stared at the steaming mess before me.

'Spaghetti?' I queried.

'That's right,' said the con serving it up, a tiny, rather nasty-looking queen.

'But we had spaghetti for dinner last night,' I said.

'Yeah,' says he, 'but it wasn't pink, was it?'

This was true. Pink food dye had been added to last night's leftovers. 'Waste not, want not,' as the saying goes. I was learning how rules and regulations were interpreted by those in power.

During the first week of my stint inside I cut into some mashed potato and hit a cockroach. I was pleased to see it was dead but it was a shock all the same. Oh, how I longed for one of my mam's Sunday dinners, with individual Yorkshire puddings balanced precariously on top of a mountain of roast beef, roast potatoes, peas, sprouts, carrots and gravy made from the juice of the joint. The cockroach did it for me, as far as prison food was concerned. From that moment until the day of my release I did my damnedest to eat only what I could afford to buy from the shop, which was usually a packet of Ryvita and a tub of Dairylea cheese per week, and whatever I was given by Tommy, the elderly maintenance fitter who looked after me with bits of grub. I lost two stone in the short time I was in there and without Tommy's generosity I would have been in an even worse state.

My first few weeks in Strangeways were unreal – I felt as if it wasn't happening to me. I wandered around in a kind of daze, looking at other cons in a detached, observing way. I was lucky no one gave me a clout. Then one day it hit me: you're in prison, this is all real, you can't go home when you want to, you're surrounded by rapists and murderers, bandits and other criminals and that's it. There's nothing you can do about it. Worse than that: in society's eyes you're one of them, just the same. The truth hit me like an anvil falling on to my shoulders. I was pretty near rock-bottom. But at least when you get there, there's only one way to go.

Strangeways was on twenty-three-hours-a-day bang-up back then, which meant I was in my cell for all but a single hour every day, which I spent walking around in circles in the exercise yard along with all the other inmates. This sub-human regime was against Home Office guidelines and led to constant tension and volatility among the prisoners, but it made life easier for the officers so that was how the nick was run. If you landed any gig that got you out of your cell for a few hours you were considered one of the lucky ones. I sewed mailbags for a couple of weeks, which was inadvertently hilarious as it resembled a scene straight out of an Ealing comedy, with a room full of tattooed, rock-jawed, beady-eyed villains trying to do delicate seams. Big thick hands, much better suited to throttling sub-postmasters, struggled to hold the tiny needles. I wanted to laugh, but of course I didn't dare. It would have been lights out for me. Then, because of my engineering background, I was put on to the prison works detail. I was nervous about this as I wasn't sure what I'd be asked to do and whether I'd be able to do it. The old fear of failure reared its head again.

Come Monday morning, all the inmates on works duty, twenty or so, were assembled on the wing. A senior prison officer called out the names and we were led away in groups of between two and six to different parts of the nick. I was taken down to the maintenance workshop, a small place with a low-level window and its own open front door. Crucially, it was beyond the wing and felt to me like the outside. The leathery-looking guy who ran things in there was called Tommy. He could only have been in his late forties but he seemed very old to me. He wasn't unlike my dad to look at, and they had the same wry smile and throaty laugh. Tommy was kind to me, which was way more than he was obliged to be, and that was precious: an act of human kindness was uncommon in that nick.

Tommy was a maintenance contractor rather than a prison officer, so the rules governing his employment were different. The prison's workshop was just like the cathedral-like fabrication shops at Parsons, though on a much-reduced scale. He'd have that morning's newspaper and would let me read it, an unbelievable treat. Best of all, though, he brought food in, ostensibly for his own consumption, and we'd cook it on his makeshift stove. A couple of rashers of bacon and an egg, with a bit of fried bread as well! Oh, my God! Talk about a life-saver.

The strangest thing Tommy knocked up on the stove was a kind of fondue: he crumbled a whole packet of cheese into a soup bowl, then added enough milk to submerge it. He placed the bowl on top of a pan of boiling water and the contents eventually turned into this gooey, bubbling mulch. Then we dipped bread into it with plenty of butter. It looked awful but to me it was the most wonderful dish I'd ever eaten and I gobbled it down gratefully. I tried not to gulp it too fast but Tommy knew I was starving. He'd laugh and tell me, 'Go on, Geordie, get it down you, son.' He had no need or ulterior motive to do these things for me. I had nothing to give him in return, other than my heartfelt thanks. It was purely an act of kindness on his part, and had he been caught giving me any of this stuff he would have been sacked, no doubt about that.

Because of the brutal nature of the regime, I rarely encountered much that resembled compassion. If you happen to be out there reading this, Tommy, your kindness made the difference and I thank you from the bottom of my heart.

The need to spend everything I earned (about ninety pence a week) on food meant I had to make some difficult decisions. For as long as I can remember I've always needed to start the day by cleaning my teeth. I can go without a shower if I have to, but I cannot function without a scrub of the old dominoes. Out of toothpaste one day, I had to decide between Colgate and Dairylea. I went for the Dairylea and figured I could use salt to clean my teeth. I did this until one day there was no salt, only some Vim-like sink scourer. Out of desperation I used it. As soon as I started brushing I knew I'd made a bad mistake. My gums bled and it took the top layer of enamel off my teeth. After that it was back to the salt.

There was the odd practical joke, and one day I found myself on the end of a good one. On the way to work one morning I overheard two inmates talking about how much they were looking forward to having chips with their dinner that evening. I asked them about it, and they told me about the protocol. Those on works duty could have chips with their meals any time they wished. They just had to put their name down with the prison officer at the end of the working day.

Chips! Oh, my God. My mouth watered and my guts rumbled at the prospect.

About ten hours later I was on the wing landing with all the other inmates on works detail, waiting for the roll call. The wing prison officer was a dead-ringer for Fulton McKay's Mr McKay from *Porridge*, tall, thin, ramrod straight, with his cap peak pulled down over his eyes. Just before the names were read out, I stepped forward and announced to him loud and clear that I'd like to put my name down for chips in the evenings. There was a moment's silence, during which I died a thousand deaths as the penny dropped. The other inmates were pissing themselves as the prison officer made his way towards me. 'Chips?' he asked.

I gave a half-hearted nod.

He looked at me from under his peak. 'Get back into the line before I have you sent down to the block!' he growled.

Food, or the lack of it, played a big part in my time inside. I was always hungry, and I'd fantasize about big dinners washed down with a half-decent mug of tea. Boy, was I going to have a slap-up meal when I got out. In the meantime, though, there was only the tasteless, inedible rubbish they served up three times a day, which I avoided – and was right to, never mind dead cockroaches.

I was taken into the kitchen one day, under guard, to

mend the belt chain on the bread oven. It ran trays of dough in and, moments later, baked bread out, conveyor-style. As I welded the broken link back together I could hear singing, and . . . splashing? Once I'd finished, I asked the screw with me where all the noise was coming from. 'It's just the kitchen cons, finishing up for the day,' he replied.

Job done, time to go, and we were walking back through the kitchen the way we'd come. As I rounded a corner I saw the big steam vats used to cook all the prison's vegetables. They looked like oversized kettle drums, but right then they were filled with naked inmates having a bath.

As a Newcastle United supporter I felt very alone in Strangeways. If I'd been in Durham I dare say I would have known a few other inmates but in Mancunian Strangeways I was on my own. It was all either City or United. It was also the first time anyone called me Geordie. I became friends with a little Irish lad, Davey, a hardened con who'd been inside before. He was a real tough nut from Ballymena and had an accent even thicker than mine. It wasn't the done thing to inquire too deeply into folks' past, but whoever he was and whatever he'd done, Davey was respected by everyone and given a lot of room.

He used to say, as did Tommy the maintenance man, that I shouldn't have been in there, and it was reassuring to hear, no matter who said it. The thought of coming back scared the living daylights out of me. Punch-ups were relatively rare, though, and I managed to keep myself out of trouble, except on one particular day. The works detail was walking along the inner perimeter of the jail in a kind of squad formation, ten men deep and five across or thereabouts. All of a sudden I got a kick up the arse. I turned round and saw a guy behind me with a bleached-blond mop. He made it clear he didn't wish to discuss it amicably. A little further on, he did it again.

This went on for a while with me trying to ignore it, desperate not to retaliate for fear of losing my remission. It was becoming impossible, though. Pretty soon I'd have to do something.

Then, just as I was about to turn and lamp the fucker, my pal Davey appeared and settled in next to me. 'All right, Geordie?' he asked.

I nodded, not wishing to involve anyone else.

Next thing I knew there was a crack and I looked behind me. The bleached-blond was lying on his back, out cold. He was picked up by the guards and thrown back into the formation. I never heard from him again.

As happened fairly regularly, I was moved into a different cell; this one contained two other guys. When the screws did this the resulting pressure-cooker atmosphere was intense. You were thrown into a cramped cell with total strangers guilty of God-knew-what, and everyone was unsettled. It often boiled over into violence. One of my new cell-mates was a really weird guy, a Londoner with lank dark hair and wild, staring eyes. He would stare at me for long periods, saying nothing. It was unnerving, especially trying to get to sleep. He'd mumble on about northerners, how they were all a bunch of fuckers and cunts. Ever fearful of doing anything that might result in losing remission and being locked up for one day more than I had to be, I said nothing. It was very stressful, just waiting for something to kick off. I was sure it would sooner or later. So I waited, trying to be as ready for it as I could be.

One day I came back from work to find the crazy-eyed guy was gone. He'd received a 'Dear John', slang for a lover's goodbye letter, and had apparently flipped out. You wouldn't normally wish a 'Dear John' on anyone but I was mightily relieved when I found out about it. He'd been put in a strait-jacket and sectioned. Hallelujah! After that the atmosphere picked up a bit.

A rare fond memory I have from my stint inside is of listening each Sunday night to a dramatized version of *Les Misérables* on Radio 4. I tuned in my tiny tranny and for an hour was transported from my cell to the streets of nineteenth-century France. The sound effects were simple but evocative: the clip-clop of pursuing soles and heels, the scraping sound of metal over stone as manhole covers were prised open. Jean Valjean led the law a merry dance week in, week out, and I was transfixed. The whole nick listened to the radio and the BBC was a lifeline in terms of keeping us up to date with the world outside. More than that, it *was* the world outside, and precious to us. The BBC was fast becoming an important accompaniment to all my ups and downs, just as it had been when I listened to all those voices and melodies as a kid at my aunts' house.

Years later I was offered the part of the Innkeeper in *Les Mis* and refused it, not because of the part, which was great, but because of the audience. I wasn't familiar with the show so I thought it a good idea to go and see it. Seats were hastily arranged. I went along one evening and was horrified at the behaviour of blue-rinsed American women, the bulk of the crowd, who called out to no one in particular whenever a thought entered their minds. It's the same when you go to see a movie in America, constant yak and natter. Anyway, come the death scene of one of the young lovers: hushed auditorium, backlit figures appearing in ghostly white behind gauze. Then, a great whoop as an American woman suddenly bellows, 'Oh, gee, a wedding!' That was enough for me. If I'd been on that stage I would have pelted her with anything to hand. As a revolutionary I might have been toting a chunk of rock, or a rifle with a bayonet! So, not a good idea, I figured. Best left.

At long last my short spell inside ended and it was time to go home. As it was August bank-holiday weekend I'd be getting out on the Friday morning with a number of other inmates. I never slept a wink the night before, yet when the time came to leave a great sadness came over me – not about my release, for I was desperate to be shot of the place and free again, but for all those who would remain behind, the innocent men I'd met, the friends I'd made. They'd be banged up in their poxy cells that night, and I even felt a bit guilty at having gained my liberty while they were left to languish. I dare say one or two of the poor bastards will be there still.

I was given back the clothes I'd been wearing on the day I was sent down, jeans, a leather jacket and, best of all, my own shoes. I pulled up the jeans, only to see them drop straight back down and come to rest round my ankles. Then I was handed my bits and pieces, along with a giro for about forty pounds and a travel warrant good for the train ride home to Geordieland. I was going home. I felt like I wanted to cry.

At nine a.m. they let us out. I'd dreamed of this moment for the last few months, imagined how sweet it would taste. With a single step I was back on the street, taking in all the traffic noise, breathing deep lungfuls of Mancunian air, walking away from that horrible prison and into the light morning drizzle. Suddenly music, which had all but left my life and my mind, entered my head and I started singing, very quietly, to myself. I crossed the road and reached the other side. It felt strange, as though I'd escaped. I half expected a voice to shout, 'Hoi! You!' It never came, though. I had a great urge to look back, to take one last glance at the place, but I wouldn't allow myself to do it.

All of a sudden I realized I didn't know which way I should be walking. I'd just followed all the other ex-cons as they crossed the road – that was what I was now and would always be. It turned out quite a few of the other lads were headed for the railway station. As I walked along the pavement with them, the most unpleasant prison officer I'd encountered inside was walking towards the main gates. This guy, his face clouded with bitter unpleasantness, had shown himself to be a sadistic, racist bully. As he walked towards his next shift, with his peaked cap pulled down over his eyes, his shoulders hunched against the wind and rain, he looked across the road. With a triumphant cackle, he shouted, at no one in particular, 'Ah, you'll be back.'

It almost stopped me in my tracks and sent a cold shiver down my spine. Was he right? Or was it just bile? Many of my companions fucked him off in short order, but not me. For the briefest of moments, that scumbag embodied the devil.

I looked at him and thought, No, mate, I'll not be back. I'll fucking die before I let that happen. I shouted it inside my head. I wanted the devil to hear my resolve.

6

On the train home I had a cold beer, which tasted very sweet indeed. Just the one, though. I was very aware of the danger drink might now pose. The last thing I needed was to get pissed, have another mindless punch-up and find myself back inside. Thoughts of returning home and how it would be were whizzing around in my head. My emotions were running like a rollercoaster. I determined to keep them in check and I was all right until the train pulled on to the high-level bridge and I caught sight of the Tyne, my river, with its big, broad, murky-grey waters and its old north bank, the quayside where I'd spent many happy childhood days. I broke down and cried.

My pal Ray was waiting for me at the station. His reaction on seeing me gave me a bit of a start. He was obviously shocked at the deterioration in my physical condition. Looking me up and down, he simply asked, 'Are you all right?'

I nodded, but the nod was a lie: I didn't feel all right. My head was certainly a long way from all right. I felt as though everyone was aware of where I'd been living for the past few months, as though I had a sign round my neck that read 'PRISON'. I hadn't and they weren't, of course, but such was the stigma that a spell in prison brought with it back then that I felt that way for months, if not years.

Also, I'd come back skint, a penniless failure, and my failure was major, big-time, there for all to see and have a good laugh at. The same thing had happened a few years earlier, after a hot, sweaty summer spent working in the kitchens of Torquay hotels. What had started out as a great idea in the pub had quickly ended in ignominy, with me returning home potless, reduced to begging and cadging from my parents and friends. I hadn't a penny to my name and I hated it. The fear of not being able to pay my way in life has always pushed me into action of one sort or another: I would do almost anything to avoid being in that situation. To my mind there is no worse feeling in the world than being on the end of hand-outs, no matter how well-meant. I'm not sure when it started, maybe with my mam and those pop bottles, but by this time the unbearable fear of being, or staying, poor was very powerful. Now it was as if everyone could see I had nothing to my name. Much better to be in the business of giving.

Illogically, this fear of ending up back at the bottom haunts and drives me still; it occupies ridiculous amounts of my everyday thoughts, even though in financial terms I'm beyond the need to worry. Even my dreams feature disasters that result in me going back to the north-east cap in hand, humbled and poor, to be mocked by all those I left behind for having had the temerity to give the fame game a shot. Smart Alec! Who did I think I was? Having spoken to various people about this over the years I know I'm not alone in feeling the way I do, but I'd much rather feel and dream differently.

Ray drove me to my sister's place in Whitley Bay, on the Newcastle coast. My mam was there with Val, my brother-in-law Mac and little Sarah. It was an emotional reunion with lots of tears. Not knowing what else to do for me, my mam had made me the most wonderful meal, as any mother might for their son in such circumstances, and she'd spent hours getting it all ready. Once I was seated she set it lovingly before me: a great dinner plate struggling to contain all of my favourite things, roast beef, roast potatoes, vegetables, gravy, all topped off with a load of little Yorkshire puddings. But after all those weeks living on near-starvation rations I found the sight of that food overwhelming and I couldn't eat it. She began to cry, wrongly assuming she'd failed me.

I left the house and went for a long walk in the rain. I walked for hours along roads and lanes, eventually returning when it was nearly dark. Then I had a couple of slices of toast spread with butter, a treat I'd been deprived of during my stint inside. I had tears in my eyes as the toast melted the butter and it ran down my fingers and either side of my mouth. Never has a bit of burnt bread tasted better.

I'd expected to have my hair cropped off in a basin cut when I was locked up but, thankfully, that hadn't happened. You could pretty much have it as long as you liked. I did get talking to the wing barber, though, a big, likeable lad called Tony, whose own hair was rapidly receding. Years later I met him at an AC/DC gig at the Wembley Arena. He was on security, and I was a guest of the band. I couldn't immediately place him and, out of courtesy, he didn't want to remind me. Then I remembered and we had a good old laugh about how things had changed. He wished me well and I him. Back on a hair note, I'd deliberately let my barnet grow in the hope that when I did get out I wouldn't look like an ex-con fresh out of the jug. Soon after I came home I went to a barber's in Newcastle city centre for a tidy-up but they made such a mess of it I ended up having a bloody basin cut to sort it out.

I was on my uppers. As hard as I tried – and, believe me, I did try – there was just no landing a job. It seemed that no one wanted to employ a guy fresh out of prison. If only I'd finished my apprenticeship at Parsons, I could have gone back on the tools. But towards the end of my time at the factory the welding had affected my vision so I was none too keen on revisiting it. I struggled to make ends meet – but there were some funny moments along the way.

After much bullshitting and fib-telling, I landed a gig pipe-fitting on the massive petrochemical plant at Seal Sands, near Middlesbrough. On the Monday I was given a set of plans with pipework information and left to get on with it. I was used to engineering drawings but not on this scale. The pipes were very small bore, nothing like the monsters I'd worked on as an apprentice, and were labyrinthine. I looked at the drawings, mystified, hoping to see something familiar. But they might as well have been written in Swahili. No matter, I'd busk it. I looked at the plans all morning and couldn't work out what was required. Then a load of fittings arrived. I looked at them for a long time, too. I was beginning to sweat. I'd hoped to be paired with someone who would help me get through the worst of it, but I was on my own.

Then I had an idea. There was a JCB working just outside the window of the room I was in, digging out a deep trench, making ready for the drains to be laid. I gathered up the fittings and, when I thought the driver wasn't looking, slung the lot out of the window and into the trench. Every time I received a delivery of fittings I simply slung them out of the window for the JCB to gobble up. The foreman visited occasionally and was puzzled that there had been no deliveries to this part of the site. I just shrugged. I got away with it for a fortnight before the inevitable. I was paid, though.

It was a lean time, when my parents helped me as best they could and Ray gave me a bit of work here and there, but time dragged, just like it had inside. The difference was I now understood the crime of wasted time. It was unbearable to be sitting around with nowt to do and no means of paying my way. I hadn't been the most driven of people before I was locked up, liked lazing around, lying in bed, but prison made me realize that wasting time was the biggest crime. It was my choice, in my hands, and from the moment I got out I was determined not to squander any more.

To this day I cannot sit around doing nothing. I find it hard to relax and chill out, although I'm a lot better than I was. It's a bit of a curse, and when it spills over into family life it causes arguments. The kids don't understand the precious nature of a moment, and why should they? They're young, and understanding comes with the passing of time.

I was a healthy, willing, able and reasonably sensible young man, who had nothing to do. I never once considered crime as a way forward. It just didn't seem sensible. Lots of my pals were criminals, but as hard as things were for me, it never appealed. For one thing, there was obviously much more effort involved in being a criminal than in staying on the straight and narrow. The returns were debatable and, after my recent spell indoors, the potential consequences unacceptable. As for the music, my dreams of making it with a band had all but evaporated. It seemed beyond the realms of possibility. Never mind a Lear jet, I couldn't afford a pair of shoes.

Around this time something happened to me that had a big effect on what I did, and how I did what I did, over the next few years. I was sitting alone in the upstairs room of the Burton House, a tiny city centre pub, one Friday night, with a tomato juice. I'd been off the drink since getting out of prison for fear of landing myself back inside. My pals must have thought I was nuts but I didn't care: I was really concerned about it. So there I was, all quiet and well behaved, nursing my drink and minding my own business, when someone put a record on the jukebox that turned my head right round and changed everything.

99

This track started, very loud, and I looked at the juke-box, unable to believe what I was hearing. It was as if the place had been hit by mortar fire. Just under three minutes later I walked out of the pub and on to the street, my body literally shaking with excitement and anxiety, my mind blown. I was in an altered state. It was scary. I'd had to clear out of there quickly as I honestly feared I might throw a table through a window. That was the effect this incredible cut had on me. The lyrics, mocking and scathing, had been spat out with undisguised hatred; the incendiary guitars, like detonating bombs at the chorus, seemed to sum up exactly how I felt. I went back in and looked at the credits. The track was called 'Anarchy In The UK'. The band was the Sex Pistols.

Soon I'd learned about what I'd missed that summer, the punk explosion, the safety-pins, the ripped clothes, and the new bands, the Pistols, the Clash, the Damned. There'd been a full-blown revolution and I'd missed it! At least, I'd missed the beginning. The whole punk ethos suited me down to the ground. I was thrilled there was a movement out there whose prime motivation seemed to be 'wreck and destroy', and I bought into it with the zeal of the religious convert.

All the smashing and banging was right up my street and the swearing was music to my ears. I've always cursed and sworn a lot, and although I've toned it down over the years I was worse than any trooper back then. Of course, I wasn't actually doing any damage, I was too worried about getting banged up again, but that night my heart and soul were won over. It wasn't so much that my attitude changed, more that a whole swathe of society had caught on and caught up. They felt the same as I did. But my 'FUCK OFF!' T-shirt was a statement too far for most of the pubs on Tyneside, and I felt I had to get back to London. Before I could, though, I met two Geordie brothers whose antics, in their own way, were as anarchic as anything the Pistols came up with.

Joe and John Watson were a couple of real rough diamonds, tough cookies out of Shieldfield with no airs or graces; Joe was the elder by a couple of years. He was a glazier specializing in leaded and stained-glass windows and had always wanted to strike out on his own but hadn't the means: in the late 1950s the banks and lending institutions weren't as keen on handing out money to blue-collar grafters as they are today. John was a coachbuilder at the Co-op, but he hated mending the milk floats, the reek of sour milk knocking him cockly. I'm sure that was how things would have stayed had John not won the pools. It wasn't a massive win, in the thousands, but it was enough for him to give Joe the stake he needed.

Joe set up on his own, trading as Jos. Watson, Glazing Contractor, and from the humblest beginnings, which saw him carrying bits of glass on the bus as he had no other means of transport, he built the business into a large and successful concern. By the time I was washed up on their shores he and John were steaming ahead, employing a couple of dozen. And what a workforce! More eccentric than any motley mob ever dreamed up in a work of fiction.

There were Syd and Billy, the two pensioners perched above the bait cabin with all the leaded-window gear. Looking like the two elderly buffers, Waldorf and Stadler, from *The Muppets*, they'd peer down on us plebs in the factory below and sneak a nap whenever they thought they could get away with it. Billy, who'd worked as a manager in a past life, considered his current employment beneath him and was particularly grumpy.

Then there were the glaziers: dodgepots Bob Smith and Terry Matfen, the likely lads; Charlie Ollie; John 'Rowley'

Carter, who had, by a long chalk, the worst-smelling arse in the world; miserable John Sutton, a.k.a. Sooty, with his full set of gleaming white false teeth; silver-haired, hot-water-drinking Harry Sellars, who'd always backed the day's big winner but never provided proof with a betting slip. Based in the factory were little Tommy Miller, foreman John Muckle and chippie Billy Dixon, star turns all of them.

Then there was John Watson, or Sir John as we called him, by his own admission the oldest swinger in town; and, to top it all, madcap Joe, with his look of constant surprise, his big mug of tea swilling and spilling and his thick-rimmed glasses forever sliding down his nose. Whenever I watch Ozzy Osbourne in his reality series on the box I'm reminded of Joe. In both facial expression and bad language, Ozzy's a dead-ringer for my former boss. Every day was an adventure, a crash course in merriment. Best of all, the crack was incredible. In time, all this stuff would find its way on to the telly. But I'm getting ahead of myself.

When I was released from prison my mate Ray Black was working for his brother-in-law, Jimmy the Ripper, at the woodcraft shop on Chillingham Road. The bulk of their work was in remodelling doors, cutting out the inner wood and inserting in its place glass panels. There was a huge demand for them and Ray was kept busy. His brother-in-law bought all his glass from Watson's so Ray was down there two or three times a week. Compared to how most factories were run, discipline in the Watson domain was non-existent, or seemed to be. In its place there was a kind of organized chaos. Ray became good friends with the Watson brothers, particularly John, who was single.

I met the brothers one Saturday afternoon in the bar of the Heaton Buffs club. Ray had set it all up, had mentioned his pal to them, told them of how he was down on his luck and needed a break. I remember that afternoon clearly: I had not a penny to my name, and was terrified in case someone asked me to get a round of drinks in. The Watsons looked for all the world like a couple of tramps. Joe had on a shabby old cardigan, covered with bits of putty, and a pair of jeans with turn-ups so high they reached his knees. John was different: he was altogether more crusty. I was confused, because Ray had told me they were wealthy, maybe even millionaires. They were both slightly deaf and wore hearing-aids which weren't always in full working order, so the pair were in the habit of shouting. The first thing Joe ever said to me, in a very loud voice, was, 'Ginger says you've been in jail for bashing people up. Is that right?'

It sounded so awful but that was how it was, whether I liked it or not. I nodded. The whole bar was looking at me. They couldn't have failed to hear. I felt like a leper. I think it must have been some kind of test, that Joe wanted to see how I reacted. Goodness knows how I came over.

Joe told me that Ray, whom he and John always called Ginger on account of his red hair, had mentioned I was looking for a job and had assured them I was a straight-up, honest lad. Was that right, he asked. I nodded again, grateful for the testimonial. Ray was going out on a limb for me here and I was determined not to make him look like a fool. I wouldn't let him down.

Joe looked at me over his thick glasses, up and down, then he looked at John. It was crunch time. John shrugged an affirmative. Joe looked at me again. Did I want to come down on Monday morning and sweep the factory floor? The pay would be a couple of quid a day.

Did I? Oh, boy! Yes, I did, I said, and thanked them for the opportunity. I'd sweep their floor cleaner than it had ever been swept before. I was ecstatic. It was the first positive thing to happen for me since I'd got out of jail, the first time someone outside my circle of family and friends had shown a little faith in me. The Watsons knew my background and were willing to take a chance on me. They didn't need to, these two wealthy brothers, but they had. It was only sweeping the floor, but what a boost it gave my self-confidence.

One more thing happened that day, which said a great deal about Joe. As he was leaving he came over to me. Very quietly, without anyone seeing, he pressed a five-pound note into my hand.

I started at the glass factory on a Monday morning in late 1976 and remained there, off and on, right up to 1982. I received an indication of how it would be one day in that first week. I was sent out in a van to help John 'Rowley' Carter with a delivery. We had to drop off a large number of double-glazed units for a man called Wakinshaw. I accident-ally pinged – broke – one of the units while putting it down. I was crestfallen: I'd only been in the job a matter of days and I was certain I'd be sacked when Joe heard what had happened. They'd consider me a liability. Rowley told me to forget about it: he'd say it was pinged when we went to get it off the van. When we got back to the factory I found Joe waiting for me. He already knew about the broken unit and whose fault it was. Mr Wakinshaw had kindly called up and told him all about it. As it was lunch-time we all went into the little office where everyone sat down to eat. Joe put the kettle on. Rowley told him exactly what had happened. Joe asked me about it and I told him it was down to me, then waited for the inevitable.

John, sitting there with his tea, said to Joe, 'So, Wakie rang you up and shopped the lad, did he?'

'Aye,' said Joe.

An awfully long pause followed as I wondered where and how I'd get another job, then John said, 'Fuck him!'

To my amazement, Joe replied, 'Aye,' then got to his feet and left the room.

I was confused. Were they referring to me or Mr Wakinshaw? This bloke was a long-standing customer, and I'd been there all of two days.

It turned out they had meant him, and he was never made welcome there again, certainly not by me. There had been no need for him to shop me the way he had and, luckily for me, the Watson brothers didn't like it. I'd been honest with them and they appreciated that. It was a valuable lesson in how I should conduct myself in those parts and with those people, and a lesson in the virtue of being straight. It felt strange to put my trust in the boss, but I recognized goodness and responded in kind.

Watson's was a place were fairness was the order of the day. As long as you could do something you were allowed to get on and do it. Of course, not everyone was interested and thrived the way I did, but the opportunity was there if you wanted to take it. It didn't matter who you knew, or who your father was. Not only were you allowed to take on all kinds of different challenges, you were actively encouraged to. For me encouragement is the single most important thing we can give to others, especially those younger than ourselves.

Joe would often, half jokingly, tell stroppy customers they'd better behave themselves because I'd been in prison for fighting. Although I found it hard at first, this out-in-the-open approach eventually took away the awkwardness I felt about my recent past.

In no time at all I went from sweeping floors to cutting glass, making leaded windows, installing plate-glass shopfronts, bevelling and polishing edges, cutting out circles and drilling tiny holes. It was fantastic: the work was interesting and challenging, with no union or management bullshit. Joe was respected by all the guys under him because he'd done it the hard way. Those years were the best working times of my life – and I include all the jobs I've had since. It was a revelation to find a place where you could have such a laugh with the boss. He'd have a beer after work, he'd drop you off on your way home, he'd loan you a van or even his car. He'd even accompany the workforce on trips to the races at Gosforth Park. Over the next few years Joe Watson became almost like a father to me. I appreciate the patience he showed me and his sound advice.

With the confidence, job security and personal encouragement the Watsons gave me I was soon back to my best – or worst: I was back on the drink, and this time with a vengeance. I felt once again as if there was ground to make up and went for it big-time. The fighting had finished a long time ago – or, at least, the kind of mindless mayhem I'd been involved with before. My days of traipsing around the country with the football crowd were over. I was almost a model citizen. I didn't want anything to happen that might cost me my job. I loved working at Watson's. But try as I might, I could never quite shake off the bother. I'd woken up to the simple fact that it was wrong, but the sheer enjoyment I got from the taste of beer was another matter entirely and it was a thirst impossible to quench, although I did try. Drinking heavily made me more inclined to argue, with anyone, so that was the problem – and it *was* a problem. For someone like me, drink was never the best way of staying calm. It's worth noting, I think, that I was never one of those poor souls who could neither live with the drink nor without it. I could and often did go for weeks without a pint, but more often than not I was on the sauce.

The quantities were not only daunting but downright dangerous. I'd think nothing of downing sixteen pints over the course of an evening. That's two gallons, or ten litres. As we all know, a litre of water weighs a kilo, so my poor body was taking on board up to ten kilos of chemical-loaded lager every twenty-four hours. And I'd wonder why I felt rough some mornings. I put it down to the flu, never the drink, an early example of self-delusion and denial, which became a recurring theme where drink was concerned. Today I'd struggle to carry ten litres of alcohol, never mind drink it, but back then I thought myself immortal. I bounced off moving cars and fell off high walls without so much as a scratch. Never a day off sick. With the drinking came more extrovert behaviour: I was a loud bugger at the best of times and must have been an intimidating sight when in full, foul-mouthed flow. But I was happy, and slowly getting back to where I'd been before I got locked up.

John Watson was a one-off, absolutely unique. He had never married and was a confirmed bachelor with a lifestyle that revolved around beer and dancing, which he loved. His wealth ran to many hundreds of thousands, but he'd as soon fly to the moon as go on a luxury holiday or buy something luxurious. He couldn't stand what he considered to be osten-tation, flash. To him, money represented primarily security, and I think that rubbed off on me, though I have no problem with burning a large hole in the stuff. John wasn't big on personal hygiene, not fond of washing, so he was a bit of a minger, truth to tell, a crusty old dinosaur from a bygone age. His digs were dreadful, beyond imagination. It would have taken a flame-thrower to clean them properly. But he had a priceless turn of phrase any poet would have been proud to call his or her own, and he'd often reduce us all to tears with the rough-edged, blue beauty of his language. It's difficult for me to describe his gift with the written word, as it was all about the sound of the words he'd choose – I based and modelled an awful lot of Oz in *Auf Wiedersehen, Pet* on John, and although I never dared to tell him I think he had an inkling. And all this wonderful wordplay was no accident. John knew fine well what he was doing and the effect it had on people, and he derived as much pleasure from it as anyone else. His natural gift for emphasizing certain syllables, his speech-rhythms and cadences, all wrapped as they were in the broadest Geordie brogue, transformed the most mundane sentence into something hilarious.

I made a lot of money while I was working with John, although it was peanuts compared to what I was earning from television a few years later. John was in charge of the factory floor and he looked after all the glass supply orders. As it was a builders' environment, there were always lots of cash transactions. Some days would see us take hundreds of pounds at the till, and occasionally it ran to thousands. John paid me a daily bonus, in cash, depending on how much we'd sold that day. It was usually twenty pounds, but often much more. It was hard-earned, though: we got through caseloads of glass. We often raced each other to see who could get through the orders fastest. I loved that side of the job, the sporting challenge. And John always had his radio blaring the current hits, so the days fair flew. On top of my weekly wage, around £150 take-home, I'd make at least that much again in bonuses. Add to that the money I made from jobs at weekends and I'd be regularly trousering up to £500 per week, a lot of money for a single bloke in his early twenties and an absolute fortune compared to where I'd been a year or so before. I always had at least a hundred quid in my pocket for emergencies.

The name 'Nail' was bestowed on me by John Watson. I

was atop a big case of glass one day, newly arrived from the USA and needing to be racked in the big bays at the north end of the factory. The crowbar was the best way to get those things opened and I set to. The big wooden side of the crate fell to the floor taking a good bit of straw packing with it. I hopped down and landed in the worst place possible: on the edge of the lid. Because of the straw I couldn't see what was underneath and I impaled myself on a six-inch spike. It went straight through my foot and out the top. I made quite a noise and John ambled over. He looked at this peculiar sight, then laughed. 'Ah,' he said, 'the nail!' From that day on I was known as the Nail. It became my nickname. As I wasn't working officially at the time I told the hospital, to which I went for a tetanus jab, that I'd had a gardening accident.

Another incident that everyone has sad cause to remember illustrates just how special John was, and Joe, for that matter. I was on my way to work on a grey December morning, travelling by taxi, having slept in. Just before we arrived at the glass factory the cabbie turned to me and said, 'Have you heard about John Lennon getting shot?' Still half asleep, I assumed it was one of those dreadful cabbies' jokes. I said, 'Go on, then,' and waited for the crap punch-line. But there wasn't one. The guy just said, 'He's dead.' Like everyone else around the world, I was shocked, stunned and sickened by the news. With John Lennon's murder the world became a little darker and a whole lot poorer for his passing.

For those, like myself, whose lives were inextricably entwined with the music of the Beatles, it was a traumatic event. That day a part of my big dream died. I felt as though I'd lost a brother. Oh, other stars had passed away, lots of them, and some who'd been influential in the musical and cultural revolution of the 1960s, legends like Brian Jones,

Jim Morrison and Jimi Hendrix, but when John Lennon, a man who'd spent a lot of time and money campaigning for peace, and whose 'Make Love, Not War' message had had an impact on my own thinking, was brutally killed as he signed an autograph for Mark David Chapman, it seemed as though an era had ended, and that maybe the opportunity for me to break free was now lost. Much as I loved the punk movement, John Lennon's death depressed me.

At the factory I found a dejected-looking John sitting alone on the cutting bench. Next to him was a bottle of Harvey's Bristol Cream and a cup. The radio, turned up even louder than usual, was blasting out Lennon and Beatles songs. John Watson was a real music-lover, and the Beatles were his favourite band. Our working days revolved around music and the mood was greatly informed by whatever sounds emitted from the radio.

Without a word, John handed me the cup and I took a slug. For a long time we just stood there. It seemed such a waste of a special life. There was no anger, just sadness. John was unequivocal as to how we should properly pay our respects: there would be no work that day. People came in for glass only to be told by John that we'd not be serving. He got quite cross with disgruntled builders but he felt that in the circumstances working was out of the question. It would have been disrespectful to the great man's memory, and that was that. It's a day I'll never forget, one unique John honouring another.

John and Joe Watson, two brothers I met in a pub, looked out for me and looked after me when I was most in need of a leg up. They'd taken chances with kids before and had their fingers burnt, but they saw something in me they thought worth encouraging and had faith in me when no one else did. I like to think I repaid that faith in all I achieved later on. I know they both got a lot of pleasure out of telling customers about my working on the cutting benches. A few years after *Auf Wiedersehen, Pet* I even went back and spent a happy day cutting glass for old times' sake. I learned so much from them and I consider myself a better, more rounded human being for having known them and their kindness, compassion and encouragement. Proper Geordies, great blokes both.

As much as I loved working at the glass factory, I was still dreaming my big dreams, so when Rob Lockhart, a pal from Manor Park schooldays, suggested we go to London and put a band together, I jumped at the chance. Not only did the Watsons give me their blessing, they told me my job would always be there for me, and even sold me one of their company vans, a Commer commercial with the engine in the cab – *that* turned out to be a mixed blessing! As the singer I needed a mike and a PA system. By rights the band should have split the cost of that but no one else had any money, so my dad loaned me £600 – he had recently been made redundant and that was most of what he had left from his pay-off – and I put in the rest towards a big loud rig. Rob and I managed to talk Colin Stuart, a pal of ours who'd been the drummer with a local band, Greenie, into coming with us – much to our disappointment, my pal Tommy didn't fancy moving his drums away from home. After a year or so with the Watsons I set off for London to make it as a rock 'n' roll star.

We had the use of a house in Glebe Street, Chiswick, owned by the mother of a very bonny girl Rob was friendly with called Sabrina, and we all lived there. We began rehearsing above a pub on the river and took on a talented bass player called Gary. It was very exciting. I was now in a bona-fide band and sometimes we sounded really good, but we were playing R&B music, a hard sell at that time with punk ruling the roost. Maybe if we'd stuck at it a little longer we'd have made some headway but we all enjoyed our beds and the drink too much. We liked the idea of being in a band but not the day-to-day reality.

I was out one evening at the Lyceum ballroom, watching a show featuring guitarist Chris Spedding, when I met Johnny Rotten. He was just about the hottest star on earth and I was amazed he'd take time out to talk to me, but he did, and he was a scream, dead funny. We had a few drinks and I told him of the effect that 'Anarchy In The UK' had had on me in the pub a year or so before. At the end of the evening he gave me a telephone number and said I should give him a call. I did, and was amazed to hear his voice at the end of the line. We went out on the drink a few times and things got pretty lively once or twice. Our unlikely friendship ended when he pulled out a wood-handled corkscrew one evening and waved it in my face. I took it off him and told him he should be a bit more careful who he waved it at: it might get stuck up his arse. I don't think he liked that much.

That summer of 1977, the year of the Queen's Silver Jubilee, I received an unwelcome blast from the past. There were street parties going on everywhere with flags fluttering, booze and food aplenty. I'd somehow ended up in Fulham. I was in a bar, on my own but having a lovely old time on the drink. As I lifted yet another pint of Young's Ram and Special to my lips I clocked a guy standing with a team of maybe half a dozen across the room. He clocked me at the same time. For what seemed an eternity but was probably no more than seconds we stood there, trying to remember who the other was, trying to place the face.

Then it hit me. It was my Cockney friend from Strangeways, the Geordie-hater. Thankfully, I got there a moment before he did. I dropped my pint on the floor and ran from the bar. He was after me in a flash – they were all after me. We were out in the road now and I was running as fast as I could, passing all the smiling happy people. I had no idea where I was going. It was near dark. I felt sick with all the beer I'd drunk that day, but I had to keep running. I could hear their feet clattering along behind me, hear their voices, gruff Cockney voices, saying, 'We'll catch him! We'll fucking kill the cunt! He's slowing down – we'll have him any minute!' It felt as though I was running through treacle, and they were right, I was slowing down. They'd be on top of me any second. Was this where I was destined to die? In the gutter of a London street, hundreds of miles from the safety of my own city and my home?

I made it to the end of a street, rounded the corner and careered into a group of young men and women, smartly togged out in formal evening dress and clearly pissed. At my impact they cheered and tumbled backwards. They were going into the main entrance of a mansion block. There was a party going on somewhere inside. They invited me along and I gratefully bundled myself through the double doors. I was gasping for breath but my new pals seemed oblivious to my state.

Moments later I was in an elegant apartment with a load more well-dressed folk, all staggering around singing 'God Save the Queen', the traditional version. There was a stack of beer cans standing about six feet high and I was told to help myself, get stuck in. A well-spoken young man offered me a canapé from a silver platter so I tucked into a cocktail sausage with a bit of pineapple. Just moments earlier I'd been running for my life, and now this. It was an odd end to a scary encounter.

After a valiant effort, the band came to nothing and we were all potless. It was an experience I'd known before, and I still didn't like the feeling one bit, especially after having had plenty of money in my pocket not long before. We ended up doing removals, carting furniture around in the Commer van. As a last resort we decided to try to get work on the US bases in Europe. Colin had played them, knew the circuit and the agents, but their needs were different from our dreams. The first thing they stipulated was that we had to have a female singer, something for the GIs to look at, so we took on an American girl who was living in London. Gaye Perez was a tiny, bleached-blonde, fighting plump, prom-queen type, a Mormon, and completely bonkers. Soon after joining up with us she announced that there would be a period every month, lasting about a week, when she wouldn't be able to sing. That made planning gigs difficult. Another time, she lost her voice and insisted the only way to get it back was to have it blessed by the local Mormon cleric. Rob and I shook our heads, but Colin took her round to the tabernacle where the guy did his thing and she came back cured.

The hoped-for gigs on the US bases didn't materialize, but we wanted to keep the band going. We ended up going home to the North East, where we did some gigs in the clubs, but the band fizzled out. I was disappointed: for someone who'd long nurtured a dream of making it in the music business it was a let-down. But we were right in the middle of the punk explosion: if we'd followed our instincts, sacked the bird and taken the band down a more raucous, riotous road, goodness knows where we might have ended up.

I went back to working with John and Joe Watson at the glass factory but it wasn't long before Rob and I were making plans for another band, and this time it was going to rock. We'd make sure of that from day one.

In the late 1970s I made a great leap forward in terms of my own personal security. At that time there was a boom in the north-eastern housing market. Older Tyneside properties without any mod cons or even inside toilets were at long last being brought up to date with money from the local council. Renovation grants were plentiful and lots of houses were being done up and sold on at a healthy profit. Many of the builders who bought their glass from Watson's were in on the boom and Ray thought it would be a good idea to get on the bandwagon. I agreed with him, but how? Where would we start and, more importantly, what would we use for money?

As luck would have it, my sister Val, who'd gone from teaching English and drama to presenting local radio programmes for – you guessed it – the BBC, wanted to get rid of a pair of Tyneside flats she and her husband owned in Sandringham Road, their first marital home. South Gosforth was a desirable neck of the woods in which to own property. Val had a couple of young kids to bring up, and although working on the radio was cool, the pay at Radio Newcastle wouldn't have been all that much. On top of that, she's always had strong socialist beliefs and I think maybe the idea of being a landlord didn't sit comfortably with her. I had no such scruples: I saw a chance to get ahead and grabbed it gratefully.

Sandringham Road is made up of terraced properties on either side of the road, brick-built under slate roofs, converted into flats, two-bedroomed downstairs and three-bedroomed upstairs. My sister was looking for the princely sum of £4000 for the pair, a ludicrous amount nowadays but a lot to us back then. We were determined to get on the property ladder so we mustered a couple of grand deposit from our savings and Val kindly allowed us to pay the rest in instalments. We were now landlords and, using the deeds to the flats as collateral, we borrowed and bought more. Soon we had quite a few places dotted around town. A few years later we sold those flats for £40,000, a ten-fold profit, and felt we'd made a killing, which we had, I suppose – but when you consider those same flats now sell for anything up to £150,000 each, we'd have done better to hang on to them. I loved the challenge of doing up those old places and I'd have been quite happy as a property developer. I still dabble, but back then fortune or just plain good luck had me marked down for something other than landlording.

7

Another nasty accident in the glass factory marked the time I met someone who would change my life beyond recognition. It was the spring of 1980 and I was taking a sheet of Deep Flemish glass, notorious within the trade for its unpredictability, off a delivery wagon when it shattered. I had a piece of rubber between my hand and the glass but when the sheet went, with a loud crack, it sheered straight through and took off most of my little finger. There was blood everywhere and the bone was clearly visible, so I was off to the hospital. I hated going up there, always felt such a lead-swinger, but it was a Saturday morning, which meant I could go straight from Casualty to the pub and watch *Grandstand*.

I duly reported to the Royal Victoria Infirmary and a nurse darned my finger with the greatest care. I was in there for over an hour. Then, suitably stitched up and bandaged, I made my way across town to the Portland Arms, my regular city-centre watering-hole. Pint in hand and paper tucked under one arm, I sat down in the corner by the window. The sport was on the television. I lifted my beer to my mouth for that first gulp of the day and felt a rapid ping-ping-ping as, one by one, the stitches burst. More blood everywhere, and back to the hospital. The nurse was none too pleased to see me back so soon. Once she'd restitched me she put an aluminium splint over my finger, which looked great but was a right bugger to live with. I had it on my finger the day I met Miriam.

Miriam Elizabeth Jones had come to Newcastle from her home in Caerphilly, South Wales, to study for a degree in creative art. She was just twenty when we met and was as different from me as it was possible to be. She was petite, gentle and delicate; I was big, clumsy and rough. She was fair; I was dark. She was well-spoken and articulate; I was foul-mouthed and tongue-tied. She was pretty; I was most definitely not. She was reasonable; I was unreasonable. She was civilized; I was not. She was placid and non-violent; I was aggressive and violent. She was middle class; I was working class. Miriam always thought before passing comment; I just opened my gob and ploughed right in. She was considerate; I was inconsiderate. Unlike anyone else I knew, she was completely non-judgemental. I was the opposite. If you're thinking I've gone overboard here and that I'm describing some kind of saintly superwoman, you'd be dead right. She was, and is, exactly that. Anyone who knows me well will attest to two things: that I've changed beyond all recognition since I met Miriam, and that that change has been for the better.

She was, by a country mile, the loveliest human being I had ever met, and after twenty-four years I still regard meeting Miriam as the best thing that ever happened to me. Why was the chemistry right with Miriam, and not with any of the other women I'd met? Why was I, of all people, the one for her? I can't offer up a reasoned answer, and I suspect that no one really knows why these things go the way they do. I just got extremely lucky. Again. I'm certain I'll never feel such a depth of love for anyone else and I don't want to put it to the test. If you love someone and they feel the same way about you, then you are truly blessed. Whatever I amount to, whatever I've achieved, it's because of her. Without Miriam I'd be nothing.

In retrospect I see that this was the beginning of a golden

period in my life. Those five years between 1977 and 1982 were extraordinary. Working for the wonderful Watson brothers was a lot of fun and gave me the opportunity to regain some desperately needed self-esteem. Entering into a relationship with Miriam, which proved all the doubters wrong in that it endured, gave me enormous self-confidence. She always encouraged my constant stream of ideas where others rushed to dismiss them as either hare-brained or beyond me. If someone as lovely and eminently sensible as Miriam had faith in me, and that faith was real, I could move mountains. Anything was possible.

Like many a long-lasting relationship, ours wasn't blessed with the greatest start. Miriam was working in the bar I used as a local, the Millstone in South Gosforth. The place has changed now, it's all open-plan and brass on the walls, but back then it was a basic bar with a dartboard and some seats. There was a lounge and a snug, but the bar was where you went to drink and curse so that was pretty much where I lived for a few years. How Miriam ever got past those first few encounters I'll never know. As I was getting through about sixteen pints a night, God knows what I talked about. But talk I did, because I fancied this lass behind the bar. That she seemed unaware of me only made her more desirable. Then I never dreamed we'd still be together twenty-four years later, with two fine sons, a cat and a house on top of the hill. I'm pretty sure she didn't either – no, I know it for a fact. The very idea of me, six foot three and a half of hooligan, shacking up with five foot five inches of art student was beyond the realm of possibility. Back then, it was beyond anyone's imagining, with one notable exception.

Her hair was the first thing I noticed, that lovely long fair hair. It reached all the way down to her bum. She had a boyfriend at the time, a nice guy called Mark to whom I took an instant dislike, but that was on the way out before she and I became an item – as they now term the process of getting to know and love someone.

On 28 June 1980 I went along to Miriam's twenty-first birthday party in Jesmond with a crate of beer and big Peter Knox – that one notable exception and a friend to us both. Big Peter, or Farmer Pete, as he was sometimes known, looks like a cross between Robert Morley and Henry Cooper, with rosy red cheeks. He was the local milkman, kind of by default, as he lived on a farm, Castles Farm, right in the heart of South Gosforth. Over time the housing estates grew up around it and it's now long gone. Like me, Peter was a major music nut and Newcastle United daft, toon-potty. To celebrate our getting to an FA Cup final one year (we lost to Liverpool; horrible day) he dyed his hair black on one side, white on the other. Unlike me, and just about everyone else in our roistering crowd, he was someone who took all people as they came and judged them solely on their merits. No preconceptions or prejudices – it didn't matter to Peter if you were a student, a navvy or a company director, and all of those types used the Millstone at that time. If they were all right, then that was enough for him. He was the conduit between those vastly differing groups in that bar and, because of him, the barriers came down and we all got along together, playing darts, going out on pub-crawls. Peter was a special guy with a special eye. All who knew him, and they numbered hundreds, loved him, and those who were lucky enough to know him well loved him all the more. He and Miriam were big pals and very close.

My own take on the whole 'students = spongers' thing was disappointingly predictable. I just went along with the widely held view. The truth was that it was based in envy, an unattractive trait. I envied students their fun and their opportunity to learn, to broaden their minds and become bigger, more rounded people. And I envied them their contemporaries. As much as I loved my own mates, I envied students the stimulating conversation I knew would never be part of my own life. My pals weren't equipped for it and capable of it and neither was I.

The downstairs flat Miriam was renting in Hazlewood Avenue, Jesmond, was not very well looked after by the landlord. It's become a bit of a cliché but most of the landlords and property owners who rented to students were neglectful. Ray and I used to let our properties mainly to nurses, as the Freeman Hospital was within striking distance of most of them, and we always tried to look after them properly. That night Miriam's bog burst, sending shit-coloured water flooding through the entire place. Happy birthday. Not long after, she happened to mention that she and some pals were looking for a new flat. As luck would have it, we had one available for rent, a three-bedroomed place in South Gosforth, so they took it and moved in. I was always hanging around the place just so that I could be in her company, helping her to paint walls and stuff. She never once asked about my past. What a breath of fresh air. I'd never met anyone so reasonable in my life.

At this point in my life I was drinking heavily but I liked to think it was under control. I drank no more nor less than most of my pals, and it was always the ale, nothing else. I could work without it affecting me unduly, although there were times when I was still half-cut from the night before and handling glass. One day at work I had a black-out, had to drop a big sheet of plate glass. It was a near thing so I went to the doctor. He took my blood pressure and told me it was abnormally high. Did I smoke? No. Did I drink? Well, yes, but only the Guinness. How much Guinness? When I told him how much I got through he had a fit. 'I thought it was good for you,' I said.

'Half a bottle a day, maybe,' he said. 'Certainly not two gallons of the stuff.'

I just loved the taste. The dense texture took a while to get used to, but, as with most things alcoholic, I got there in the end. I'd also convinced myself it was as good as a meal, saving me the bother of cooking or carrying-out.

Our first date. How we got through it only God knows. I'd asked Miriam if she'd like to go for a drink and she'd said yes. I couldn't believe my luck. Off we went to a pub called the North Terrace, a real spit-and-vomit job with sawdust on the floor. I asked her what she'd like to drink and she replied, 'A pint of Bass.'

I looked at her for a moment. Was she joking? No, she wasn't. 'Why would you want a pint of Bass? Are you a lesbian?'

'No,' said Miriam, showing me more patience and courtesy than I deserved. 'I'm thirsty.'

I couldn't get my head round it. I offered her two half-pints but she wasn't having any of that. I said, 'I'm sorry, but I'm not buying a bird a pint.'

She settled for a can of Stella. The ring-pull wouldn't come off so I gave it a manly tug and tore it off, managing in the process to take a chunk out of one of Miriam's delicate little hands. She still has the scar to this day, a memento of our first evening *à deux*.

Our first meal indoors. Oh, God, it's all of twenty-four years ago yet I remember it like it was yesterday. It was in the Sandringham Road upstairs flat. After spending hours in the galley, Miriam served up a lovely plate of . . . 'What is it?' I inquired, regarding what was before me with suspicion and poking at it gingerly with my knife.

'It's ratatouille,' she told me, with a smile.

I poked about some more, flipping over unusual bits of veg. 'Where's the meat?' I wanted to know.

'There's no meat with ratatouille,' Miriam explained patiently. 'It's a vegetarian dish.'

I laughed, incredulous. 'There has to be meat, man! You can't have a meal without meat!'

You could, and this was proof, Miriam explained, although why she didn't chuck me out at this point I'll never know. After looking at it for a while I asked for some sliced bread and made ratatouille sandwiches. As I recall it my toes are curling. Forgive me, pet.

Christmas 1980 was going to be 'meet the parents' time. When I told Joe Watson I was planning to head to South Wales he loaned me his brand new Ford Granada. I don't know anyone else who'd have done such a thing for me. Off we duly went, with me worrying about what Miriam's parents would make of me. The trip turned out to be wonderful, with most days spent either in the local pub or at home drinking wine. Miriam's parents, Jack and Jean, took people as they found them, and they made me most welcome. It was a lovely Christmas.

As well as a more balanced diet, Miriam brought me something else that was sorely missing from my life: rational thinking. I was forever getting into arguments that led to brawls. Most of the time it was no more than a cuff or a punch here and there, or a chair thrown at someone, but it happened far too regularly. I was no super-tough guy, nothing special, and I lost plenty of these little tiffs. Now the disconcerting thing about it is how easily and thoughtlessly I followed those patterns of behaviour. Today I bore my kids to death about it, trying to make sure they avoid mindless violence. As they rightly remind me, they aren't me, and for that I'm truly thankful.

One day after yet another set-to in the pub, Miriam said to me, 'You know, if one person thinks one thing and you think another, it doesn't necessarily mean they're wrong.'

'What else can it mean?' I said.

'Simply that you have differing opinions.'

I'd never had anyone take the time to explain this to me, and it was a revelation. From that day on I didn't feel quite the same need to crack people's heads. I wasn't completely cured of wild rages and needless punch-ups, though. It took me years to bring that under control. Part of the reason for that was that I considered myself inarticulate and, for fear of being made to look a fool, I tended to head off any discussion I felt wasn't going my way with a punch. I still feel ill-equipped and ill-at-ease in discussion but it seldom ends in a punch-up. I'm too old for all that now.

Around the end of 1980, with Miriam's encouragement and help, I put another band together. We called ourselves the King Crabs, but people tended to refer to us as the Crabs. It was your classic four-piece beat combo, supercharged with an injection of punk. Quite a powerful cocktail, both aurally and visually. Loud in every sense, and deliberately so. Although over the years the line-up changed with members coming and going, it was initially and most often thus: I was lead vocalist, Rob Lockhart was the guitarist, a young, good-looking lad from South Shields called Simon was our bass player, and my old pal Tommy was on drums. Miriam made us some oversized crab claws, all painted up and perfect, which we wore on our hands for publicity photos. They looked really neat. Our roadies were Peter the Hair, my pal Jeff and daft Alan, whose arse we stencilled with a Batman motif, to be revealed at the end of the show bathed in spotlights while we rocked out to a version of the theme from the 1960s television series. I often took a riding crop to his arse and he'd be lucky to finish the evening uncut. It was totally wild from day one, which is exactly how it should be. That's why you join a band. As a live act we were a pretty heavy handful.

We based ourselves out of Colin the Shoe's big terraced house next door to the family planning clinic up near the general hospital on West Road and from there declared rock 'n' roll war on the world. Our dreams were the usual big ones, far beyond anything we'd ever realistically achieve, but that didn't stop us discussing what we'd do when fame came and how we'd handle the pressure. Rob was going to have a big American convertible to tool around in. I wanted a Bentley. Tommy just wanted to shag loads of girls, but he was doing that anyway so it wasn't much of a dream. So we dreamed. And why not? Hadn't the Animals got out of this place nearly twenty years earlier? Hadn't Lindisfarne swung together a decade before? And Brian Ferry, and Mark Knopfler, and Sting, and just recently Brian Johnson? Yeah, they'd cracked it, all of them, so shut your mouth! You could escape via music: they'd proved as much. Win or lose, we were determined to have a bash.

As I was the only one working at the time we used one of the Watson's vans to lug our gear around – not the Commer! – but the smell of putty was unbearable, and I felt like I was still at work. Then after we'd been gigging for a while we bought a twin-wheel Ford Transit, your classic band-wagon. That was an exciting day. All the established local bands used a Trannie and, with their squat appearance on the road, back windows blacked out, they resembled mean-looking scarab beetles. I really felt like we were going somewhere when we got that van, really felt like I was in a proper band. Until, that is, Peter the Hair, out of sheer boredom, decided to paint it, windows, wheels, the lot, in a bright flamingo pink.

With a paintbrush. Jesus, what a sight. I dreaded getting into it. Also, we were easily spotted by police patrol cars and always getting a late-night pull.

Our gigs were riotous local affairs that often spiralled out of control, spilling over into mayhem and sometimes lawlessness. We were not the finest of musicians but what we lacked in ability we made up for in passion and commitment. We were loud and dangerous. Sets consisted mostly of R&B standards, by the likes of Muddy Waters and Howlin' Wolf, but after our arrangements, additions and changes had been made the originals were nigh-on unrecognizable. The audiences took their lead from us and I'm afraid we set an appalling example. I once got a gig closed down because I thumped a synthesized drum with my nob. It seemed that every time we played a gig there was a near riot. It made for some great word-of-mouth publicity but it was also a headache: there were often arrests, with members of our team having to be bailed so they could play a gig. In no time we'd built up a loyal following, mostly of men who liked a drink, and we had the best fun. We were never allowed anywhere near the working-men's clubs, a mainstay for most local bands back then: the content of our act was just too extreme for them. We did, however, get to play one weekly residence.

In a portent of how local times were about to change, the Benton working-men's club had gone bust. After it had stood empty for a long time the building became a private boozer-cum-club owned and run by Derek Brown, a lovely man. He had previously managed the legendary Club à Go-Go on Percy Street in the city centre, which in the 1960s had been a permanent home to the Animals and a temporary staging-post to whoever came through on tour, everyone from the Stones and Jimi Hendrix to Tom Jones and Long

John Baldry. Consequently Derek had seen, heard and done it all, so he tolerated us and our excesses with good grace. I think he liked the way we really didn't give a flying fuck about anything – but the fact that we filled the place to bursting on an otherwise quiet Sunday morning might have had something to do with it too.

We'd often play a double-header with the Dance Class, my pal Tony Mac's band. They were friends of ours and very good indeed, playing sets made up of all their own material with real style and gusto. There was, however, a rivalry between us that often got out of hand. One of the things we used to do was prepare flour, tomatoes and eggs to pelt at them when they were on. We got them proper on one occasion. It was very bad. While the chaps were on the stage belting it out we distributed the ammunition among the audience. At my signal, we let them have it. A hail of flour, eggs and tomatoes hit the stage, covering everything, bodies, guitars, amps, curtains, the lot. The band ground to a spluttering halt and retired, beaten. No one could have continued.

On another morning Derek was celebrating his birthday. Something extra-special was called for. Half-way through the set we stopped and called him on to the stage. Up came poor, unsuspecting Derek. I announced it was his birthday and a big cake was brought on. I asked the audience to accompany me in a round of 'Happy Birthday'. Off we all went, with Derek beaming. At least, he was until I hit him with the cake. It wasn't planned so I caught him unawares. The look of shock on his face made me feel a little guilty, but the almighty roar that went up in the room banished that. He took it like a trouper, I have to say. We were eventually banned from playing there because our gigs were so unruly.

The worst experience I ever had was having to fight a guy

before we could play our set. It came about because of a near-riot we'd been involved in at Middlesbrough Polytechnic. Booked as support act for a London-based punk outfit, we'd taken to the stage, only to be spat upon by members of the audience. Now, if there's one thing I will not countenance it's someone spitting at me. Apart from the health implications of someone sending a gobful of their germs in your direction, for me it's the lowest, most despicable thing a man can do. When I see a footballer spit at another I'm amazed they're ever allowed to play another game. I'd ban them for life. So that night I explained, in no uncertain terms, that we'd prefer they kept their phlegm for the headliners, who'd no doubt appreciate it. Off we went again, with the same result: hockle everywhere. At this point, concerned at the real possibility of swallowing a gobload of someone else's gob, I told the now-baying crowd that if it happened again we'd be off the stage and among them. A mistake. Off we went again, and once again we were coated in spit. I jumped off the stage into the audience. Fighting followed, the stage was invaded, the PA columns were toppled and the gig was cancelled. But not before Rob had caught some young guy square on the side of the head with his Fender Telecaster. Guitars like that are very heavy and it almost took the guy's head off.

Cut to weeks later, and a gig in Middlesbrough. Rob and I got there late, having stopped off for a beer *en route*, to find the gear still in the van. The boys explained to us nervously that some guys were waiting to see us indoors. Half a dozen well-built men with no necks to speak of and inky pictures all over their arms explained their mission. One was the uncle of the lad Rob had hit with his guitar, and they were demanding redress. I went out into the car-park and fought this bloke. He was a stocky little bastard, broad-shouldered, and looked a right handful, so before he'd had an opportunity to get himself squared up, I kicked him as hard as I could in the bollocks and that, thank goodness, was that. They buggered off and we played the gig. By then fighting was all but a thing of the past for me, but there was still the odd occasion when it couldn't be avoided. And I know this isn't a very enlightened view, but for me there are some people out there who just merit a slap.

What ultimately turned me away from brawling was Miriam. She never once said, 'This is wrong,' or 'I'm not having it.' There was no ultimatum as there would have been with me, had the boot been on the other foot. She just felt I was letting myself down. I couldn't argue with that. Here was someone willing to support, encourage and love me. I would have been mad not to take notice of what she felt. In the eyes of the girl I loved, I was letting myself down. I wasn't having that.

There was never any money in playing music at this level. Once we'd taken out the cost of petrol, fines, tickets, PA hire, food and, always the biggest outgoing by far, booze, there was never anything left. In fact, most days found us well in the red. It didn't matter, though. We did it because we loved it, and it allowed us the chance to indulge in some serious artistic expression. Most valuably, it allowed me to find my feet as a performer. Paradoxically, although I didn't like the thought of what I got up to on stage and considered it the worst kind of showing off, I liked the feeling that being up there, centre-stage, brought with it. I still have that ambivalence with regard to performing.

With her background in the arts, Miriam helped me out with ideas and needlework on my stage costumes, and I'd occasionally blag one of her dresses if I was short on choices for the evening. This became a bit of a talking-point. They do say, 'Put an Englishman in a dress and he'll be happy,' don't they? I have to admit that the freedom, so to speak, was comfortable and enjoyable after all those years trapped in tight jeans. After a few beers at the bar, in costume, I would take to the stage, in my dress and a pair of ox-blood Dealer boots, to shout and bawl for an hour or two. It raised a few eyebrows but I didn't care: it was all about eliciting a reaction.

Once I was driven through the doors of a gig and up on to the stage on the back of a motorbike, a big Kawasaki. At least, that had been the plan: we hit the door far too fast and crashed into a table of drinkers, sending them flying. Another of our outings saw us fighting with a load of young farmers during the interval between sets, only to be back onstage twenty minutes later with split lips and bruises. After a first half when all the girls were dancing, in marked contrast to their beaux who'd just looked on, I was at the bar, about to take a drink, when one of the tuxed-up young tossers said to me, 'That was a load of shite!' I hit him. What else can you do in such circumstances? The next thing you know it's Dodge City.

Eventually it was obvious that the band wasn't going anywhere and I'd come to an impasse in my life. Since that leg-up from my sister, Ray and I had acquired quite a bit of property, but I was bored. I felt I'd achieved little in real terms and wanted to do something substantial, leave my mark in the sand. I didn't know what I wanted to do, or what form it might take, but I was restless and knew I'd have to do something before I drove myself, and everyone around me, mad. I felt as if I was in limbo, stuck mid-stream in a river of my own making. I'd had this idea that a different life existed locally, one in which conversation sparkled, sophisti-cated women drank from martini glasses and that property-developing would gain me instant access to it. I didn't want to go back to where I'd worked so hard to get away from, yet I wasn't thrilled about where I'd landed. My imagined world didn't exist, at least not in Newcastle, so I was stuck in the middle and restless.

Normally this would have been a difficult period for me, as my choices tended to be extreme. This time, though, I had my Miriam to guide and support me in my decisions. And this time, although I couldn't know it, something unbelievable was just round the corner.

8

It was dawning on me that all my mad male-dominated antics ran contrary to the way I wanted to live, the way I was when I was with Miriam. It wasn't just that making a noise and smashing things up felt juvenile and immature: it no longer felt natural. It felt more comfortable – and natural and lovely – to be with Miriam, but I wasn't willing to throw the habits of a lifetime down the pan just like that. Too much fun. I struggled for a while, trying to find my feet.

Because of my dad's strongly held socialist beliefs, I'd been brought up to understand and appreciate the value of trade-union representation, and my time at Parsons had made me aware of union power. Although my dad was never one to bang on about party politics at home and was no militant, he was clear about the working man's place in our society and he believed the only way for folks like us to get anything like a fair crack of the whip was through weight of numbers and proper union representation. In terms of the working man's progress, nothing was given freely and nothing ever won without a struggle. And, boy, did my dad like a struggle! Not long after he was taken on at Reyrolle's, after the war, he had been voted in as union shop steward and, by his own account, was such a bloody pest that the management decided to offer him the foreman's job just to get him off their backs. He took it, along with a much-needed pay rise, to the disgruntlement of his former workmates, but felt he was best-placed in that post to see that everyone's needs were accommodated, both workforce and management. Not everyone felt the same, but my dad could live with that. He was a thick-skinned bugger.

I'd been a member of the Boilermakers' Union since I was sixteen but by my early twenties my union ticket had lapsed. So when I was told, rather stroppily, that I should be in one of the performance-related unions, I didn't mind; I've never liked being told what to do but, like most outsiders, I wanted nothing more than to come in, and the sense of inclusion that membership of an official body might offer appealed to me. Why not? I thought.

My first port of call was the Musicians' Union, known to all as the MU. My first mistake was to assume they'd want me. They didn't. A rule existed back then, or so I was told, that excluded singers, who weren't regarded as musicians. I told them I was a dab hand with a tambourine and played harmonica on lots of songs, but to no avail: if I really wanted to be represented, the variety branch of Equity, the actors' union, was the body I should approach. This seemed bonkers to me but I went along with it. I knew my sister Val was involved in some capacity with actors, though I wasn't really sure what she did. I discussed it with her and we decided that I'd apply along with Rob Lockhart. I was miffed about the MU, but Val put a positive spin on things: she told us that in Equity we might get called up for a crowd scene on a telly advert – you could get thirty-five quid per day plus your meals, just for standing around. That seemed like a fantasy scenario but as I recalled my brief stint on *Get Carter* I reminded myself that the most unlikely things could and sometimes did happen. All we had to do was fill in a form and come up with proof of paid employment in the form of a half-dozen contracts – not difficult as long as you had access to a photocopier. Val agreed to propose us both at the next branch meeting.

After I'd attended that first meeting I never wanted to go to another and I never did. It was held in a big back room in a working men's club somewhere, filled with smoke and stern, unfriendly faces. Grey and grim, typical of union politics at the time, the place was full of people who weren't very good at the job, in this instance entertaining, and seemed to busy themselves by making life as difficult as possible for everyone else – especially the likes of me, outsiders with the temerity to seek admission into their jealously guarded little world. At an allocated time you had to stand up and answer questions put to you by folk behind makeshift desks.

It didn't take me long to work out the lie of the land in that back room: as with the Boilermakers', there was no reasoning, no middle ground, no sanity, just rhetoric and dogma. This was the early 1980s, Thatcher's time and a last hurrah for the closed-shop, for loud-mouthed Militant bullies and blatant favouritism. These people were running scared and were bound to do all in their power to see to it things stayed that way. I hated everything about it. Two weeks later I learned I'd been accepted. What do I know?

In a few hectic weeks I'd pretty much forgotten the idea of getting a day's work on an advert and was involved with life's priorities, which consisted of dealing with falling ever more in love, drinking, playing in the band, holding down the now part-time day job at Watson's and making a fist of Ray's and my property venture. I was now living with Miriam and it was both wonderful and frightening. She allowed me to be the person I wanted to be, rather than the one I was expected to be, and I was happier than I'd ever been but terrified that she'd see sense, jump ship and leave me on my own. I honestly thought it was only a matter of time. I never dreamed of bringing the subject up for fear I might provoke the very thing I was afraid of. I carried on working, drinking and worrying.

A few months after I joined Equity I got a message one day to call Dave Holly, the local Equity rep. He was a regular guy I always felt comfortable with and he told me there was an open casting session for extras needed in a television series about to be made by Central Television. Did I want to go along? I was surprised. 'Why me?' I asked Dave.

'Because of that stuff you wrote on your union application form,' he replied.

Shit, I thought, what did I write? My mind went blank. Was it a load of old bollocks, about to rebound and embarrass me? 'Er, what stuff, exactly, Dave? Which bit?'

'The bit about your having extensive experience in property renovation and the construction industry.'

'Oh, that! Right.' I gave a huge sigh of relief as that stuff was all true. I'd avoided the worst, most unbearable thing: getting rumbled, being embarrassed. 'So, when is it?'

Dave gave me the dates when the television people would be in town. Right. I told him I'd think about it and let him know.

I didn't fancy it. I mean, what were the chances of folk like them offering someone like me a job? Zero, I reckoned. I'd had my luck, been an extra, done my scene with Mr Michael Caine, no less. Leave it at that. If I went along with this charade I'd be winding myself up for disappointment and, worse, the dreaded rejection. The way I saw it, if I didn't go they couldn't tell me I was no good.

Miriam, God bless her, thought otherwise. 'You should go,' she said. I promised her I'd think about it, but in the end it wasn't difficult just to forget about it.

Weeks later, Dave Holly called again. He spoke to Miriam this time. Was Jimmy up for going along to meet the television people? She'd ask and get back to him. We talked about it, and I said I felt the same as I had before: nowt would come of it and it was a waste of time. Miriam insisted I went along, and as I was permanently terrified of falling out with this lovely person who'd blessed my life, I thought I'd better do as I was told. But in this area I had no self-confidence. It would lead nowhere, I thought. A day and time were set, but I was determined to watch them pass without putting in an appearance. I just had to keep quiet about it. With a bit of luck Miriam might forget. Ha!

On that fateful day I was working on one of our properties in South Gosforth along with Johnny Fail – revitalization, it was known as, and revite grants were available. It entailed knocking down and removing an outside toilet and I was up to my elbows in filth and dust when Miriam arrived to remind me of my appointment with the television people. Like she was ever going to forget. It was for four o'clock that afternoon and if I was going to make it I'd have to knock off there and then, get showered and changed. I told Miriam I was enjoying myself and didn't want to stop, which was true: there's something very satisfying about going to town with a sledgehammer.

Miriam would have none of it. 'Go,' she told me, in no uncertain terms. 'Get washed, get your arse across town and at least meet them.'

I tried one last time, one last spineless bottle-out whinge.

Miriam looked at me and said I must go. 'You never know what might happen.' As a big Bowie fan, she was convinced we could be heroes, even if it was just for one day.

Half washed, half changed, scruffy, nervous, anxious and angry, I arrived for my interview having left my car on a double-yellow line. I entered the building, an old schoolhouse near the city centre, and parked my arse on a chair. One other unfortunate soul was sitting there, shaking. I said nothing, just stared at the unfriendly plaster wall. I felt as though I was about to be arrested and charged. And who'd be behind that door, ready to ambush me? What kind of smug, patronizing people awaited me? I'd no idea but I could hazard a guess: half a dozen cravat-toting poofters, most likely, who would take one look at me, shriek and recoil in horror.

The door opened and Shaky was called in by an elderly man with grey hair and a kindly smile. The door closed behind him and I was alone. I so wanted to go home to where I would be safe, and where I knew and understood what was under my feet. This was new terrain for me. I was getting more and more wound up. I'd be bound to have a ticket by now. The big clock above the double doors at the end of the corridor was telling me it had gone four. I was on time, they were late. It got to five past and I said, 'Fuck it, I'm off!'

I got to my feet and the bloody door opened. Shaky came out looking none too happy, passed me on his way out, and the man with the grey hair and friendly face was asking, 'Er, Jimmy Neil?'

'It's Nail, actually.'

'Nail?'

'Well, actually, it's not Nail . . . Oh, fuck it, it's too long a story.'

'Well, er, would you like to come through, Mr, er . . . Nail, is it?'

I had to decide whether to tell this friendly old man to fuck off or go in there with him. He was waiting. Ah, what the hell! I was there now. I'd only get a row if I went back and told Miriam I'd come all this way, got this far, got a ticket probably, and bottled it at the last minute. She'd say

I'd let myself down. She had faith in me. Maybe I should have a little myself. I took a deep breath and went in.

It was a massive room, an old classroom. In the middle, two oblong flat-topped tables had been pushed together to make an L shape. At the shorter end, the old man introduced himself as Barry Ford, Central Television's senior casting director. I'd no idea what that was but I nodded. Next to him was a guy in his mid-forties, wearing glasses with thick lenses. This, Mr Ford told me, was Martin McKeand. He'd be producing the television series they were now casting. I nodded another hello. To their immediate left was a guy in his mid-thirties, who was introduced as Roger Bamford, the director. I nodded yet again. Hmm, not a single cravat between the three of them. I'd no idea who was in charge or, more importantly, who had the juice, as Steve McQueen used to refer to power, who was calling the shots. So I did what came naturally and felt right: I stayed quiet, acted surly and hoped I wouldn't make a fool of myself.

Martin McKeand kicked it off by asking me about past experience.

'In what field?' I growled.

'Acting.' He smiled.

'None.'

'No experience?'

'No.'

'None at all?'

'Well, school plays and the like, but nowt since then.'

'Commercials?'

'No.'

'The stage, then?'

'Nope.'

'Nothing at all?'

'That's right.'

I could feel what little chance there might have been ebbing away like a fast-receding tide. Barry Ford and Martin McKeand did their best to make the situation more bearable with a bit of chit-chat, but the other guy, the director, had said nothing all this time. I turned to my right and faced him. 'Is there something wrong with my face, pal?'

'I beg your pardon?'

'I said, is there something wrong with my face?'

'No – er –'

'Well why have you just sat there for the past ten minutes staring at it?'

'I, er –'

'You see, where I come from, if somebody stares at someone else like you've just been staring at me, that merits a smack in the mouth.'

'Oh, right, er –'

'So I'd be grateful if you didn't do it.'

'Right.'

Poor Roger, he must have wondered what the hell was going on.

Bridges well and truly burned, I figured it was time to make my exit. 'Look,' I said, 'I've got nothing in common with people like you, I don't like the look of you, and I'm parked on a double yellow, so if there's nowt else, I'm gonna fuck off home. All right?'

'All right.' Barry Ford nodded.

I left the room without either a goodbye or a backward glance.

Later I learned that as soon as the door closed behind me, Martin McKeand had shuddered and Barry Ford had taken his thick black felt tip pen and obliterated my name from his list, saying, 'Well, I never want to see him again. He was evil!'

Roger Bamford, however, told them he thought he might

have found one of his leading men. I can only imagine the looks on their faces when he said that! They must have feared their director had lost his mind. Roger assures me they displayed a mixture of abject horror and bamboozlement. It still makes him chuckle even now, all these years later.

I finally got back to my car. No parking ticket. Unbelievable. It must be my lucky day, I thought.

I got home and told Miriam all about it. Guess what? No cravats! I'd tried my best, I fibbed, but it was a waste of time: they hated me on sight, probably before I even got in there. She said she doubted that.

Never mind, back to the shelter and security of the sledge-hammer and the outside toilet. Back to what I knew. Not hiding, exactly – I was there for everyone to see – but away from any kind of responsibility. In contrast to my cowardice, actors, a group I considered poncy and pansy-like, were putting themselves on the line like that every day. That's real bottle.

I was working during the day and most evenings, cutting glass, refurbishing properties to rent them out, and there was the band to fit in, socializing, dinner dates with Miriam. Things were so busy I forgot all about the television people.

For weeks my life followed the same semi-chaotic pattern; organized chaos. There was one constant, though: work. I've never been comfortable not working. Every day when I wake up I think straight away about what can be done to avert the disaster, financial or otherwise, I imagine to be just up ahead. I used to believe it was a kind of working-class curse, to do with guilt at being so lucky and fearing it will all be taken away one day. It's true that every day I have cause to bless my good fortune but it's not that, thank goodness. The real reason, I believe, is to do with time, and how precious it is – prison, of course, had brought home to me that it shouldn't be squandered: it should be packed full of as much action and doing as you can cram in. If you're free to choose what you're going to do, then choose carefully. Ask yourself who you really want to spend precious time with: your soul-mate? Your buddies? Your kids? And ask yourself what you want to do: listen to birdsong? Walk along the seashore? Do it. Don't put it off. All those individual moments will not come your way again. For us, right now, the clock moves in only one direction.

So there I was, working away on having a fun life and generally succeeding, when the phone rang. It was Barry Ford of Central Television. 'Regarding the interview you had.'

'What about it?'

'Well, we were wondering if you'd be interested in coming down to London to read.'

'Read what?'

'Some lines.'

'What kind of lines?'

'Lines of dialogue, scripted lines.'

'Oh, right. And who's going to pay for that little trip?'

'We would.'

'Really?'

Tony Mac was in London with the Dance Class on real business, rock 'n' roll business. They'd just signed a deal with A&M Records. I was so envious of their good fortune but they deserved it: they were mustard, a fantastic little band. A day down in London would allow me to meet up with them and get drunk.

A week or so later I was on the train. I spent the entire journey in the buffet car, drinking. I stumbled on to the platform at King's Cross. A taxi ride took me to Regent's Park and a building named Cecil Sharpe House. I was shown down some stairs to a waiting room. Tim Healy was there reading a script and another guy was doing his best to hold a newspaper in shaking hands. I said the briefest hello to Tim. Although I was aware he worked on some occasions and in some capacity with Val at the Live Theatre Company in Newcastle, he and I didn't know each other, and of course I was so grumpy I just wanted to chin everybody I saw. 'What's wrong with him?' I asked Tim, nodding in the direction of Shaky in the corner.

'Nerves,' he replied, 'he's nervous.'

'What about?' I asked.

'About the audition. About the job.'

The lad stood up, went over to a sink in the corner of the room and vomited.

'And it's got him like that?'

'Yes.'

Tim understood but I couldn't believe it. If a job's doing that to you, it's time to find another.

The door opened and it's my man Barry Ford. He forced a smile, then asked Tim if he'd like to come in. In went Tim and it's just me and Shaky. I read my newspaper for a while and wondered how long I'd have to be there before I met up with the Dance Class chaps. They were at an hotel adjacent to Euston station so it wouldn't take long to get over there, once this was all done and dusted.

Now Tim was out and would I like to come in? I followed Barry Ford into a big room, low ceiling, dimly lit. What hair he had was tufty and messy, it needed a tidy-up, the way older guys' hair often does. My old pals Martin McKeand and Roger Bamford were sitting behind another desk. They greeted me with a warm but noncommittal hello. They were friendly, but I was nervous. What did they want from me, I wondered.

I sat down in front of them. Would I read some lines of dialogue for them? Yes. They handed me some pages. I looked at the formatting. It was not something I'd seen before, but was not over-complicated. 'Do you want me to read it all?'

'No, just the bits for the guy named Oz. We'll read the other parts between us.'

'Right. Shall I kick off, then?' I asked, checking my watch.

'Please do.'

The lines on the page read easily and were effortlessly funny. We went through a couple of pages and I was getting the hang of it, going with it. Then there was a little chuckle from the darkness over to my left, which threw me a little. 'Who's that?' I shouted. Dick Clement and Ian La Frenais, the writers, identified themselves. I shouted into the darkness that I'd come a long way, I was trying to read here for these people and having other people sitting in the dark chuckling wasn't helping matters. Someone mumbled, 'Sorry,' but they were still giggling. I carried on for a bit, and then they asked Tim to come back in. We were to read some scenes where Tim was Dennis and I was Oz. It seemed to go all right, and I was soon off to Euston and on the chuck with the chaps.

I travelled back on the train with Tim Healy. He was convinced we'd landed the parts and was very excited, talking about what it would do for us, how great it would be. I was a little more cautious and circumspect. As with my arrest and trial six years earlier, I had told no one, not even my parents, about all this television business, and planned to keep it that way unless and until something firm came of it. Still, there was no harm in day-dreaming. A job on the telly? That would be something to talk about in the pub.

So, then, home once more and back to what passed for

the daily grind: constant work interspersed with lots of laughs. Good times I still remember with fondness. A few weeks passed, long enough for me to forget about it all over again, and then my old pal Barry was on the phone, asking me if I would like to come down to London next week, this time for a screen-test.

My first thought was the train strike, which was scheduled to go off at that time. 'I'll not be able to get down until that's over,' I said.

'We'll fly you,' said Barry.

At this I got a little tingle, an inkling that there might just be something for me in all of this. Until now it was beyond fantasy, the idea of me landing a part in a television series. So much so that I'd not mentioned it to anyone except Miriam. But I knew what a screen-test was, and the message was now plain: I was in with a real chance. Of landing what, though? As far as I knew, this whole thing was probably about a couple of scenes, maybe half a dozen, in a single episode of a series. Any more than that was beyond contemplation. I simply hadn't considered it. Stuff like that didn't really happen . . . did it? Could it? I couldn't think about it because the idea was overwhelming. My dreams had always been big dreams but I was a realist, and the parameters of my dreams had always been based on music and, more recently, property. This would be a walk on somebody else's wild side.

I discussed these latest developments with Miriam and she agreed: it was right and proper to get a little excited, there was a chance of something, goodness knows what, but something. So I worked and played and waited for the next big day. Big days were becoming a regular thing now, and each one was outdoing the last.

In the meantime and the real world the Rolling Stones

were due to play a concert at St James' Park. We went along with a load of pals, including some of the boys from Dance Class, and had a wonderful evening. As we walked through the city centre on our way home, I was talking excitedly to Dave Taggart, the Dance Class vocalist, when a seagull shat right on top of my head. There must have been upwards of forty thousand people on the streets of Newcastle at that precise moment, jam-packed together, and yet, out of them all, fate had chosen me to be the recipient of that flying fucker's crap. I was absolutely livid. Taggart, however, saw it differently. 'Shit for luck,' he said. 'Don't you know stuff like that's supposed to mean good fortune?' I told him I'd happily do without any more luck of that kind.

I was booked on a plane at seven thirty. Tim Healy was travelling down for the same screen tests so he kindly offered me a lift to the airport. He'd pick me up on Gosforth high street at seven and from there it would take ten minutes, no more, to reach the airport. Just enough time to park, check in and buy a morning paper.

I slept in.

I woke up at ten to seven. I jumped out of bed, got dressed and was running up the street in seconds, fastening shirt buttons and pulling up trousers. No mobile phones back then to let people know where you were. Feeling sick, I got to the high street a few minutes after the hour and there was Tim, God bless him: he'd waited. I wouldn't forget that.

We made the flight, just. As we got on the captain apologized to the rest of the passengers for the slight delay, one or two late arrivals. There was much tut-tutting from pinstriped business types as we made our way to our seats, but I didn't care: I was on and then we were off.

On the flight down it was vodka and tomato juice for breakfast. I wouldn't pay it the compliment of describing it as a Bloody Mary, but it hit the spot. I was getting to know Tim a little better now and he was convinced we were going to get the parts of Dennis and Oz. I didn't argue with him: he knew much better than me the way these things worked, but I was determined to keep my head in the real world for as long as possible, thereby minimizing the disappointment when it finally came our way. Or maybe just my way. Whatever.

We got to the studio, a poky little place somewhere near Oxford Street, a little late, of course, and everyone was waiting for us. Perhaps for the benefit of newcomer Nail, they were trying to give the impression that time didn't matter and everything was relaxed and fun and ooh-la-la, but it was obvious to me that time did matter.

After a beer Roger led me out on to a studio floor. A weird feeling. Lots of big grey cameras, cabled up, the type I'd seen gliding around the *Blue Peter* studio. Sound men with their microphones dangling from the end of boom poles. Props men, this men, that men, not enough room to swing a cat! In one sense it was completely unreal, in another all too real. Roger introduced me to everyone but I'd forgotten all the names in an instant. In my head I was constantly running my lines, over and over again. I began to get a little nervous.

Something had been bothering me since all this began: ever since the first meeting in Newcastle I'd been swearing profusely and no one had seemed to mind. Or if they had they hadn't mentioned it. Now, with a scripted set of words to adhere to, I felt tongue-tied.

Roger put an arm round my shoulders and said, 'Oh, by the way, if you want to swear, just go ahead.'

'Really?'

'Really.' With that he was off to the gallery.

The effect this had on me was surprising: I felt no need to

swear. The fact that Roger had paid me the courtesy of offering me the choice rendered it unnecessary. So for my very first stab at performing dialogue in front of a camera, I delivered the text to the letter. It was a long time before I did that again.

The scene I remember performing that day was one where Tim and I were standing against a bar counter, drinking and shooting the breeze. No problems there! I'd supposedly spent all my hard-earned money on a watch, rather than sending it home to the wife like everyone else. As Dennis, Tim doubted the authenticity of my fine new timepiece, asking, 'Is it any good?' to which my reply was, 'It works underwater, Dennis!' When I delivered it there was a chuckle from behind the camera nearest to me, which put me at ease. The chuckler was Roy Simper, senior cameraman, a cool guy, a class act and much older than me. I listened to everything he said from moment one by way of suggestion and advice. He'd ask me politely to move a little this way or that so the light would be just right. I appreciated the help and determined to take on board as much as I could. Roger kept telling me to take no notice of everything that was going on around me but that was impossible: it was fascinating to witness at first hand how it all came together.

Another remarkable thing was that most of these people were from a very different social class and background from me, yet it didn't appear to matter: most were friendly, none was less than polite and, joy of joys, some of the women swore like troopers! I couldn't believe that.

Had it gone well? I thought it had: I'd said my lines, with no swearing, and people had laughed. More importantly, as far as I was concerned, so had Tim Healy, but it was hard to tell. No one was very direct about anything; instead they were vague, but in a positive, encouraging way.

147

The screen-test over, Tim and I headed for Gatwick from where we were to catch our plane home the next morning. We had a very late night on the drink and the darts and ended up missing the flight. I made it home to Sandringham Road around lunchtime. Understandably Miriam wanted to know all about how it had gone but I was knocked out, knackered and simply had to have a kip. Within minutes of lying down on the settee I was deep in sleep.

Somewhere in the place between dreams and reality I could hear a phone ringing. It felt as though I'd only had my eyes closed for a moment when Miriam was trying to wake me up. It was the television people.

'What do they want?'

'To speak to you.'

'Ask them to call back, pet. Me head's thumping.'

I went back to sleep. An hour or so later they were on the phone again. This time I got up and wandered through to the dining room where the phone was. No cordless jobbies back then. It was my mate Barry on the line.

'Jimmy, I'm delighted to be able to confirm that Central Television would like to offer you the part of Oz in our forthcoming series, *Auf Wiedersehen, Pet*.'

'Smashing, Barry, that's great, but would you mind calling back in an hour? I've not been in long and I'm having a kip.'

'Oh,' said my mate Barry, deflated. I guess he'd assumed I'd be doing hand-springs and offering him eternal thanks. Any sane person would have been grovelling down the telephone, but I was still drunk from the night before. Anyway, he'd ring back in an hour. I put the receiver down and went back to kip. Or tried to.

Lying on the settee it suddenly hit me: I've got the job! I'VE GOT THE JOB! It was going to be a year-long gig. Crikey! A whole year away? Where was that seagull? I wanted to go out and kiss the fucker! I've looked for it on and off ever since, but no joy. I guess you can only be blessed with such good fortune once in your life. Any more wouldn't be fair, would it?

Miriam and I danced around the room, delirious. I didn't know what the gig was, exactly, probably a fleeting appearance, then gone again, but I was going to be on the telly. This was a truly life-changing moment. Our heads were spinning with the excitement of it all.

Even then it was impossible for either of us to imagine the sheer scale of what lay ahead. As of that day, my life, as I'd known it, was over, had gone for ever.

9

Although Ray and I owned a fair few properties by now, our plan to use any profits to buy more places meant ready cash was in short supply. In fact, when I got the good news from London Miriam and I had about sixty quid between us to last the week. In the circumstances there was no question of what would happen next, though. We went straight down to the pub.

At five thirty as the doors were unbolted (this was long before Britain caught up to the rest of Europe with the advent of all-day drinking) we went into the Brandling Arms, intent on celebrating our good fortune and finding a friend with whom we could share our news.

There was only ever going to be one person already at the bar: big Peter was quaffing his usual Black Velvet – Guinness and cider – his milk deliveries long finished. He nodded his usual greeting, 'How, James. How, Mirras,' as Miriam and I bounced towards the counter.

As was his habit he offered us a drink, always did, but I said, 'No, Peter, thank you, these ones are on us.'

'How come?' he asked. In about a minute flat, without a pause for breath, I told him I was off to work on the telly, in London, for a whole year, and what did he think of that?

Peter looked at me, eyes wide, then at Miriam, then back at me. Maybe he was expecting us to tell him it was a wind-up. Of all the things I thought he might say, 'Fuck off!' had not been high on the list. He just didn't believe it. Or maybe 'couldn't believe it' is more apt. Whatever, him being the first pal to be told of our good news, Peter's reaction took some of the wind out of our sails.

In fact our news elicited a similar reaction from almost everyone we told. I told my dad as he sat in his armchair, his feet up on the gas fire, watching *Coronation Street*. I was standing behind him as I retold my story and by now I was hoping for a positive reaction. He never took his eyes off the screen, and only when I'd finished did he turn towards me. Looking at me as though I'd gone bonkers, he said, with a dismissive half-laugh, 'Aye, I'll believe it when I see it, son,' and with that he turned back to the telly.

I suppose it was only to be expected but the lack of enthusiasm and encouragement was a blow and threw my already shaky self-confidence off-balance. But nothing was going to get in the way of that golden opportunity, and I told myself so every time a negative aspect appeared or was pointed out to me – which happened frequently.

My new pal Barry Ford had told me they would be sending me the scripts within days, and I eagerly awaited their falling through the letterbox on to our clippy mat. Receiving a script through the post is still a thrill. Not that I receive all that many, but hey-ho! Anyway, when they did arrive I nearly had a seizure. There were thirteen, sixty-odd pages long, stacked one on top of another like half a dozen telephone directories; and Oz was everywhere, in almost every scene, with so much to say, reams and reams of dialogue, speeches here, speeches there. I panicked, lost it. I told Miriam I'd have to ring them back and say it was off, I couldn't do it, couldn't memorize all that lot. Impossible. Who did they think I was, bloody Laurence Olivier?

With great patience, Miriam, the voice of reason, explained to me that you didn't have to memorize it all, just chunks: they filmed it in parts. 'So calm down. You can do it. You can.'

'How do you know about all this?'

'Because my father is head of Light Entertainment for the BBC in Wales.'

I should have known this. Miriam and I had been together almost two years. Most likely I did know, but as it had no relevance to my life and world I'd given it no thought. Now I would, though. Now I'd bless Jack and, even more, his daughter.

Miriam sat with me day after day and explained how it all worked. She read other parts while I read Oz, tried to memorize, tried to learn, tried too hard as usual. She explained the meaning of television terminology, all the industry slang and instruction in the scripts, which to me read like so much double-Dutch. But what a buzz: I was doing something new and it was exciting. Although the dialogue was not always easy to learn, mainly due to the sheer amount, it was almost always easy to deliver. It sounded so natural to say. Didn't seem anything like the stuff you normally heard on the telly. It had something else, too, something I unconsciously latched on to straight away: it somehow allowed me to deliver it in a way that was, if not strictly musical, then definitely rhythmic, almost rap-like. It had a groove and I'd stumbled on a way of doing it that seemed effective. Over and above anything else, though, the scripts were a great read, hugely enjoyable. You couldn't go through them without laughing.

I wasn't aware of it at the time but I'd been given some of the best scripts ever to have been written for television. I was already on the way to being spoiled.

We'd have to move, we decided. No way round it, other than my going down to London temporarily and having Miriam visit, and that was never on the cards. Miriam wouldn't have put up with it, and anyway, we were two young people head over heels in love, excited and ambitious, our minds filled

1. My mam, Laura Johnston, aged twenty-three, with her aunt 'Belle'

3. Proof of my dad's secondment to the American navy

2. My mam and dad on their wedding day, August 1941

4. My dad, Jimmy Bradford, fourth from the left, convalescing in hospital during the Second World War

11. 'The prize guys': that's a polka-dotted Mickey Hutton showing off in the middle!

12. 'Sir John', Majorca, 1978

13. Miriam at the door of 127 Sandringham Road

14. Pestering the life out of Miriam, this time in Bergen

15. Working with Johnny Fail and Robeson the cat on Sandringham Road. This was the very day I was ordered by Miriam to go into town and meet the *Auf Wiedersehen, Pet* people, 1982

CENTRAL

Telephone 01-953 6100
Telex 923041
Cables and telegrams:
Cent Boreham Wood

28th June, 1982

Mr. Jimmy Nail,
127, Sandringham Road,
South Gosforth
Newcastle NE.3

Dear Jimmy,

    Thank you very much for coming to our reading for "AUF WIEDERSEHEN, PET" last week. We all enjoyed meeting you and would like to talk to you further about the part of "OZ".

    We would like to do a Screen Test at the end of this week or the beginning of next, with you, Tim Healey reading the part of "DENNIS", and Kevin Whateley who you didn't meet last week reading the part of "NEVILLE". We would like you to learn by heart the separate scenes, and also to read through the whole of Ep.3.

    I am enclosing a copy of the script for all these.

    I don't know if you and Tim Healey are in contact with each other but if so you might wish to work together on this, I am sending a similar letter to Tim. If you have any questions please contact me, or Sue Foreman at 01-953-6100, we will come back to you as soon as we have a date and place for Screen Test. I hope this might be on Monday next dependant on the Rail Strike situation.

    Yours sincerely,

Enclosed is Rail Warrant
to be used for Screen Test -
when date known.

MARTIN McKEAND

16. The beginning of an awfully big adventure: the letter from Central Television asking me to come down to London for a screen test

17. Kevin W., Tim H. and I rehearse our lines, *Auf Wiedersehen, Pet*, 1982

18. With Gary Holton, serenading a beer bottle, *Auf Wiedersehen, Pet*, 1982

19. Roger Bamford (second from left) issues instructions to David McDonald (centre) on the back lot at Elstree Studios, *Auf Wiedersehen, Pet*, 1982

20. Relaxing in Düsseldorf, *Auf Wiedersehen, Pet*, 1982

21. Sexy or what?

22. As Chris Fairbanks looks on, Tim Spall explains studio sound recording to the novice,
Auf Wiedersehen, Pet, 1982

23. Pat Roach looks on as I go for a bit of the soppy stuff. In the doorway, first AD David McDonald. So that's where all the pies went!

24. The same evening. Front Row: Tim Healy, Tim Spall, Miriam, George Wiggins and Sue Forman. Behind Miriam is director Roger Bamford and a baby Rafe Spall

25. Our first London home: 2 Gothic Cottages, Golders Green, 1982

26. Restaurateur Peter Langan,
Hollywood Hills, 1982

27. With Alan McKeown, Hollywood Hills, 198?

28. Chihuahua, Mexico, 1982. That 'McCulloch' sign had a lot of weird significance, both at the time and in the years to come

29. Geordies on skis? Miriam and me, Lake Tahoe, 1982

30. Kevin, Pat and Tim H. relax between takes, *Auf Wiedersehen, Pet*, Belgian–German border, 1982

31. Gary Holton and Ian La Frenais,
Auf Wiedersehen, Pet, Hamburg, 1982

32. George Wiggins, the only photographer I fe
really comfortable with, Germany, 1982

33. Everyone looking
suitably bamboozled,
Auf Wiedersehen, Pet,
Hamburg, 1982

34. A baby-faced
Kevin Whately and
Gary Holton wrestle
with their props,
Auf Wiedersehen, Pet,
Hamburg, 1982

35. Kevin and Gary, proving
that actors can – just about! –
walk and talk at the same
time, *Auf Wiedersehen, Pet*,
Hamburg, 1982

36. What on earth has he got down the front of those knickers? My favourite
'Oz' photograph, Elstree, 1982

37. Miriam getting her long hair blown about, Pacific Coast Highway, California, 1982

38. Me and Miriam with Tommy Cooper, comic genius, Elstree, 1982

39. Any jobs going, mate? Cricklewood, London, 1983

40. Miriam with baby Tom outside St Mary's Hospital, Paddington, London, February 1985

41. Father and son 1: me and baby Tom, London, February, 1985

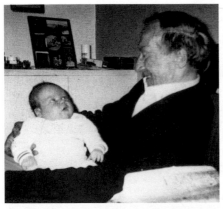

42. My dad with his first grandson, our baby Tom, Penfold Close, Newcastle upon Tyne, 1985

43. Welcome home, Tom: the Spalls, Pippa Markham and Michael Vale toast the arrival of the new baby, February 19

44. Sharon, our lovely nanny, with Miriam and Tom, Dicey Avenue, London, 1985

45. Me with baby Tom and Joe Watson, Newcastle upon Tyne, 19

to bursting with the kind of dreams you have at that age. We were going to take on the world and win! This was an adventure in which we'd both play an active part – adventures are a lot more enjoyable when they're shared.

To help me acclimatize to my new circumstances and surroundings, the good people of Central Television had sorted me out some temporary digs near the studio. I wondered what kind of place it might be; a big mansion, high-fenced and guarded, maybe, or an hotel penthouse. I was about to get the first of many lessons in the difference between reality and perceived reality, as regards UK television.

Tim Healy and I drove to London in his little red Triumph Spitfire, arms hanging out of the windows, suitcases strapped to the back. Turned out he'd been right about our landing the job. I remember the journey so well, with the sporadic downpours coming through the Triumph's tatty fabric top, dribbling all over my strides, and Tim telling me over and over that this thing, this *Auf Wiedersehen, Pet* thing, was going to change our lives irrevocably. I thought he was full of shit, just talking bollocks. I had to think that. So much for intuition.

We were going to be filming this series, this *television series*, for fuck's sake!, at Elstree studios. *Elstree!* That was where they'd made the James Bond pictures! And *Star Wars*! I was going to be working there. I – Geordie boy Jimmy, the same Jimmy who according to his teachers would amount to nowt, or less than nowt – was going to be making a television series, and playing a major part in it! I still didn't quite believe it.

I managed to find my digs, not far from the studio, and here was reality-check number one: my luxurious living environment was a poxy little room with a scruffy sink in a house just off Borehamwood's main shopping street. Miriam planned to join me as soon as all the loose ends were tied up in

153

Newcastle and then we could set about renting a house – that the studio would pay for! The sooner the better. What an adventure. No thoughts of buying a place locally, mind: this was still a one-year diversion, after which I'd go back and take up where I'd left off with Ray and the rental properties.

My digs were a hoot. Every morning I'd sit at the tiny Formica-covered kitchen table listening to the bleary yak of half a dozen British Telecom engineers as they discussed their upcoming day climbing poles and soldering cables. God knows what they made of me, most probably took me for a terrorist or a criminal on the lam. I felt like an undercover agent on a top-secret mission. Daft bat! I didn't dare tell the other lodgers what I was doing for fear of being laughed at. No one else had believed it, so why should they be any different? If you were one of those dour buggers sitting around that Formica table back in 1982 with a big surly bloke who never said anything but ate a lot of toast, that was me.

Before all of that, however, I'd to meet my fellow cast members at the 'read-through'. It's an important part of the process and is usually the only time the writers will hear their work performed all the way through by the cast until it's broadcast. By and large, read-throughs are a bit of a chore for most actors as they require you to play your part without actually allowing you to do so. You're usually stuck in an uncomfortable chair round a big table with other actors, most of whom you won't have met until then, along with various heads of department, the casting director, the producer and, in the words of the immortal Rumpole, he (or she) who must be obeyed: the director, all-powerful, the big cheese, the guv'nor. Theoretically, the stronger your position in a project, that is, the bigger your part, the easier the read-through should be, but it doesn't seem to work that way. Invariably there's a good deal of mucus in the room, what with everyone attempting to clear their throats before giving their all, darling. On occasion read-throughs can be excruciating, depending on who's running them.

My first took place in a small studio space next door to a pub. At this point pubs were still my markers for finding my way around. Of course, the new recruit was there almost an hour early. I had no idea what to expect. Seven uncomfortable chairs, which reminded me of the type you're forced to sit on in school, had been arranged in a sort of semi-circle so that their occupants would directly face the numerous production staff and executives. No pressure there, then. After making sure there were no prearranged places or pecking orders to observe, I plonked my bag down next to the chair in the middle. Not for me an end seat. No, sir, safe and secure was how I wanted it to be. Needed it to be today. Anyway, I was here first, so there.

The cast trickled through the door in dribs and drabs, without fanfare. They were offered tea or coffee and the way they were all greeting one another it seemed that everyone knew everyone else apart from me. I felt like the outsider. Of course, it was just the way theatricals tend to greet one another, but I wasn't to know that. Tim Healy I knew. Kevin Whately I didn't. He was friendly and polite, if a little on the quiet side. Hyper-sensitive Nail, of course, took this to be aloofness, standoffishness. In no time at all I had Kevin prejudged and pegged as a misery. It wasn't the last time that day I'd get it wrong.

Pat Roach arrived. I recognized him from his wrestling on Saturday-afternoon television, but in the flesh his dimensions took my breath away. I'd never met anyone that big before – he had a good couple of inches on me. What a physique he possessed! Amazing definition, and perfectly proportioned. I kept glancing at him whenever I thought he wouldn't notice.

Pat is one of the most softly spoken guys I've ever known and gives off no aggressive vibes, but back then I thought, Whatever this guy has to say, no matter whether he's right or wrong, whether you agree or not, just nod. From very early on, Pat took to calling me Big Jim, which, coming from him, still makes me laugh.

Chris Fairbank was quiet, like Kevin, friendly and polite. He seemed a little more wound up. Like everyone else in there that day he must have been nervous. More than anything I remember the voice. Out of this little bloke's mouth emanated this incredibly rich, big, deep, sexy voice, like Sinatra's. It sounded like gravel on velvet. When he began reading Moxey as this stammering Scouser I was flabbergasted.

Gary Holton exploded into the proceedings. I already knew of him, of course. Gary was a rock singer. I'd seen him at the Mayfair with his band, the Heavy Metal Kids. He'd done a lot of acting as well, playing the Artful Dodger on stage as a kid, and had television and film work under his belt, including a role in *Quadrophenia*, which had been directed by Franc Roddam, who originally dreamed up *Auf Wiedersehen, Pet*. I couldn't believe I was working alongside a bona-fide rock singer, but there he was, laughing, joking, smoking, swearing, larger than life and putting out more energy than half a dozen acrobats. Whether that energy was his own or whether it was borrowed for the day is anyone's guess. With his jet-black barnet, his wild pecking head movements and his crackling, cackling laugh, Gary looked like an oversized crow. As soon as he found out I was a fellow musician he and I got on like the proverbial blazing building. He was great company from the off and it was impossible not to like him.

So there we all were, everyone apart from the one actor who was apparently running late. His chair, right next to mine, stood empty. I remember thinking, How disrespectful. On a day like this! All these people! I wouldn't like to be in his shoes when he does pitch up. He's bound to cop it. God, the anxiety. I felt bad for him and we hadn't even met. After waiting a while, an executive decision was taken to begin without him. We all took our chosen pews, me safe in the middle of the semi-circle, my tidy ordered scripts on my lap, my pencils sharpened and ready.

Martin McKeand began by introducing himself as the show's producer and suggested everyone should give a brief explanation of their function in the production.

It was all going along swimmingly until the door opened and a skinny young guy entered in a state of chaos. Late and flustered, his hair was bleached a cheap-looking yellow, his tight pants were candy-striped and his scripts were in loose pages under his arm. He issued a 'Sorry, everyone. Got held up in the traffic,' in broad Cockney tones. Apples and pears and Pearly Kings and Queens? Oh, God, save me from all that bollocks.

The most surprising thing about all this, however, was everyone else's reaction to it. No one seemed annoyed. Indeed, if anything, the rest of the production staff were fawning over this shabby peroxide *arriviste*. It was as though he was doing the production a favour by just turning up. Why all the fuss over him? I wondered. Just who exactly was this walking rainbow, this well-late, psychedelic shambles who was being worshipped by one and all?

The new bloke, the Cockney, plonked himself and his shambles down in the empty chair next to mine. With a big smile and a hand outstretched, he said, 'All right, mate? I'm Tim.'

I scoped him beadily, this bloke who, unbeknown to me, was already the hottest talent in town. He would go on to be recognized as one of the finest actors of his generation. 'I'm Jimmy,' I grumped.

The reading finally began and it soon became apparent why everyone had been extraordinarily lenient with the latecomer. He was incredible, unbelievable, even in that classy company. Once or twice over the years I've been in the company of truly gifted individuals and there's no mistaking what they have: it's a pure thing and it rings out like a bell. And talk about bringing the part to life! What he did with Barry that morning had everyone cracked up – but there was so much more besides. There was pathos, humanity, honour, pain. You name it, Timothy Spall rolled it out that morning for all to see, hear and marvel at. I'd never experienced anything like it and I had to fight the urge to down tools and watch him. It was a privilege to be in the room that day, truly thrilling.

Was I a little envious of all the fuss and attention Tim had received? I don't think so, though I might be kidding myself. He seemed so . . . well, normal, I guess. Down to earth. There were no airs or graces, there was no big fuss. From the first moment he uttered those lines in that most memorable dialect, Tim, without spelling it out, made it clear there was nothing mystical about the process, nothing I need be scared of. You could either do it or you couldn't, and he reckoned I could, I'd do just fine – told me as much that day, which did my confidence the world of good. The rest, he reckoned, was down to working, grafting, preparing. Preparation, Tim said, was everything. He always said that God is in the detail, and he was right about that, just as he was right about a whole raft of things.

Having said all that about Tim, what was immediately clear was that this was an ensemble piece. I'd been fortunate enough to land the part of a character with many great punchlines, and even I could see they worked gangbusters. What threw me, though, was the generosity of the other actors, the total lack of envy or resentment. They'd happily set up a situation and, having delivered the pay-off, I'd bask in the glory of all the off-camera chuckles. This, a kind of reciprocal, shared creativity, was new to me and I was wary of it for a long time, unable to puzzle it out. It seemed as though everyone, the entire cast, got a buzz out of it when a scene went well, not just me. Of course, those chuckles were brought about by the successful execution of the whole scene, not just the pay-off. I had a lot to learn about the true nature of teamwork.

Half-way through the day, and much to my annoyance as I was enjoying it all so much, we broke for lunch and trooped off to the pub, where I was in for another eye-opener. Any preconceived notions I had about those working in the television industry not being able to hold their own in the neck-oil stakes were soon dispelled. Man and woman alike, these people could drink for England! I felt like I'd died and gone to heaven. Surely, though, it wouldn't continue this way. Nah, it couldn't. Nothing could be so much fun for grown-ups. Never mind, the eternal fatalist figured, get it down your neck before someone realizes they've made a big mistake.

Back in the studio we finished all too quickly and my first read-through was over. I'd enjoyed it. I'd met a bunch of people who would be figuring large in my life from now on, socially and professionally, and we'd all had a great day. As we dispersed there was a real sense of anticipation and excitement. I couldn't believe I was going to be paid handsomely for doing this. Why, it was as easy as falling off a log.

A few words on the subject of my being paid handsomely. Because I didn't yet have an agent, I had agreed my own deal terms with Barry Ford representing Central Television. The contract ran to no more than a couple of typed pages and was easy to understand. Maybe I should have sought professional legal advice but for me it was simple. I asked him how it worked and he told me his version of how it worked and I took him at his word. The show was an ensemble piece, which meant there was no single leading character, and because of this, Barry said, very large fees, the ridiculous amounts you see written up in the newspapers, were out of the question. Central Television were proposing to pay me £600 per episode, plus all my expenses. In total it added up to about twelve grand for the year. Not one to accept a first offer, I managed to get Barry to agree to £650 an episode. Did we have a deal, then? Yes, I said, we did, not wishing to look a gift horse in the mouth. By and large it sounded fine and I was happy. One last question. Would anyone else in the ensemble be getting paid more than me, I asked. Absolutely not, said Barry. I took him at his word, but I warned him if I found out different he'd be sorry. He was.

I made my way back to my grotty Borehamwood bedsit, wondering where all the other actors' mansions were situated. I thought back over the day. What a blast! In that rehearsal room, I'd had a feeling that this oddly named telly series had real potential. Back then I was big on real: it had to be real or it meant nothing. I'd been nervous about going into the read-through but it had been fine and I'd acquitted myself fairly well. The rest of the guys had cut me a lot of slack and Tim Spall, kind man that he was, had taken the heat off the new boy very cleverly. In all the years I've known him I've never felt the slightest bit envious of his prodigious talent as an actor. Part of the reason for this is that inside a scene Tim never feels he has to win, or try any scene-stealing monkey-business. I just count myself lucky to be around when blokes like him are doing their thing.

Elstree Television Studios, it transpired, consisted of a

motley collection of run-down buildings just across the road from the more illustrious Elstree Film Studios, but for me it was still a revelation. Behind the security gates was a galaxy of famous faces, faces I'd only ever seen on television or a movie screen. I'd certainly never dreamed of meeting their owners, not in a million years, and yet now I was working, drinking and mixing with those famous faces. They had voices, too. And on occasion they'd say my name.

The corridors at Elstree were lined with framed photographs of all the famous stars who'd worked there. You name them and, believe me, they were on those walls, every movie and television star from the thirties through to the eighties. Too many to list. As I wandered along, I'd gaze at the mugshots of Richard Greene, Kenneth More, Roger Moore, Douglas Fairbanks Jnr, John Mills and many more, determined to make a go of this television business and not let Geordieland down. Nobody, but nobody, was ever given a chance like the one I'd been given – my director Roger Bamford had taken a gamble the likes of which would nowadays be unthinkable – and I wasn't going to piss it down the drain. Who knows? I'd catch myself thinking. With a little bit of luck, a little bit more luck, I might even end up on one of those walls myself one day. Talk about enough never being enough!

Just going to work was a highlight. I wanted to tell everyone where I was going and what I was doing. Being me, I'd usually get there around nine forty-five for a ten thirty kick-off and head for the assistant directors' office, a little cubby-hole just off the main corridor. Usually Dave McDonald, Francesco Reidy and Simon Flood were already there, mulling over the day ahead. It wasn't the norm for an actor to join them in their daily deliberations but I wasn't to know that and they never told me so I called in there rather than at the canteen, where the rest of the chaps could usually be found tucking into a subsidized breakfast.

What made my time in the ADs' office somewhat unusual was that they'd be doing their preparations over a glass of Buck's Fizz! How civilized, I thought, how cool. I didn't know it was actually Veuve du Vernay we were quaffing. Hey, it tasted fine to my untutored tastebuds. Now things have changed in the industry: it's a lot more sober and, some might say, a lot less fun, but back then an awful lot of booze was consumed and such situations weren't frowned upon. Indeed, guzzling Buck's Fizz and anything else alcoholic was actively encouraged. Everyone was at it, the management included. No matter how all this eventually turned out, I knew one thing straight away: I was going to enjoy the working conditions.

The first few weeks were thrilling and terrifying in equal measure as I tried to learn fast. I'd always been good at that but there was so much to take on board. Nor was it a matter of my looking dumb, or even of failing. That didn't bother me just as long as I was as good as the next guy. I wasn't, of course – in fact, I was way off the pace and must have been a nightmare from the others' point of view, a little like a rogue attacker on a football team: individually talented but in terms of tactical team-play a nightmare of unpredictability.

But wait a minute! Suddenly everyone was telling me I was better than the next guy at this stuff, better than all the guys. I had to hang on to my ego, but even with all the sycophantic bullshit that was being pumped my way, and the alcoholic fog, I always knew where I was: at the start of a journey with a long way to go and a whole lot to learn.

I discovered a world inhabited not by cravat-wearing poofs – oh, there were the odd one or two, but there'd been the odd one or two back home in the Bigg Market – but by real hardened bevviers and party animals and people who swore even more than I did! I'd never met such an open, full-on crowd before. And the world of television was and is, by and large, a meritocracy. As long as you can do the business on the day, you're in. It was just like Joe Watson's. The sound of your voice, your accent and your looks weren't held against you. They could even be an asset. I liked that. Yes, indeed. One day I was telling Spall I couldn't get over how happy I was, how comfortable I felt with it all. He said, with a smile, 'It's because you've come home, mate.' I didn't understand him at the time, but he was right.

The year I spent filming *Auf Wiedersehen, Pet* at Elstree would have passed as extraordinary by anyone's standards. I learned all about blocking and dollies, gaffers, close-ups, wide shots, establishers, going again, and about camaraderie, the like of which I hadn't encountered even at Watson's. It seemed these television people wanted nothing from me except my company, and that's what they gave in return. It was an education hanging out with my new colleagues, some of them razor-sharp, others as dim as a forty-watt bulb, some left of centre, others right, some straight, some gay and some in between. I had never known such an intoxicating environment and I drank freely from the cup, expecting at any moment to be rumbled and sent packing.

Two months into the filming, when I was starting to get a handle on things and enjoy myself, work came to a halt for six weeks. Don't ask me why – other shows were scheduled for studio time, I'd guess. It would never happen nowadays. Alan McKeown, one-time crimper to Michael Caine, was now the boss of Witzend Television Ltd, the independent production company contracted to make *Auf Wiedersehen, Pet* for Central. A business partner of Dick Clement and Ian La Frenais, Alan made the fateful mistake of saying casually to me one day (or was it night?) in Munich, 'If you're ever in Beverly Hills, you must come and stay.'

A few weeks later Miriam and I arrived in Los Angeles after sitting crunched up in Economy for the eleven-hour flight and jumped straight into a yellow cab. Travelling in from LAX along the freeway was like entering a great big film-set, with all the buildings and trucks, cars, motorcycles, neon and bright sunshine screaming, 'America!' Everything was larger than life. I half expected to see Peter Fonda or Dennis Hopper riding along on their hogs but no joy.

In what seemed like no time we'd left behind all the glass and concrete that bordered the freeway and were now going up through Beverly Hills and into the Hollywood Hills. On the flats, those few ultra-expensive acres either side of Sunset Boulevard at the foot of the hills, stood fantasy palaces of all descriptions, from the sublime to the truly bizarre. The one and only thing they all had in common was their price tags: they must all have cost an absolute fortune. Movie stars lived a few yards from where we were, behind high fences. Jimmy Stewart's spread was pointed out to us, a beautifully manicured place with a classic picket fence just as you'd expect of the man who cleaned up the West. He was probably in there at that very moment chowing down his dinner. Grits and coffee? I doubt it.

Sometimes words are redundant and you're reduced to gawping. So, just like all the other tourists, we gawped. Then we were travelling up Benedict Canyon and it looked as if we were in the wilderness, the swank flatlands of Beverly Hills turning in no time to real slopes and gradients.

8816 Lookout Mountain Avenue. I ask you, does that not read like Hollywood? It certainly did to me. Errol Flynn, my boyhood hero, had lived just up the hill. Standing outside his former home one day, just a high whitewashed adobe wall with a door to one side and a letterbox, its ordinariness made reality unreal. It was hard to get my head around the fact that my man Flynn, movie star, swordsman, swinger on curtains and swashbuckler supreme, had lived, parked his cars, eaten his meals, shagged his girlfriends and slept right there. I felt unworthy so I left.

After a couple of days at the McKeown residence, Miriam and I rented a signal-red Ford Mustang and hit the road. And, oh, boy, what roads! Whatever else might be said about America, it's by far the best country in the world to enjoy motoring. Empty, open roads underneath the ultimate big skies. Roadside diners straight out of the movies, with vintage jukeboxes, all-day breakfasts and customers who would match any Hollywood casting call. We clocked up over a thousand miles in less than a fortnight, heading north first, to San Francisco, then due east to Lake Tahoe, where we did some skiing and hot-tubbing, then down to Las Vegas, where a wonderful double room was twenty dollars, a steak the size of a discus ten dollars, and a waitress made Miriam's month by asking her if she was old enough to drink. From Las Vegas it was down through Arizona's incredible landscapes to New Mexico, where I bought some lovely Tony Lama boots, got drunk and ate nuclear-strength chilli that froze my face for a couple of days.

Back in England it was more of the same glorious fun. We finally finished filming *Auf Wiedersehen, Pet* in the summer of 1983. I tried to sit back and take stock of where I was. What a truly incredible twelve months I'd had.

Filming on *Auf Wiedersehen, Pet* ended, and I wasn't prepared for the terrible feelings of withdrawal I experienced. The joy of being around a television studio every day, heavily involved in the making of a drama series, in the company of creative, talented people I had come to know and like, was suddenly gone. It was a shock to the system and, of course, I handled it badly. After spending twelve months being told by everyone and his uncle that the sun shone out of my backside, I was out of work with nothing to do. It was my first taste of the massive come-down that hits you when a long gig is over. Overnight I went from being out all day and busy to being indoors and bored. I've never done bored very well, and my drinking increased again. This was on top of the hike it had taken on starting *Auf Wiedersehen, Pet*.

The morning after the wrap party I woke with a sore head. I looked at the clock: it was just gone nine. I stirred Miriam with a question: didn't she have her fifth attempt at passing her driving test booked for nine thirty? Yes! We were up, dressed and out of the door in five minutes flat. I dropped her at the test centre in Hendon. She, too, was still suffering the after-effects of the previous evening's revelries, and I was going to suggest she leave it but, as I was behind the wheel myself, I thought that might have a somewhat hypocritical ring. An hour or so later she returned. She'd passed.

With a lot of work on our part and a little help from our friends, we had our first proper London home, 50 Maygrove Road, West Hampstead, and I was proud of what we'd managed: it was lovely. All the main rooms had floor-to-ceiling curtains Miriam had run up. That girl! She seemed able to do anything and everything. She certainly knew how to turn a house into a home. Whatever happened now, we'd have a place we could either use or sell on.

There was a kind of golden period just before the first series of *Auf Wiedersehen, Pet* was transmitted, and life was pleasant and calm. I had never dreamed of being a television star, but I was living a dream of sorts. Money was plentiful. I went out on the drink and wandered the streets unmolested.

Covent Garden was one of our preferred watering-holes, and Maxwell's diner a particular favourite. We'd perch on high bar stools, guzzle super-cocktails like there was no tomorrow and finally stagger out into the street to hail a cab. Bound for north London, safe and warm, we'd sit in the back and cuddle. We were two well-heeled young people madly in love with each other, we had no ties, we were living in the most happening of capital cities. We were happy to the point of completeness and needed no one else's company. Back then we had the greatest of times.

Just before the *Auf Wiedersehen, Pet* series aired, a brush with fame proper came my way when I was offered a guest spot in an episode of *Minder*, which was being directed by Francis Megahy, who'd co-written an episode of *Auf Wiedersehen, Pet*. I played a Northern Irish gypsy, and was in the bar with Dennis Waterman and some of the crew one lunchtime when a female fan approached and asked Dennis for an autograph. He was a big star back then, as big as it got, on UK telly. Instead of signing a bit of paper, he pulled a glossy postcard-sized signed photograph of himself out of a pocket and handed it to her. I remember thinking, How big-headed, conceited and presumptuous to be carrying photographs of yourself around. Although I understand it now, it was a lesson in how I wouldn't be conducting myself with members of the public if ever I made it big. Mind you, I was so naïve back then that when fame came I answered every single fan letter I received – in longhand, can you believe? – until they were arriving in mailbags like the ones I'd sewn years before. At that point I gave in and hired a secretary.

I went along to the Bafta building on Piccadilly for the press launch for the series, blissfully unaware of the tidal wave about to hit my shores. The place was packed and the bar was open, so I skipped the screening and got stuck in. When the episode finished there was a stampede in my direction. The press people almost had me on the floor in their eagerness to get the story. I was hemmed in – which no one enjoys. They were all shouting at once, telling me how I was about to be the next big thing on British television, how I was going to be a major star. It was a frenzy. I'd never seen or experienced anything like it before. Where were the Central Television press officers? I was under siege, being asked so many questions by so many people that I became a little unnerved and decided to retreat to the bog to regroup and gather my thoughts. As I stood at a trough, relieving myself, a reporter appeared right next to me and started asking questions. Angry now, I told him to leave it out or I'd give him a smack. That circus was merely a taste of things to come.

Shellshocked, I went home and waited for my big day. Then, on 11 November 1983, *Auf Wiedersehen, Pet* was transmitted.

Everything in the press had been positive that Friday, so at just before nine in the evening I sat down with Miriam and a few friends, crossed my fingers and experienced the unusual feeling of watching myself on television. At the beginning of filming it had been a novelty to see myself on playback but that had long since passed. This, though, was very different. It was going out across the country. The announcer's disembodied voice was talking about us – about me, for goodness' sake. The fact that the episode was book-ended by similar programmes brought a useful perspective: you could get an idea of how good, or otherwise, it was. I was biased – I'd loved it from day one – but it seemed to stack up well. It was weird to see myself in the broader context of the episode's story: until that point I'd only seen the scenes that involved me. Surprisingly, it was hugely disappointing – not the programme, I loved that, but its brevity. A year's hard work, and it was gone in an hour; at least the first part of it was. It was also cast-iron confirmation that the adventure was over.

At the end I wanted to phone a lot of people but my first call was to my mam, to see what she'd thought. Of course, she was more concerned about all the swearing I'd been doing than anything else. What would the neighbours say? I explained that I was only saying and doing what I'd been told to say and do and she let me off with a gentle tut-tut.

That evening was also a big thrill, and I was more than a little proud of what I'd achieved. I'd jumped in blind, with no idea of what to do, and had pulled it off. That was very satisfying. However, you're only new once and that night I was brand new, so it was the beginning of the end, with only twelve more weeks to go. Miriam and I said goodnight to our pals, polished off a posh bottle of Louis Roederer champagne and went to bed.

The next morning, a Saturday, I walked along to the end of the street and on to the Kilburn High Road to get a newspaper and read a review of the show, if there was one. All of a sudden all these car horns were honking. I wondered what all the fuss was about, until I saw people hanging out of their cars pointing, waving and shouting – at me. People in the street were coming my way, lots of them. I ran home with a mob on my tail, got in and locked the door. People were climbing up the railings and peering through the windows. I hid behind the settee and wondered what the fuck had happened.

Fame had happened, and I was woefully ill-prepared for it. I didn't know what to do. Everywhere I went there was madness. It was more than fame, it was hysteria. People believed Oz was me and I was him. I tried to explain he wasn't real, but they didn't want to know. As far as the general public was concerned, Oz was real. I looked like him, didn't I? I sounded like him, didn't I? Well, there you are, then. That was my first indication of the power of that box in the corner of the room.

Not long after, I hopped on a bus in Newcastle to go the couple of stops between one pub and another. Silly not to get a cab, I guess, but it shows how, even then, I still wasn't fully aware of the series' impact. An elderly woman toting a sour puss and shopping-bags had been staring at me ever since I got on. Eventually, eyes narrowing, she spat, 'Anyone can do what you do!', then got up and off. It hurt so much I wanted to tell her to fuck off, but of course I couldn't do that. Then I wanted to say, 'If that's the case, pet, why isn't everyone doing it?', but I couldn't do that either, so I just sat there, struggling to work it all out. A while later I told Ian La Frenais about it. He said, 'Kid, the people who know, know. As for the rest, forget them.' The bile was what upset me. I'd only been trying to entertain people, for goodness' sake. Friends have told me such reactions are a sort of back-handed compliment as to how convincing you are in a part, but back then I couldn't see it that way and it drove me mad.

I went home to Newcastle several times immediately after the show had been on. I wanted to bask in the success but I also wanted to share it and the excitement somehow with my old pals. It didn't really work out, though. Back in the Newton Park one evening, with Scotty and Harry B, Bobby Shields and little Phil all looking at me as if I'd just landed from Mars and me not liking it, it was obvious things would never again be the way they'd once been between us all. Just as well, in one sense, as we'd shared some pretty wild times. It was the strangest vibe, with me at the bar looking across at them, and them, all seated, staring at me. After all the madness and destabilizing nonsense I'd just been through,

I'd so wanted this reunion to be rock-steady, the way our friendship always had been. But that was impossible. The chaps felt I'd changed since the show's success, while I felt that, because of my fame, their attitude to me was different. No doubt it was a bit of both, and when I look back it's understandable. What had just happened to me, the sheer scale of it, was not only out of the blue, it was almost beyond comprehension. For better or worse I couldn't make a move without people shouting, screaming and staring, always staring. It was sensational, and although there was a down-side for me personally, it had put the Geordie nation right on the television map. And all of a sudden builders were cool. What an achievement that was. The guys on the sites now walked with a swagger. I should have been a local hero, and I suppose I was to most folks, but not to my old mates. I was struggling to make sense of it all myself, so goodness knows what they made of it. It was an odd, rather uncomfortable evening.

I was an actor now. It said so on my Equity card. I had a London agent, Pippa Markham. I'd been on the telly in a show that had been an enormous, if unexpected, success. The folks back home couldn't argue with that, although many were almost as mystified and bemused by it as I was. I'd assumed the phone would ring off the hook with offers from Hollywood and beyond. I'd assumed wrong. There was an awful silence. Pippa had done her best to explain how the whole thing worked: becoming famous overnight brought with it problems from a casting point of view and the industry's perception of you. A lot of people would suppose you were a one-trick pony. Then, again, there was the fame scenario: one job into my new career, I was already in a position that prevented me taking another gig without creating a stir and possibly detracting from the new piece. On top of that there was artistic snobbery. 'Successful? We don't want any of that!' A lot of industry people couldn't stand the idea of how things had happened for me, though no one ever said it to my face. Today, because of the poor financial state of the television industry, that attitude is not so much in evidence, but it was prevalent back in the 1980s. Pippa's job was to get me past these stumbling-blocks. It wouldn't be easy. Maybe I *was* a one-trick-pony. At that stage I didn't know. I'd had a great year, but I'd been very lucky. I wasn't sure about acting as a regular job. I'm still not sure about it.

And I was known to just about everyone in the UK because *Auf Wiedersehen, Pet* was a phenomenal success. Most actors climb the ladder of recognition a step at a time, becoming gradually well known over a long period. In my case there were no half-measures. Just . . . BANG! One day, a Friday, I wasn't famous, and the next, a Saturday, I was.

When it happened I felt confusion and anger. I'd grown up in a community where someone staring was usually asked 'Who the fuck are you looking at?' or worse. That kind of reaction, the only one I knew, was of no use to me now. I couldn't very well threaten the whole nation – although in drink that wasn't beyond me. I struggled with the situation for years. It pushed me into drinking even greater amounts, brought huge pressure on my family life and eventually saw me end up in therapy.

I've spent an awful lot of time trying to work out why it was such a problem for me and have come to realize there's no simple answer. It's a combination of things, both real and perceived. I do not like being stared at, partly because, like most people, I'm insecure about my looks. They never bothered me until I became well known. It hurts when you read in newspapers about how ugly you are.

Nor do I like being singled out for special attention. I'd

had enough of that at school. Praise sits uneasily on my shoulders. I differ from today's fifteen-minute fame-seekers in as much as I do not see my occupation as involving anything outside what I do for a living: I go to a film set, ply my trade, then go home again. I do not go to showbiz parties or seek mention in the gossip columns of tabloid newspapers. I do not appear in glossy lifestyle magazines. I do not like what I see as unreasonable intrusion into my life, be it from the press or the public. I do not like the fact that I can't do anything without being noticed and pointed out. Of course, it could be argued that the people who are noticing me are the same people who watched me in *Auf Wiedersehen, Pet* and who took me and the show to their hearts, but that's of no comfort to me. Just the opposite, in fact. I'm not ungrateful for the wonderful things success has brought me, but the general public, fed a daily diet of non-stop rubbish by the tabloid press, tend to have certain preconceived ideas about what famous folk are like, and how they should behave. In my experience they are way wide of the mark.

All this bred in me the desire to prove I was more than the public saw and more than they thought they knew. 'What you see is what you get', so the saying goes. That may well be, but what you see is not always all there is. I felt I had to prove to the world, or at least our corner of it, that Roger Bamford had been right to take that chance on me. I was beginning to formulate a plan as to how I might do that. It would take a long time, but I was all right with that. I wasn't going anywhere else. Certainly not back to Newcastle. That would have been to go backwards, I reckoned. And there it was again, the overwhelming need to go forward, to prove myself. But to whom? It was almost twenty years before I knew the answer to that one.

I'd realized very early into the *Auf Wiedersehen, Pet* shoot that, by and large, actors have no power over the course of their own destiny. Oh, we can kid ourselves that we're indispensable but all the money-men have to do is order the writers to type, 'Suddenly, there was an explosion!' and we're down the road. The only way to take some control of your own destiny is to own the show. It was a grand idea, you might think, for a then novice to be harbouring, and I didn't understand just how big a number I was about to take on. If landing the *Auf Wiedersehen, Pet* gig, and all its subsequent success, had been unlikely, establishing a successful independent production company was even more so. But the way I looked at it was, someone has to be the person with the successful production company so why not me?

There was also the little matter that I did not wish to be 'working for the man', something I'd always had trouble with in the past. About a month into filming *Auf Wiedersehen, Pet* I wrote a comedy script based on the characters I'd known and worked with in Watson's glass factory. It was rough round the edges and never got made, but I still have it. I also began to plan my production company. I had my first go at it with Roger Bamford and Tim Spall: we called it NBS Productions, but it never got much further than alcohol-fuelled creative meetings. Never mind: the stationery had looked good. More importantly, I'd made a start and I was sure there would be opportunities in the future.

The show's success meant that I had lots of lucrative offers for commercials and endorsements, and I could have cleaned up financially, but Pippa felt, rightly, that it was not a good idea. One of the things I was more than happy to do, though, was introduce the Gary Moore Band at the Hammersmith Odeon. I had no problem with that one: Gary had been a big favourite of mine since he burst on to the scene with the Irish trio Skid Row in the early 1970s (check out the incendiary 'Unco Up Showband Blues'). The gig was part of a tour to promote the album *Victims of the Future* and I'd already been out and bought it.

I went down to the Hammy early, was let in through the stage door – always a thrill – met the promoters and Gary's management people, had a bit of a natter and mooched about the way fans tend to do. Then it was time to do my bit, so it was down with the house lights and out I went. The reception I got when I walked on to the stage was a shock. The place went bonkers, with the audience chanting my name and cheering me. I was not a little embarrassed – this was Gary's show.

At the after-show party I told Gary what a fan I was of his work. I also met Lenny Henry, and we subsequently became big pals. The three of us had our picture taken together and I remember seeing it in the paper the next day.

But it was time to see if I could get another job as an actor. I'd been lucky with *Auf Wiedersehen, Pet*, I knew that – right place, right time. The challenge now was to find out if I was up to more than that. Rightly or wrongly, a great many jobs weren't open to me. Landing a bit of Shakespeare was unlikely back then, as was bumping into Jeremy Irons at a casting. Among the jobs Pippa did send me up for was one of the lead parts in a movie entitled *Morons From Outer Space*. The screenplay had been written by Mel Smith and Griff Rhys Jones, who would also be playing leading roles, and the part I was up for, Des, a foul-mouthed intergalactic space traveller, was hilarious on the page, brutally crude. It was to be shot in and around Pinewood Studios, home to 007 and the *Carry On* films among others, and would be directed by . . . Mike Hodges! My old mate Mike from *Get Carter*. I couldn't wait to see him again and have a catch-up.

Off I went to Pinewood for an interview, which was

referred to as a meeting. That tends to be the way in this business, so that fragile egos aren't bruised. I drove through the big main gates, feeling like I do when I drive through the gates of BBC Television Centre – I'm always kind of amazed they let me in. I parked up and reported to the production office. I was shown straight into a big inner office and there he was, my old mate Mike. He'd not changed a bit. There was the posh cloth cap and the beard. He shook my hand. 'Good to meet you,' he said.

'We've met before, Mike,' I reminded him. He couldn't remember. I told him when and where, but he still couldn't remember. Was he shitting me? How could he forget the big skinny kid behind Sid Butcher in that single set-up in that single scene for all of two seconds fifteen years ago?

We chatted. Mike congratulated me on the success of *Auf Wiedersehen, Pet* and asked whether I felt I'd be able to carry off a co-lead in his picture. Thrown by the terminology, I told him I'd just done thirteen episodes of *Auf Wiedersehen, Pet* and, by all accounts, I'd managed all right. 'But that was television,' he said. 'This is a movie. It's different.' He talked about comedy in a very serious manner. I blustered something about how I'd be fine, but all my confidence had evaporated. What *was* the difference between television and a movie?

I asked Tim Spall. He just laughed and said, 'It's slower, mate, that's all. You'll be fine.'

I got the part. I couldn't believe it – I was going to be in a proper film, one that would be on a great big screen at the cinema and people would pay to see it. And, unlike *Auf Wiedersehen, Pet*, this one had dialogue peppered with 'fuck'. Even better. When would all this wonder end? Not for a while yet, I hoped. Miriam and I celebrated with a knees-up. More drink.

My happiness was short-lived. At the read-through I was in for a big shock. I sat down at an enormous table in a Pinewood suite with the producer, Verity Lambert, Mike Hodges, various heads of department and all the leading actors involved: Mel and Griff, Joanne Pearce, Paul Bown, James B. Sikking and yours truly. Jim Sikking! He was just out of *Hill Street Blues*. Even more impressive, he'd killed Lee Marvin at the end of John Boorman's *Point Blank*. But although I was nervous in this company, I couldn't wait to get started. We came to my first line, which contained 'fuck'. I read it and elicited a laugh from the assembled company – a huge confidence boost, until Mike stopped the read: 'That line's been rejigged.' What he meant was, the 'fuck' had been cut, as it had from every other line in the script. My face fell. I was told that this was because someone at EMI, the film's financiers, had decreed the film must have a U certificate to maximize appeal to its potential audience. I was gutted, and felt somewhat cheated. This was not only a major let-down, as it cut the balls clean off my character, it was also a big mistake: Mel and Griff were never kids' comedians.

If that was a disappointment, then the news Miriam gave me around that time was the opposite, probably the best I'd ever had. She was pregnant. I was so proud. The idea that someone loved me enough to bear my child was profound. I felt complete.

With Miriam pregnant, my mam came down to stay with us for a while and enjoyed the odd day out at Pinewood. I was dying to have her visit the set and see me doing my stuff. I figured she'd be so proud, and so she was, but I hadn't considered what it might be like if you weren't at the hub of the action. I'd never been on a set as a visitor. Unless you are actively involved, a film set is about the least glamorous, least interesting, least dynamic place you could wish to find yourself. In the course of an average day's filming for television – eleven hours – you'd expect a yield of around five minutes' finished footage. On a movie the daily yield can be as low as twenty seconds, the equivalent of 1.5 seconds of screen time per hour worked. It's no cavalry charge.

I well remember a morning on one of the big sound stages with about a hundred of us on a polystyrene spacecraft up at one end of the building and, at the other end, sitting in the corner, my mam knitting something for the baby with Mel's mother reading a book. Between takes I wandered down to check she was all right and bask with her in the glory of being in a proper film. After all the let-downs and all the grief, her boy was a hero at last. 'Can I ask you a question, son?' my mam said. Of course, I told her. 'Does anyone ever do anything?' she asked.

Dialogue-butchering aside, I had a great time on that movie, although the socializing almost put paid to my relationship with Miriam. In those days Mel used to like the odd late night and I'd regularly roll home in the early hours very much the worse for wear. Then, after a couple of hours' shut-eye, I'd head back to work. I was hanging out with Mel Smith, no less, eating meals and drinking drinks with him, lots of drinks, and Miriam was having to miss out on it. I was carried away with my own success, I suppose, but that's scant consolation to those left at home.

She and I did, however, manage the odd evening out. The production took us for a meal to Le Manoir aux Quat' Saisons, Raymond Blanc's famous restaurant just outside Oxford. *Nouvelle cuisine* was at the peak of its popularity when about eight of us sat down and ordered. After what seemed like an age, the vegetables arrived. A waiter lifted the lid of a serving platter to reveal, with a flourish, two small potatoes and a carrot. I looked at it, distinctly underwhelmed. 'I think you must've dropped some on the way,' I said. The guy just stared at me. The main course was lamb, two bits the size of a fifty-pence piece. What really put the tin hat on it, though, was Mel being told he couldn't order any more wine. It had turned eleven p.m. So we had to jump into our waiting motors and whiz all the way back to London simply to get another drink. The bill for that meal was over £1100. Now that's what I call service.

Coincidentally, Griff and his wife, Jo, were expecting their first child at the same time as we were and we bumped into them in a corridor at an antenatal tour of St Mary's hospital in Paddington. Griff seemed in a bit of a state and explained he'd hailed a cab on the Kilburn High Road, intending it to bring them both to the hospital, but as it had pulled over it had knocked down an elderly lady. Griff had put his overcoat over her and waited for an ambulance. When it arrived it had taken away the lady and his overcoat. A little later we found out that she had been brought in to St Mary's A and E – now long gone. She was going to be all right, and Griff retrieved his coat.

After our tour I offered Griff and Jo a lift home. When we got to their place they invited us in for a cuppa. On his way to the front door, Griff put his hand into his pocket, and froze. A moment later he pulled out – not his keys – a set of bottom dentures, with traces of a cooked breakfast still stuck to them. We all stared at them. 'Whose are they?' I asked.

'I don't know,' said Griff. We stood there, mystified, until Griff said, with a gasp, 'Oh, my God . . . They'll belong to the old lady!' We figured they must've been knocked out on impact and someone had picked them up and popped them into Griff's coat pocket, which, of course, had been over the lady.

So many things were happening, and there was so much excitement in my life that I didn't notice the way drink had become so much a part of it. Too much a part. I was never really a daytime drinker – makes you too sleepy. I was never a vomiter or a staggerer, so I could look all right when I was blotto. Champagne and wine, my new tipples, didn't do me any good: I drank them the way I'd drunk beer – by the pint. The results were predictable: arguments, fights . . . one day I had a terrible punch-up with one of my closest pals, John Gordon. It kicked off in the Rasa Sayang restaurant in Soho's Dean Street, then spilled out into the main road. As we went at it hammer and tongs, a crowd gathered. Sensibly, John decided he'd had enough and walked away, leaving me swinging wildly at the empty air like a carnival bear. I remember hearing someone say, 'Isn't that the bloke off the telly?' Much more worryingly, I found myself, late one evening, on the bonnet of Miriam's car with a poker in my hand, jumping up and down, completely crazed, as she tried to drive off and get away from me. She was pregnant. I shiver at the – vague – memory.

Of course, it would have been sensible to moderate my drinking. 'Moderation in all things,' my dad would say, but he could never practise it and neither could I. My alcohol consumption was not out of control – at least, I didn't think so at the time – but the consequences of drinking so much were becoming grave. I was going to have to ask myself some big questions.

In January 1985 we moved, just in the nick of time, out of Maygrove Road and into a much larger house about a mile away in Dicey Avenue, Willesden. In February we were blessed when our first son was born. After thirty hours of labour, Thomas Owen Jones hit the scales at seven pounds one ounce. I was lucky enough to be present at his birth and it was, by a long way, the most wonderful moment of my life. Miriam and I were truly in love with each other, and now the physical manifestation of our love was in my arms, alive and wriggling. Tom was part of us both, yet totally his own person. I was on a cloud for days, absolutely euphoric – I'm in tears now as I write about it.

There was, however, one major and unforeseen negative to this most joyous of times. Miriam was on a public ward, and we were plagued by pissed-up parents coming in and recognizing me. Even with curtains round the bed it persisted. I'll never know how I never smacked any of them. The hospital were very apologetic about it and in no time we were home, but I vowed that such a situation would never arise again.

We all have defining moments in our lives and this was the point at which I began to realize drink was not the great thing I'd always taken it to be. It didn't go with my being a good father. In fact, it came a distant second. I still loved it, though, and old habits die hard. The taste of the drink, and the crack that went along with the drinking, had been ever-present in my life since I was in my teens and they were hard *amigos* to say goodbye to. So, for a little while longer, the drinking continued apace.

A couple of days after Tom's birth Miriam arrived back at Dicey Avenue with our brand-new baby, swathed in a shawl, and her mum, Jean, to find all the windows in the house wide open. She asked me why that was and I explained the baby would need fresh air. 'It's February,' she said. 'He'll freeze to death!' A poor start on my part but I tried hard to listen and I did get better. We began life as a family and it was great, better than anything I'd known before. Certainly better than pub life. We tended to treat Tom as though he were a porcelain doll, but he was a tough little lad. He even survived me sitting on him one day, though the guilt nearly did for me. As we were preparing to go to the première of *Morons From Outer Space* in Leicester Square, Miriam decided Tom was too brand new to leave with a babysitter so we wrapped him up and took him along too. My name might have been up there in lights but Tom stole the show that night and he was in all the papers the next day.

With my first movie safely in the can, I sat back to await what I imagined would be yet more glowing reviews. After all, they'd loved me in *Auf Wiedersehen, Pet*, hadn't they? Why should this be any different? That weekend, the *Observer* gave our effort all of one line. It said simply, 'Die before you see this movie!' The rest weren't much kinder. The film had its faults and it was no masterpiece, but it didn't deserve that kind of smart-arse dismissal. I'd taken my first cold bath at the hands of the critics and it wasn't a pleasant feeling. Mel and Griff are two tip-top geezers we see far too little of on the box now. Sadly *Morons From Outer Space*, through no fault of theirs, inhabited a place that was neither adult, kids' nor juvenile humour. It missed the spot and just about finished off Mel and Griff as film-makers almost before they'd started. Not for the first time, a really good opportunity had been squandered by anonymous executives who had called it wrong.

For five years Miriam and I had loved, looked after and out for each other. No one else was part of the equation and that was how we'd wanted it. With Tom's arrival, everything changed. Two had become three. That's not to say we didn't want a child: we had been desperately keen to start a family and fully committed to the idea. But things were different. It's a well-worn cliché, but nothing prepares you for first-time parenthood. Some changes were obvious and easy for me to see, while with others it was a long time before I was even aware of them. We went through the same ups and downs I'm sure most couples go through with regard to lack of sleep, lack of time, lack of sex, etc., but it was an age before I grasped just how profound a change we'd both experienced. A child is a blessing, the most precious of them all, but it's also a challenge, and nature's way of telling you to grow up. Some heed the call, others don't. I'd like to think I knuckled down and took my responsibilities seriously, but I didn't see a lot of stuff – and I should have.

I thought my end of the deal was to earn the money, and Miriam's job was to look after the kid. Why did I think that? Because I knew no better. That was how it had been when I had grown up. I thought I was doing plenty, more than my share, in bringing home the bacon, big-time. I should have looked at everything around me and considered Miriam's opinions and feelings, but I never did – or not nearly enough. I couldn't see the important things through a fog of alcohol and ego. You live and learn, thank goodness, but the fame and the baby and the drinking were having an effect on our relationship. We were now in a place neither of us had either planned for or expected, and although, in retrospect, we coped well with it all, no one could go through all of that and come out unscathed. And although I didn't recognize or realize it then, drinking was an important means by which both of us let off steam. We dealt with pent-up anxiety in a shouting match, and then, of course, there was the making up. Always great. So, there was a pattern to our lives in which booze played a big part and, by and large, it worked, I thought. Never considered asking, mind. But I knew it couldn't go on like that indefinitely. No one in their right mind would put up with it.

*

After a lot of soul-searching and talking it over with Miriam, I agreed to do a second *Auf Wiedersehen, Pet* series for Central Television. The reason I hesitated for so long was not, as was widely reported in the newspapers at the time, because I wanted more money than the rest of the boys: that has never been the case. It was to do with the fame. I knew if I did the show, another thirteen episodes, I'd be perpetuating the recognition thing that was causing me so much grief. It was a conversation with Kevin Whately that turned me round. During a telephone call we were discussing the merits and pitfalls of going again when Kevin said to me, 'You know, Jim, for most actors, scripts like these only come along once in a lifetime, and that's if you're lucky.' He was right. I'd never considered it like that, because I wasn't an actor – not in the way other actors were. I was someone who'd landed somewhere by accident and circumstance, not someone who'd worked for a long period to achieve a certain status. Suddenly I felt guilty about being so unenthusiastic when most actors would have cut off an arm for the opportunity to do what I was being begged to do. In the end, the chance of working with the guys again was too much to pass up. The crack was always great among us, and I'd missed it. I'd missed them too.

10

After the success of the first series it was almost inevitable there'd be another. It gave me immense satisfaction to recall all those so-called 'proper' actors who'd been making their 'proper' drama shows at Elstree while we were there. With one or two notable exceptions, such as Michael Elphick, they'd been dismissive of our efforts: 'Who would ever want to watch a drama series about bricklayers?' I don't know how many times I overheard that in the bar, and it was the opinion of most of the management and executives too. It bred a kind of siege mentality among us, an 'us against the rest' type of thing, which perfectly suited my simmering persecution complex. All the detractors and knockers simply occupied the space vacated a decade or so earlier by my teachers at Manor Park School. Moreover, it helped to forge a special bond between the main cast of a kind that I've not encountered since and which endures to this day.

This time out, we were going to be building and carousing in sunny Spain. Not straight away, mind: Central Television wanted a cheaper show so the first eight or nine episodes were set in and around their brand-new studios in Lenton Lane, Nottingham. In terms of money earned and profile, it was great – Pippa negotiated almost ten times the wages I'd been paid the first time out – but it would mean being away from home for the best part of a year. Instead of the two of us together, as we had been the first time, Miriam wouldn't be with me every day. To my eternal shame, I never considered it from her point of view, or Tom's, and didn't think to discuss it with her. Not only was that unfair and wrong, it was a big mistake: I missed out on a lot of one-to-one stuff with my Tom, nappy-changing and pram-pushing, stuff I should have been involved in and enjoying.

In 1985 Margaret Thatcher was running the country and, with the help of Nicholas Ridley, MP, was in the midst of ruining the mining industry. It was a period of sustained union-bashing, either overdue or unprovoked, depending on where your political allegiances lay, and broadcasting companies were determined to wrest control from the workforce. In the middle of all this, the second series of *Auf Wiedersehen, Pet*, one of the jewels in the broadcasting crown, was being bitterly fought over. The end result of all this grief, with neither side willing to give an inch, was the eventual ruin of British commercial television. It's taken a while, but just look at ITV now: on the rocks and sinking, both commercially and creatively. So much for the free market.

The broadcasting unions lost, as did all the others, and it was now a post-industrial Britain. Lenton Lane was an all-new, hi-tech studio complex, and it stank, literally, the way hospitals and government buildings tend to, of bleach, polish and other chemicals. Where there had been decades of tradition at Elstree, there was only stark, bland newness. My first day there was a scary indication of how life was going to be. On arrival, I approached the posh main reception desk, behind which were two smartly dressed security guards. I'm sure their job must have been a chore at times, but you expect common courtesy.

'Yes?' asked one guy. 'What can I do for you?' I was there, of course, to help make the second series of *Auf Wiedersehen, Pet*, arguably the most eagerly awaited show of the year, so they must have known I was coming in, but you go through the motions. 'Name?' I gave it and he looked down a list on his clipboard. 'Dressing room five,' or whatever number it was.

'Can I have the key, please?'

'No key.'

Where was it? The guy shrugged. 'One of your lot must've stolen it.'

One of my . . . Oh, I eventually twigged. Actors are also notorious thieves, right? Because you'd want to steal a dressing-room key, wouldn't you? To organize a late-night party in a building you couldn't access, or maybe weigh it in for scrap.

So how was I supposed to get into my dressing room? I asked. The guy shrugged again. I'd had it by this point so I went to the dressing room, kicked the door off its hinges and started to get changed.

A little while later the security guard turned up, accompanied by the studio manager who looked at the splintered door frame in amazement. 'Who did this?' he demanded. Did what? I asked. He spluttered: he was going to call the police, have me arrested for criminal damage. Didn't I know that door was brand new? That this whole studio was brand new? Why, it was the flagship regional . . . His face was going a dangerously deep red. I explained to him that should he do as he was threatening and have me arrested the financial consequences of my not being available for work would be about eighty grand for a day's lost studio time. That was why I had wanted to get in. That was why I had kicked down the door. I honestly felt I was making a valid and important point, but in hindsight I suppose I could have made it in a less violent way. Next day the door was mended and they had a key ready and waiting.

Sadly, it was more of the same all the way through the

shoot. The management folk weren't television people, so they had no idea of how magical the process is. When you're asking something special of people, as they were of us, you have to make those people *feel* special, because if you don't they'll not believe they can give something special and the result may be mediocrity. They looked at us and assumed we were our characters: builders were working-class blokes, so they were bound to be union members and therefore trouble. Worse, they had no love for the craft and process of programme-making. They might just as well have been producing fish-fingers. They're probably doing that today, now the studios have been mothballed. The city of Nottingham and its inhabitants went a long way towards making up for the daily nonsense we had to put up with at Lenton Lane, but after the unbridled joy of making the first series it was a real downer.

It was mostly work, work, work, but there were some great nights in Nottingham. We'd originally been offered the Royal, an upmarket hotel in the city centre, for our prolonged stay – the best part of a year – but Tim Spall, Roger Bamford and I decided to stay at the George, a smaller, less salubrious establishment sited on a noisy corner. We three had the top floor to ourselves and kept open house, with people coming and going day and night. Roger was usually in his cot by one a.m., but it was much later when Tim and I sounded lights-out.

It was a great place, and the star in its firmament was Mary, the elderly batty barmaid. With her hair stacked up in a bouffant style and a full set of gleaming dentures, she looked after us as if we were her own, and we loved her for it. She'd always refer to herself in the third person – 'Ooh, Mary doesn't like that!' Malcolm, the beleaguered night porter, looked after our late-night refreshment requests, which were regular and substantial. Over the year the champagne bill alone must have added up to thousands. Booze was easy, hot food less so. I was forever after something hot, and Malcolm would often leave his post to nip out for a kebab or what-have-you. Spall woke me up one Saturday morning and found me, face covered in grease, cuddling a turkey carcass. Overtaken with drunken hunger, I'd gone downstairs in the middle of the night and pinched it from the kitchen. Turned out it had been for a wedding reception that afternoon. Oh dear.

Because of the worsening situation between the unions and the management, we went out to Spain not knowing if we'd even get started, never mind complete the location filming. In the end we did, but not without problems. We'd all taken our wives and kids with us to Marbella and were billeted in apartments at the Melia Don Pepe hotel. It was great with all the little ones running around, and filming went as well as could be expected in the circumstances.

It was in Spain that I ended up looking down the barrel of a gun late one night and I was lucky indeed not to get shot. I'd had a gun pulled on me once before, during an argument in an Earl's Court bar between myself, a fully robed elderly Arab, his minder and a hooker. The girl took a slap, I took exception and it went from there. It was a bowel-mover, not an experience I wanted to repeat. But drink often makes you invincible – or so you imagine.

So there I was, sleeping off the drink one hot afternoon, sprawled out naked on my Spanish double bed, which was actually two singles pushed loosely together, when I woke suddenly, aware of a stinging sensation between my legs. I looked down and found a mosquito right on the end of my knob. I killed it but it must have been there for a good while because there was blood everywhere. (The bite left a nasty scar, which remains to this day.) In the process I fell through the gap in the beds and landed on the tiled floor. In a state of some confusion and anger I went down to the bar and showed Spall what had happened to my manhood. It was a right mess, but he thought my getting a blow-job from a mosquito was very funny. In my drunk, muddled state, I decided it was the fault of those two single beds, which kept parting and landing me on the floor. I'd had enough. I was going to move rooms.

There were no other rooms available at short notice so I was forced to stay put. I could, however, change my bed – or, at least, the mattress. My own decision, and a bad one. Later that night, after a bellyful of San Miguel beer, I found a stock room and enlisted Tim's help in lugging a mattress out and along the corridor. Soon we came upon an elderly Spanish security guard having a snooze. He opened his eyes and said something in Spanish, to the effect of 'Where are you going with that mattress?' I waved him away – 'Don't worry, Pop, it's all right, we're guests.' But he was having none of it and started shouting at us, still in Spanish. I returned fire in English, and so it went on until he pulled out a gun and pointed it straight at my head, his old hand shaking dangerously. I remember noticing his fingernails had black dirt under them. I was stone-cold sober now, wide-eyed and staring. In an instant the likely outcome had whizzed through my mind: he was probably a war veteran so he'd get the sympathy vote from the local court and most likely a suspended sentence, and I'd be a dead foreigner, going home in a box. All because of a mattress. For the sake of series continuity we put it back.

Right in the middle of filming and out of the blue I suddenly had a hit record on my hands.

As a result of the reception I'd been given when I introduced the Gary Moore Band at their Hammersmith gig, Gary's manager, Steve Barnett, asked me if I'd be interested in cutting a record. He couldn't have known it had been my dream since I was a kid. A week or so later we met at Steve's home in West Hampstead with Richard Griffiths of Virgin Records, but it soon became apparent, at least to me, that this wasn't going to fly. When we got round to discussing what kind of material we might record, Griffiths shrugged and told me, 'It doesn't matter. Right now, Jimmy, you could record yourself singing the phone book and the record would sell.' As far as the music business was concerned, 'actor' meant 'novelty record'. Not their fault, just the way it was. Bernard Cribbins singing 'Right Said Fred' and the like. To be fair, that was never the suggestion, but there was no other reference point, really, and I didn't fancy it. Instinct told me to leave it and, as I've tended to act on instinct and intuition all my life, I passed – reluctantly.

As it turned out, all was not lost. Soon after that meeting, I was roped in to sing some stuff on the *Morons From Outer Space* soundtrack and, on the strength of that, Peter Brown, who managed Mel and Griff, arranged for me to spend a little down time on the Barge, Virgin's floating recording studio tethered at Regent's Canal basin. Maybe the Virgin link was connected to my earlier meeting with Richard Griffiths, I don't know. Over a couple of nights in winter, my Dance Class pals, Tony Mac and Trevor Brewis, helped me record a couple of tracks. One was a stripped-down cover of the Rose Royce hit 'Love Don't Live Here Anymore'. I remember sitting in a café with Tony one morning, having been up all the previous night in the studio. We were both rather pleased with the way it had gone.

Virgin's MD was then Simon Draper, whose wife's sister

was married to Roger Taylor, the Queen drummer. Somehow Roger got to hear my tape and offered to produce some tracks for me. I was thrilled. This was real rock 'n' roll. I remember going over to his palatial house in Kensington and being flabbergasted by the sheer opulence. This was beyond rich. Rides in Roger's Bentley Turbo to Chelsea nightclubs only strengthened my belief that I was in the right hands.

We cut some tracks and had a great time doing it. Roger played drums as well as co-producing with Dave Richards, and roped in Phil Chen to play bass. What a rhythm section! I was off and rocking. The record was released in the spring of 1985, just as I was starting work on the second series of *Auf Wiedersehen, Pet*, and struggled until Dave Lee Travis began to play it regularly. Next thing, it was in the charts. I'd got a hit record! It went to number three and sold over 400,000 copies.

But a major problem soon arose – and drove the record company bonkers: I wasn't available for promotion. If you're lucky enough to have a hit, you really should be out there plugging it for all you're worth. But I couldn't. I was filming. For a whole year. I was gutted, but there was nothing I could do. Roger Bamford kindly let me go early one day so that I could whiz to London to do *Top of the Pops*. I didn't even have time to buy clothes and had to appear in my *Auf Wiedersehen, Pet* costume. But it was the fulfilment of a long-held dream. Tony Mac was on bass, and Trevor Brewis on drums. My pals from the Dance Class were along for the ride. Oh, it was a sweet moment. While I was singing I tried to imagine the look on everyone's faces up home, but it made me laugh so I had to stop. No nerves, none at all. Funny, that.

A hit, then. Success, of sorts, in music. It had happened at last and it was a big thrill, especially for my mam. She was the toast of the Walker Road bingo. After all my talk I felt vindicated, but it would take a long time and a lot of work to establish myself in the eyes of the music business as more than just a novelty turn, a thespian messing around. I was up against a tradition of actors who'd had a bash at the old singing malarkey by way of earning a quick payday. I won't name names. You know the culprits. Take your pick.

Closer to home, Gary Holton was having terrible problems with hard drugs and trying to keep it together as best he could. The success of our show depended to a great degree on the interplay between the actors. Unless everyone was on song it didn't work. Professional pride made sure we all knew our stuff and it was usually a joy to do ensemble scenes, but as the weeks went by and Gary got steadily worse it became more and more difficult to get things done. It wasn't easy for anyone. Gary felt bad about letting everyone down, and none of us knew what to do for the best. In fact, I don't think there was anything we could have done because Gary had to do it himself and, God bless him, he tried. He wasn't the first good person to go under because of drugs and there have been many since. I tried threatening him with a good hiding, which scared him into getting his act together for a week or so, but it all just went to hell again. It was heartbreaking to witness. The last time I saw Gary alive he was in the Lenton Lane main studio corridor, crying. 'Look at this, man,' he said, and he held up a copy of that day's *Daily Star*. The front-page headline read, 'HEROIN HOODLUM'. His mum had seen it and it had made her unwell. He was so upset. He loved to be in the papers but he'd paid a very heavy price for allowing the tabloid press into his life.

We were rehearsing in Hammersmith the day the call came to say he had died. Although I was shocked by the news, I wasn't surprised. We all just packed up and went home. It was beyond even a drink.

We all had nicknames, and Gary's was Twinkle, as in 'little star'. At the end of the funeral service Harry Belafonte's 'Catch A Falling Star' was played. He would have liked that.

Gary died a month or so before we were due to finish filming, and the decision had to be taken as to whether we should finish or throw in the towel. After a lot of thought we decided to finish. We all felt that that was what he would have wanted. But it wasn't pleasant. The series had to be completed with a double doing long-shots, back to camera. It spooked a lot of the guys. If you saw the double from behind, with his wig on, it was easy to imagine it was Gary.

That year Miriam and I lost another close friend. Midway through the filming, we received news that Peter Knox, big Peter, the man responsible for bringing Miriam and me together, had died from multiple sclerosis. We made the long, sad journey up the M1 to say goodbye. The crematorium chapel was filled to bursting with his family and friends, literally hundreds of people. I saw lads I'd not seen for years – decades, in some cases. There was no reminiscing, no catching up, no crack, just shakes of the head at the unfairness of it all. Lots of hard men cried that day. I did, too. We often talk about big Peter – he was a special man. Miss you, mate.

The second series of *Auf Wiedersehen, Pet* limped to its finish in early 1986, and we were all glad to be done with it. I'd not wanted to do it in the first place and kind of wished I hadn't, what with Gary's death. It was nowhere near as pure, strong or fresh as the first, and yet in terms of audience numbers it was even more successful. It peaked with the touching tale of Oz going home to see his son, which pulled in a whopping sixteen million viewers. Absolutely incredible, but problematic for a bloke tormented by celebrity.

No rest for the wicked. I was straight off to Scotland to make a film for the BBC entitled *Shoot for the Sun*, a dark, powerful piece about drug-dealers and no-hopers, wonderfully written by Peter MacDougall. It was an education to go to those Scottish housing schemes and see kids running around in the snow with nothing more than socks on their feet. Every day we would go with our film unit to take advantage of some poor soul's misfortune, point our cameras at the poverty, then go back to our nice warm hotels for dinner and a comfy kip. The voyeuristic side of location filming has never sat easily with me, and it's one of the reasons I don't much care for it.

Peter, a whirlwind of a man with a gargantuan appetite for life, lived in London, in Primrose Hill, and his local, which doubled as a kind of office, was the Queen's. He and I spent many a happy hour in there, discussing the script's plot and sub-plots, willing each other on. Three rather curmudgeonly old men were always sitting in one corner of the bar, under the big bay window. We'd sometimes have words with them, though it was never heated – they always had plenty to say for themselves. To me they were just grumpy old bastards. I found out years later that one was Kingsley Amis.

Peter had written this piece especially for me, a great honour and a huge step for me personally. As I was playing the lead for the first time I felt it only right that I go a bit more potty, hitting the drink in even bigger measure – not so much burning the candle at both ends, more setting the house on fire, ably aided and abetted, it has to be said, by my pal Peter. Of course, I was already a big drinker, but for my Scottish adventure I pulled out all the stops and moved up a gear. The amounts I was putting away were both ridiculous and dangerous, and by the time I returned to London it was beyond acceptable. I hated waking up in the mornings with my head feeling like it had been hit with a brick and my big mouth desert dry. I hated all that morning-after guilt, not being able to remember what I'd said or to whom I'd said it. It was usually something offensive. I had developed a habit of falling, in a stupor, into the hallway of my house after a session, and would wake up the next morning covered with whatever Miriam had been good enough to throw over me, a coat or a blanket. All that stopped one morning when I woke up shivering. The front door was wide open, as usual, and a gale whistling up my arse, but there was no blanket, nothing. I went upstairs and demanded to know why I'd been left to freeze my nuts off. Miriam told me that if I could manage to get all the way across central London under my own steam, to our house and through the front door, I should be able to manage the stairs to bed. If not, tough shit. Thereafter I made it to bed.

As a result of what had gone on between the tabloid press and Gary Holton, I was now even more anti-print media and if I was asked to talk to them I didn't want to know. There was only one occasion when I relented and it had an odd outcome.

Tim Spall called me one day to ask if I'd be up for meeting a journalist. The author Daniel Farson, renowned chronicler of Soho past and present and piss-artist *extraordinaire*, apparently wanted to interview us together for a feature intended to run in the *Daily Mail*. Ha, those were the days! I'd never heard of Farson and, having less than zero interest in reading lots of things I never said in newspapers I'd never normally read, my answer was the usual 'No.' I suggested to Tim that he do it on his own but apparently that wasn't an option. It had to be both of us. It was obvious Tim wanted to meet Farson (they went on to become good friends) so I agreed, and a date was set.

Come the day and around midday, the three of us met up in the French House, a shit-hole one-room boozer with brown-stained walls tucked between two retail outlets at the bottom of Frith Street and run at that time by Gaston Leroux, a bull-necked, grey-haired grumpy old Frenchman with a wonderful waxed moustache. A haven and a rendezvous for gay men and ex-pat Frogs, it was already busy when I landed – it didn't take many to pack the single room out – and there were loads of gay men, young and old, fat and thin, most sporting Village People leather chaps and thick droopy walrus moustaches. I know the public's general perception of me is as someone who's been round the block and all that, but I'd not had any social contact with the gay community and I was a little nervous around these guys. I was with Spall, though, and my back was firmly up against a wall, so I figured I'd be all right. Gulp the grog, say as little as possible, get it over with ASAP and fuck off home. That was the plan, anyway.

Dan Farson was around five ten, heavily built and sweaty, with unkempt silver-grey hair and drink-blotched skin. He looked to me like an elderly Billy Bunter as he cast a jaundiced, haughty eye over the pub's motley clientele. He wasn't unattractive, quite the opposite, sort of slobbishly distinguished-looking, yet despite his expensive blue suit he cut a rather sad figure. His voice was rasping, pickled and posh. He was good crack, 'quite a character', as my pal John Watson might have said, and in no time at all the drink was going down a treat, vodka, beer and wine – gallons of it, courtesy of someone else, which always gave me an incentive and a raging thirst. Tim was on cracking form, regaling us with laddy-actor anecdotes, lots of which I'd not heard. We were generally having a right old lark when up from somewhere popped a little man. He was elderly, short, pear-shaped, sallow-skinned, with pinched lips, blown hair and plucked eyebrows over-emphasized with thick brown pencil. He was wearing a rather sad-looking singlet. He stopped dead square in front of me and, with a kind of slow, dirty smirk, said, 'Can I buy you a drink?'

I was flustered but I did my level best not to look it. I did a terrible job of pretending to consider his offer and, far too quickly, decide against it. 'No, thank you.' Polite but firm, I was aiming and hoping for. Unambiguous.

'Oh, go on,' he pressed. 'Just a little drink.'

People were watching us now, watching *me*. I could feel my face and neck getting all hot and going a lovely bright red. The way this fellow was smiling at me left me in no doubt as to his intentions. 'Look,' I said, 'I'm sorry, but I'm not that way inclined, all right? And, really, a bloke your age should know better than to risk a clip around the ear. So go on, bugger off!'

Thankfully, the little fellow took the hint and shuffled away. It would have been impossible not to. I heaved a sigh of relief. The conversation was back with Tim and Farson. I was making a good job of being the worst interviewee in the world. He turned to me. 'Let me get this straight. You don't like being recognized, you don't like doing interviews and you don't like having your picture taken. Have you ever thought you might be in the wrong profession?'

'Absolutely, pal,' I replied, all angry and defensive, fixing him a bead, 'but I didn't ask to be here.' Either specifically or metaphorically.

More grog – oh dear, lots more grog! – more stories, more

questions, more grump, more noise. By now I was so happy I'd even stopped shouting at Gaston about his lot rolling over in two world wars – and I don't mean 'happy' as in 'pissed', I mean 'happy' as in 'having a lovely time'. Then, fuck me, if the old bloke in the singlet wasn't back in front of me, eyebrows arched, smiling.

'Hello,' he said, looking up rather dreamily.

'You again?' I growled down at him. 'What is it this time?'

He went all coy and cuddly, wringing his little wrinkled hands. 'I was wondering . . . well, I was wondering if you'd like to come back to my place.'

What? *What?* He had some bottle, I had to give him that. If I was an ageing poofter I don't think I would have wanted to risk the likely consequences of trying to pull a nasty-looking bastard like I was back then. Or maybe I would. Maybe the danger adds to the fun. God knows.

'Your place?' I said eventually, my eyebrows standing to attention. 'To do what, exactly?'

'I'd like to draw you,' he replied, as innocent as you please.

'Draw? Ho-ho! Is that what you're calling it, these days?'

Spall was laughing at me. Ha ha, very funny. I'm not very good if I think I'm being laughed at – ever since school and those fucking short trousers. So there was big pressure on me now. If I wasn't careful I'd be punching someone. Not Shorty here, in front of me: he was far too old. It would have looked great in the newspapers, me filling in some sad old poof.

'No, honestly,' he said. 'I have a place just across the road.'

By now everyone in the room was watching, or that was how it felt, waiting to see what would happen next. My head felt like a thermometer that was going to explode real soon and splatter the lot of them with my expensive mercury. Spall was in tears now, knowing I was way out of my depth

199

and drowning. It was all right for him – he was a theatrical, hung out with poofs all the time, worked with them. He was used to them, no problem. I had rather a long way to go.

'Right,' I said, intent on bringing the curtain down on this painful vignette. 'Now listen, you dirty little bastard, I know what you're up to, and it's not gonna wash with me, right? Why don't you fuck off back over there with your poofy mates and leave me alone?'

'If you're sure?' said Shorty, the look on his crumpled old boat-race suggesting I was about to miss out on the opportunity of a lifetime. Ha! I think not. If I'm sure? 'I'm sure,' I said to him. 'Fuck off!'

Off he fucked, back over to where his pals were parked and mooching, a gaggle of pretty young leather boys, all brazen, dirty and mocking. Thank goodness, the cabaret was over and the place settled back into what passed for normal.

But Dan Farson was clearly aghast. 'Do you know who that was?' said he.

'No. Who was it?'

'Francis Bacon.'

'Francis Bacon?' I said, with a shrug and a shake of my head. 'Who's he?'

'Only Britain's most famous living artist,' said drunken Dan.

'Never heard of him,' I said. It was true. 'What about David Hockney?'

Farson dismissed this suggestion with a look of such haughty disdain that Kenneth Williams would have been proud of it.

'Well, if that's true, he should be ashamed of himself, the dirty old fucker!'

Bacon, Farson, Hockney, all of them gay, as it happens.

Easy now, no problem, but hard for me to handle back then. What a prude.

More drink was consumed, and soon I'd had enough of the interview and the French House and the whole hassle-ridden afternoon. I wanted to go home and have a lie-down. Spall and Dan Farson headed off to Langan's Brasserie in a black cab and a stupor, intent on continuing the interview. I headed for the wilds of NW2.

After I'd collapsed into an armchair and had a lengthy nap, I told Miriam all about the afternoon's happenings in the boozer.

'What was the name of the artist?' she wanted to know.

I couldn't remember. 'Bacon? Somebody Bacon?'

'Not . . . Francis Bacon?' she asked, literally stopping in her tracks.

'That was him! Dirty old fucker. Have you heard of him?'

'*Have I heard of him!* You should've gone!'

'What? Don't be daft, woman. I might've had to give him a wank. Or worse!'

'But you would've ended up hanging in the National Portrait Gallery!'

Maybe. Who knows? And though I'd dearly love to be hanging in the National Portrait Gallery, the price of admission had seemed too high.

It was time to try to learn how to be a good dad – and it was hard, even though I'd read the books and gone to the odd class. The renewed success of *Auf Wiedersehen, Pet* had brought back all the pressures I was not good at dealing with. Already uncomfortable with the whole idea of celebrity and where, if at all, I fitted into it, I began to resent being recognized by everyone, and to draw back from performing. The first time round had been great, and I'd loved it: the performances and behaviour that had got me arrested regularly were garnering praise, celebrity and massive financial reward. Now, they were making me unhappy.

I also felt trapped by a sense of obligation to those I'd left behind in Newcastle. Whether I liked it or not, I was flying the flag for all the folk on the housing estates who hadn't been as lucky as me. They told me as much. I was unable to deal with it rationally so I drank all the more to dull the confusion and pain. Gradually, my personality changed. Instead of being the outgoing, open person I'd been all my life, I became introverted and guarded, ever more suspicious of everything and everyone, a different person from the one with whom Miriam had fallen in love. I feared that if I didn't do something about it now, I would become seriously unhinged.

I still had to earn a crust, though, and the best way of doing that was by exploiting my television popularity. In television I could make loads of money, but it meant all that exposure, perpetuating the vicious circle. But with my background, I couldn't say no to the huge sums I was offered. I did a lucrative commercial for Kodak. It ran to six figures, which at the time was uncommon, and the money came in very handy as we were strapped for ready cash. But it had become no fun, the filming business, and I was moving away from it more and more. I was still quietly buying and selling houses, but not at the rate I'd managed in the past. What to do?

Early in 1987, we discovered that Miriam was expecting our second child, and we were both thrilled with the prospect of a brother or sister for our golden Tom. Having been through the parenthood experience already, I considered myself prepared for the new baby but I didn't know what else was in store for me.

I had realized that if I was going to make a go of it in the entertainment business, it was essential that I gain proper control of my work. I had never been comfortable as an employee, and ever since that first day at Elstree, when I'd stood behind the camera on the set, watching silently, I'd had a hankering to produce a show. Not to direct – that's never interested me, despite what many people thought when they labelled me a control freak. Anyone who's ever worked in the business will testify that the ultimate power-trip is in directing. I wouldn't thank you for that job. Everyone on the set has a question for you, and their question is the most important.

My idea of owning my own production company and governing my destiny just would not go away. At the time one or two actors had production companies, but it wasn't common: the broadcasting companies didn't like the idea of the kids having the keys to the sweet shop. I decided it was time to have a go. It would be a challenge – a big ask, as they say these days – but I couldn't stand all the sitting around waiting for others to give me the kind of work I wanted. I was awful indoors when I was bored. As usual, there was nothing but encouragement from Miriam, although she must have been concerned about the wisdom of such a move. My reputation within the industry was one of uncompromising directness, and plenty of people would have loved to see me fall flat on my face, but that made me all the more determined to succeed. I took a deep breath and made a start.

I had to tell Pippa Markham – another who had taken a chance on me – that I was moving on. The reason for this was a simple one. Plant & Froggatt then represented only performers, and I needed an organization that could help further my production interests. Changing agents is not a thing you undertake lightly. It's a big, nerve-racking number, all the tougher because Pippa had become a good friend to

Miriam and me. For better or worse, I believe in doing these things myself, rather than hide behind a letter or a secretary – and Pippa was ill when I called on her. I had to stand at the foot of her bed and tell her I was off. She was understanding, and even wished me well. I'm glad we've all remained good friends.

I moved from Plant & Froggatt to the much larger Duncan Heath Associates. Duncan's outfit represented producers, directors, writers and technicians as well as actors. I had met Lindy King, one of the company's talent agents, some time earlier and she'd offered to look after me, should I ever decide to move. I'd only been there about a month when she left to have a baby. Jonathan Altaraz inherited me, and we got along well right from the off.

I was also introduced to Duncan, who looked after all the firm's big guns. In terms of industry standing, I was certainly not in the premier league, but I was determined. I knew that if I was going to achieve anything beyond acting gigs, I was in the right place. DHA was loud and bustling, very different from the rather unnerving calm of Plant & Froggatt. The sprawling offices on Wardour Street seemed to be buzzing with energy. I felt lucky to be a part of it.

A job offer came in one day, so I went over to Duncan's Wardour Street offices and made my way up the stairs. A man passed me on his way down. In a right state he was, tearful, sobbing. I mentioned it to one of the agents, who told me he was a client, who was convinced his career was going nowhere and that he was destined to be nothing more than a bit-part spear-carrier at the RSC. A little while later the same actor landed the leading part in one of American television's biggest shows. You just never know.

The job offer was for a commercial in New Zealand. *Auf Wiedersehen, Pet* had been well received in the Antipodes, but, as much as I liked to travel, I didn't fancy going all the way to New Zealand just to make an advertisement. Anyway, Miriam was eight months pregnant and couldn't travel. I said no – but the New Zealanders wouldn't take no for an answer, and pestered me for two weeks. Eventually my agent suggested we put in a ridiculous list of demands, in the hope that they would leave us alone: a couple of first-class return tickets and a quarter of a million New Zealand dollars as my fee. We thought that would be that. But they agreed.

Miriam and I discussed it: NZ$250,000 – around £100,000 – was an enormous amount, and Miriam felt it was too much to turn down, but the shoot was in the same week as the baby was due. Flying was out of the question for her, so late in her pregnancy, and after much soul-searching we agreed I'd have to go alone. Miriam promised not to give birth until I got home.

But what to do with the other ticket? It had been pre-paid, so I had to either use it or lose it. Tony Mac was on the dole at the time, living up in Sunderland and having a tough time. When I called him to ask if he fancied going to New Zealand at the end of the week for ten days, all expenses paid, he thought it was a wind-up, but a few days later we were in the air.

The total number of passengers in the cavernous first-class section of the Singapore Airlines plane was three – Tony, myself and the son of the president of Singapore: Heathrow to Auckland, with a stopover in Singapore, twenty-nine hours, or thereabouts. As much champagne as we could drink and, of course, we made pigs of ourselves. The amount I got through on the outward journey nearly killed me, and that was only the start of it.

The brief Singapore interlude had us in a bit of a flap. As we came in to land, a female voice announced, 'Ladies and gentlemen, in a moment we will be landing in Singapore. The local time is *blah* and the temperature on the ground is *blah-blah-blah*. We hope you have a pleasant stay, and we would remind you that the penalty for trafficking drugs is death.' We were not trafficking anything, but it was a frightening announcement. As we waited for the door to open, one of the stewardesses asked Tony where his hat was. He told her he didn't have one. She explained to him that the airport authorities would therefore be looking to give him a haircut, so he tucked his pony-tail inside the collar of his jacket. We were glad it was a short stopover.

The ten days I spent in New Zealand were wonderful. It was rather like England was in the 1950s, all open roads and polite, friendly people. No colour, though: just white faces. That was a bit odd – I'd expected to see Maoris. The reception we got anywhere and everywhere was never less than enthusiastic. Even the bouncers and doormen at the Auckland nightclubs were courteous to a fault. 'Good evening, Mr Nail. We're all great fans of your work', etc. I'd had forks pulled out of my mouth in England by impatient people wanting autographs, so this was new and it threw me. More confusion, more booze.

There was quite a lot of down time in which to enjoy the Winnebago I'd asked for as part of the deal, and Tony and I saw a lot of the North Island. Back in Auckland we learned that Billy Connolly, a client of Pippa's whom I'd met once or twice, was doing a tour Down Under. A phone-call home secured us some tickets for his Auckland show, and afterwards we went out with him for an Indian meal. Billy told anecdotes to anyone within earshot in his broad Scottish brogue, and the waiters were all Asians with New Zealand accents. On another night I sang a slightly slurred 'Someone To Watch Over Me' with the house band in an Auckland jazz club.

I spent a lot of time thinking and worrying about Miriam and one day I had a bit of a bad turn on the set. Suddenly it was a struggle to get my breath. The local doctor arrived and told me I'd been hyperventilating. It sounded scary until he explained it to me, and the probable causes – stress and anxiety. He asked if I'd ever tried acupuncture and I said I hadn't. He whipped out his box of needles and said, 'Trust me.' All went well until he pushed a needle into my philtrum – the fluted tissue between top lip and nostrils. I almost went through the ceiling, and so did the doctor. But it worked, and I've used acupuncture since to very good effect.

The commercial was for barbecue products. I can't remember much about the week, what with the drink, the needles and everything else, but the producers told me they were happy with what we'd done. On the blower one night, I asked Miriam what was new. She told me this and that, and then, almost in passing, 'There's been a bad storm.' It was October 1987.

Job done, it was party time. Masses more booze for the big-shot celebrity, then we were off. On the return journey Tony and I hit the bar once more but this time, somehow, we surpassed our previous consumption. All the lovely food went to waste – lobster, *filet mignon*, caviar. The more they brought, the more we drank. It was complete madness. I honestly don't know how it didn't kill me.

At last we were home, and I had a chance to see just how bad the storm had been as we were driven from Heathrow to my home. To the left of the M4, looking north, every tree we passed seemed to have been uprooted or was leaning over on a westerly diagonal. It looked unreal, like a movie special effect.

I arrived home to find that Miriam had kept her word, and

staggered up to bed, leaving Tony on the settee downstairs. Immediately I fell into a deep sleep. It seemed as though I'd only just closed my eyes when Miriam shook me awake. The baby was coming. Oh, God, not now! I was exhausted and still paralytic. I had also, as a result of overdoing it with the drink on a previous flight, been breathalyzed and banned from driving. Tony would have to drive us to the hospital. Somehow I got myself off the bed. Poor Tony was in an even worse state than me, and that drive to the hospital, in the dark, through the rain, with me barking directions and Miriam gasping, terrified him.

Somehow we made it to St Mary's where, just before midnight, Fredric Daniel Jones arrived, weighing in at seven pounds four ounces. Not before some fun and games, though. We'd arranged to go private this time, so a room was ready and waiting. The doctor booked to deliver the baby was summoned and when he got there he took a look at me and asked if I was all right. I told him I was just tired after a long flight. He asked if I'd like a coffee, and I said that would be lovely. This was more like it: no having to deal with pissed-up punters. How was I to know he'd go off and make it himself? We were moments away from Fred's birth and the doctor had disappeared. Incandescent with rage, Miriam called me a number of unrepeatable names with a venom that truly frightened me.

Later, after I'd held my beautiful new son in my arms and made sure Miriam was comfortable, I left the hospital and walked along to Paddington railway station where I jumped into a black cab. A shabby-looking middle-aged man was slumped in the driving seat. Euphoric, I said to him, 'My wife's just had a baby son.' 'Yours, is it?' he replied.

I considered throttling him, but then I thought, Fuck you, mate. You're not going to spoil this beautiful day.

Soon after Fred was born I stopped drinking. I remember waking up one morning, after yet another heavy session, to find Tom beside the bed, staring at me. He must have been nearly three, but the expression on his face made me feel as though God almighty was looking down at me and wasn't at all pleased with what he saw. I'm sure it was nothing to the bairn, just his dad sprawled out asleep on the bed, but I felt disgusted with myself. It wasn't right for a kid to see his dad in such an incapable state, I thought. How long had he been standing there? What might he have heard me say in my sleep? It was probably no more than the usual cocktail of guilt and self-loathing that invariably followed a drinking session, but it coincided with my need to strike out on my own as a television producer and, most importantly, my fear of losing Miriam. We'd not discussed it but I realized that no one in their right mind would put up indefinitely with my behaviour. Maybe self-preservation kicked in. Or maybe, with Fred's arrival, I'd finally accepted my responsibilities. Perhaps it was a mixture of all those things. Whatever it was, I gave up that day and haven't had a drink since – well, one pint, the night my dad died, and a single sip of champagne to celebrate a special anniversary with Tim Spall, but nothing more. I vowed my kids would never again see me in such a mess. They haven't, and they won't.

To my surprise, I never missed the booze and I've never been tempted. People often say my staying off the sauce is really impressive, especially without the help of AA, but to me it was just something I had to do. Where hangovers had once lasted a few hours, now it was days. After my near-fatal binges in New Zealand I'd crossed a line. Drink wasn't fun any more: I'd gone off it. I believe that saved my life.

All the drunken shouting and throwing crockery had taken its toll on Miriam and me. I was determined to try to mend my relationship with her before it was too late. No one should have to put up with the kind of nonsense she did, and it shames me to think of all the horrible things I said and did. It's a funny thing, giving up the drink: everyone assumes you'll automatically become a better person for it, but the only thing that's guaranteed is that you'll be a different person, and not necessarily the one with whom your partner fell in love. We were in for a tough few years, but neither of us likes to give up, so we worked at it.

Being free of the drink was a revelation. Sometimes I'd go into a pub for a tonic water and couldn't see what the attraction had been for all those years – decades. Then I started to think about the way daily life was geared in New-castle when I was growing up, the way all police overtime was rostered around weekends, the way the courts were ready for Monday-morning hearings, the defending solicitors with their excuses that their client had had one or ten too many, the money the state made from over-indulgence in alcohol. Suddenly it was more than individual foolishness: it was organized and endemic. It was so well established that people couldn't see it. It was only with the benefit of hind-sight and sobriety that I recognized that drink is a convenient means of anaesthetizing the masses. The patronizing view of the zealous, dry convert? I'm not so sure.

I desperately wanted to establish myself as a television pro-ducer, behind the camera and out of the way, but the broad-casters made it clear that I would have to appear in the stuff I produced. I was back with the double-edged sword. By the end of the 1980s, I had come to detest being identified as and with Oz, the character who'd made me famous. I believed that he was all people thought I was capable of.

If that were so, what difference did it make? Well, in the

absence of understanding, confusion reigned. Where not long before I'd been an outgoing bloke, now I was a near-recluse, doing nothing to draw attention to myself. I felt as though my own personality had been buried beneath this fictitious creation. People would call, 'Oz!' to me, and I'd reply, 'No – Jimmy. There's a difference.' I was determined to be seen for what I really was. The real Jimmy. No artifice. No fiction. So what did I do about it? I invented a whole new persona for myself. Bonkers? I guess so, but I wasn't aware of it at the time.

One day, after I'd caught sight of my naked self in the mirror in our Dicey Avenue bedroom and noticed my breasts were bigger than Miriam's, I decided I had to get into shape. I began to work out big-time. I had to suffer, of course. My daily regime was Spartan. My diet, self-created and pre-dictably daft, consisted of nothing but raw vegetables and fruit for about four months. Goodness knows what the house smelt like. Four stones disappeared, equivalent to 112 packs of butter.

I'd lost weight and I looked very different, but something unexpected and frightening was revealed. I was standing on the driveway at Dicey Avenue one sunny Sunday afternoon, talking to Tony Antoniou, our next-door neighbour and my family doctor, when he looked at my throat and asked, 'How long have you had that lump?' Cue panic in Cricklewood.

The next day, after a night spent checking my life-insurance policies, I was sitting in the waiting room of a Harley Street specialist. I had ultra-sound and scans, in gloomy basement rooms, and was sent home. I paced around the house, anxiously awaiting the results. A week passed, but I was reluctant to chase what might be bad news. Finally I was at the end of my tether. I telephoned Tony, who advised me to call the specialist.

After I'd been passed from secretary to assistant, I eventually got him on the phone. 'Haven't you had the results yet?' he said, sounding surprised. It turned out he'd forgotten to post them to me. I decided to go into town and collect them myself.

There was good news and bad news. It looked as though whatever was inside my throat was benign, but it was pressing on my vocal cords. Not good news if you sing. Tony suggested I consult a surgeon.

Lionel Gracey was a lovely man, slim and distinguished with silver hair and the kind of reassuring bedside manner all medical folk should have. He reminded me of George Martin, the Beatles' producer. He was one of the country's top thyroid surgeons, and patients travelled from all over the world to see him. Over a cuppa he suggested an operation to remove whatever was in my neck. He and Tony explained that if the lump should turn out to be cancer, the best place you could have it was in the thyroid gland as the body could manage perfectly well without it, although I might have to take a thyroxine tablet every day for the rest of my life.

Lionel and Tony were both of the opinion that it was nothing to worry about, but I said to them, 'With all due respect, it ain't your neck.' As usual, Miriam was a tower of strength, reassuring me and telling me to behave.

A week or so later I was in the St John and St Elizabeth Hospital, St John's Wood, getting a jab, doing the count and passing out way before I reached ten. I was under for five hours, and when I came round, I was convinced I'd died. I looked up, all groggy, and there in front of me was Mr Gracey in a dinner jacket and bow-tie. I stared at him, befuddled. He smiled. 'It's all right, Jimmy. I'm on my way to a dinner party, but I called in to let you know there's nothing to worry about.' Then he warned me that I was not to talk, and that he'd prescribed everything in the medicine cabinet by way of pain relief. All I had to do was press the buzzer.

That night I woke in great pain and pressed the buzzer. A night-nurse appeared and asked me to turn on to my side. She pulled my pyjama bottoms down and stuck a needle into my bum. A moment later I was overwhelmed by euphoria. I lay there smiling without a care in the world. This went on for three days, by which time I was ready and waiting, bum bared, for the nurse's arrival. Day three she spoiled the party. No more jabs, she told me. Pills from now on. 'I want the jab!' I protested.

'You can't have any more jabs.'

'Why not?' I asked.

'Because they're morphine, and you've had your whack.'

Oh, how I loved that feeling. Total bliss. If that was what addicts experienced, I understood the attraction. It was an incredible, powerful, whoosh-type hit. What surprised me, however, was that although I'd quickly got to love those jabs, my body and mind seemed to accept it was only a short-term medicinal thing. How come I wasn't roaming the wards looking for a fix? How come I wasn't addicted?

A few weeks' recuperation at home followed, and I lay on the settee feeling sorry for myself. Lenny Henry came over to see me one afternoon and was a little shocked by the state I was in: I'd lost more weight worrying about the outcome of the operation.

A couple of weeks later I was sitting in Mr Gracey's waiting room with two well-heeled, middle-aged Arab women and their twenty-something daughters. It was all pretty anxious, with none of us knowing quite where to look. Then the door opened and Mr Gracey called me in to tell me the news I'd been praying for – yes, I prayed, just like every other coward who tries to cover all the angles when the chips are down. He explained it had been a benign cyst, and that he'd carried out a partial thyroidectomy to remove it. I wouldn't even have to take the thyroxine tablets. All I'd have to do was go for six-monthly, then twelve-monthly check-ups. I was ecstatic – I wanted to do a dance, but settled for giving him a hug. As he ushered me out, his arm round my shoulder, he said, 'Now I have to tell these ladies that their daughters weren't so lucky.' It seemed that I'd had all the luck – again.

I hit the street, walked round the corner, took a deep breath and kicked my heels in the air.

I I

By the time Ian La Frenais arrived in London, in the spring of 1989, to discuss ideas for our brand-new television series, I'd lost a quarter of my body weight, and was, quite literally, a different man. I think it frightened him a little.

I was also, for better or worse, teetotal. Knocking the drink on the head left a big hole, and I needed something to fill it. I turned to work: I'd double my efforts on all fronts, I thought. 'Driven' doesn't really do it justice: I became madly focused.

And although I was run off my feet with work and two kids to help bring up, the end of the 1980s found me feeling restless, bored and listless, trying to work out what to do with the rest of my life, what direction to take, and the answers to life's big questions. I was in my mid-thirties. I'd been away from the high jinks and adventure that had been *Auf Wiedersehen, Pet* for a couple of years, and although there'd been plenty of well-paid work in film, television and music, nothing had matched up to it.

I'd worked on some lovely projects, such as *Danny, the Champion of the World*, with a blond-streaked Jeremy Irons and Robbie Coltrane, but the crack on other gigs just wasn't in the same league. Nor was the writing quality. Kevin Whately had said as much when he was trying to convince me to do the second series. Stuff like the *Auf Wiedersehen, Pet* scripts just didn't come along very often. Did I want to continue in the fickle world of television, where you could be everyone's fave at one moment and forgotten the next? Or should I go back to the property game? The anonymity of buying and selling property was certainly a plus point. Should we stay in London or go back north? For a long while I wondered about all this and talked about it endlessly with Miriam. The top and bottom of it was that I wasn't being challenged or stretched, which I need.

Meanwhile, day-to-day life flew by. There was always more than enough to do, with our two lively sons, Tom and Fred, to occupy our every waking hour and a few of the sleeping ones, too. Incredible how two little people cast from the same mould can be so unlike each other. Tom's dominant characteristics seemed to be those of his mum, and Fred's were mine. Sorry about that, Fred. Every hour of the day brought a new discovery, and I began to understand why people make such a big deal about having children.

So, there was unbridled joy at home, but creatively I missed working with the *Auf Wiedersehen, Pet* guys. The challenge of making something substantial and special out of abstract scenarios and daft ideas in ensemble performance had been satisfying. I guess Tim had been right when he'd said I'd come home, and now my adopted home had gone, I missed it. More than anything, I missed working with Ian. The urge to write something was growing.

I'd got to know Ian over the time we'd been involved with *Auf Wiedersehen, Pet* and although we seldom saw each other, because he lived in Los Angeles, we'd developed a friendship based on our regional ties: Ian had been a West Monkseaton lad, and had a sense of humour that was similar to mine. We respected and admired each other too. He and I had had some fallings-out while we were working on *Auf Wiedersehen, Pet*, especially during the second series, but Ian doesn't let disagreements fester and doesn't bear a grudge, which is just as well for me. During our many arguments, which, nine times out of ten, I would have kicked off, he was patience itself, trying valiantly to make me see sense *and* picking up the tab for dinner. My relentless pursuit of authenticity was in itself unrealistic: television is not reality – not our bit of it, anyway – and it's not the job of comedy-drama scriptwriters to make it so. It took me a long time to understand that, and to appreciate what Ian gave me. I'm glad I can recognize it today and say a big thank-you.

From the outset, Ian had encouraged me to write, advising me to look for the good idea, the strong idea, the one that keeps coming back into your mind, and, as a rule of thumb, to write about what I knew. I'd set to work, blissfully unaware of just how difficult it would be. He also suggested that I give my characters the names of people I knew so that I could more easily envisage them talking, moving, doing. It worked a treat. The first thing I came up with was *Welcome to the Working Week*, set in a glazing factory. Structurally it was all over the place but there were one or two decent gags, one or two promising moments.

I well remember in the mid-eighties having Ian over to the house in Dicey Avenue to show him a draft of something I'd been working on and was excited about. It was hard work getting him to come out to such an unhappening postcode as NW2 but eventually he relented. I felt the content of my script was strong. I'd followed Ian's suggestion and based it on something I knew about. Now I was about to get an opinion from one of the acknowledged masters in the field. My script told the story of two English guys, a rough north-eastern musician and a softie southern manager, who journey to America in search of fame, fortune and recognition. They end up in Nashville, where all goes pear-shaped. I'd called it *Crocodile Shoes*, which was the title of a song Tony Mac had written some years before. It was a pretty little ballad with a memorable, catchy chorus. Once you'd heard it you couldn't get it out of your head, and I was convinced it could be a big hit.

As Ian read, I paced the living room and made some of my undrinkable coffee. After an hour or so he put the script down. 'Well?' I asked. 'Any good?'

'No,' he said. 'Not really.' Just like that. Didn't feel the need to elaborate.

Talk about crestfallen. Talk about deflated. Once I'd picked myself up off the floor I chucked the script into a drawer and left it there. I learned an important lesson that day. When it came to work, Ian wasn't into flattering folk for the sake of it. Inside his passport it gives his occupation as writer, and he's rightly proud of that. I accepted his opinion. It would have been pointless not to just because what I'd been told wasn't what I'd wanted to hear. I did the right thing.

There were other ideas, lots of them – too many, in fact. I was working on about a dozen different things in the hope that one or two might be picked out by broadcasters as possibles. Alan McKeown, *Auf Wiedersehen, Pet*'s executive producer and a man of great experience in the field, once gave me a useful piece of advice: 'Don't hit people with too much. One idea's enough – if it's the right one.' But how do you know which one's the right one?

I'd spent many hours working on a project close to my heart and my roots, a labour of love, you might call it, and that would be true. It was the story of the Stephensons of Wylam, George and Robert, father and son, Geordies who, like me, had been born into humble beginnings, had lived, worked, experimented and invented in a little place called West Moor, near my family home in Benton. We'd all learned about them at school but then the sheer scale of their achievements had been lost on me. They were the first railway pioneers, and their visionary efforts, stubborn self-belief and tireless endeavour in the face of mockery, ridicule and often danger had changed the world.

Having published a book about the lives of these two great men to tie in with the 150th anniversary of the 1824 Rainhill Rail Trials, Hunter Davies, fellow-northerner, journalist and author, was an authority on the Stephensons and I talked him into being involved with my idea. I set about preparing a pitch document for submission to the BBC's drama department. Hunter did most of the writing, and in no time at all I had what I believed to be an informative and exciting proposal for a ten-hour series depicting the life and times of Messrs Stephenson.

Armed with my document, I set off from Dicey Avenue and headed for Shepherds Bush Green for my pitch meeting at the BBC. I'm glad now that I didn't realize just how long the odds were against it being taken on: this project would have meant multiple crews shooting in locations all over the globe, with actors in period costumes, and steam trains. Nowadays, with the aid of widely available computer-generated imagery techniques, you could get it done quite cost-effectively, but that's by the by.

The head of drama series at the BBC was then a man called Jonathan Powell. On the odd occasion that we'd met he'd struck me as a rather miserable individual. But this was a corking project – he'd be bound to recognize that. I parked, signed in and entered Threshold House, a drab office block right on Shepherds Bush Green with long grey corridors and a strong smell of Dettol. I bounced along, filled with excitement, spurred by the conviction that I had a real winner in my possession.

Eventually, I was shown into Powell's inner office by a rather pretty young lady and found a scene that seemed to greet you everywhere in the BBC back then: piles of to-be-read scripts threatened to capsize the desks, and the people sitting behind them looked as though they were drowning.

Powell grunted hello, and asked me what it was all about. I began to tell him about my project but before I'd got far he informed me that the BBC had already done something with trains that year, so it was sorry, no, and cheerio. I'd been in his office no more than five minutes.

As I wandered down the corridor on my way out I didn't know whether to go back and lamp him or skulk off and have a good cry. The very least he could have done was let me finish the pitch. I was trying to decide what course of action to take when an office door opened, a bearded head popped into view and a rich, friendly voice said, 'Jimmy, what are you doing here?' It was Colin Rogers, a producer I'd met while I was working on the BBC drama series *Spyship* shoot in 1983. He must have seen I was upset and he very kindly invited me in for a coffee and a calm-down.

I had a good moan about Powell and Colin was very understanding. Eventually I stopped feeling sorry for myself for long enough to ask him what he was up to. It transpired he was on the look-out for drama projects to be developed with a view to their eventually becoming year-on-year series and asked me if I had anything that might fit the bill. Never one to let an opportunity pass for want of a little bullshit, I said, yes, of course I had: what exactly was he after?

Colin said he fancied developing a cop show.

I had one all mapped out and ready, I lied.

To star who?

Why, me, of course. Who better, who more unlikely, to play a cop?

OK, said Colin gamely. Did I have a writer on board? That was what these things often hinged on, and the right man for the job would be paramount.

Oh, yes. Ian La Frenais, I lied. Colin wanted to see some pages with a view to commissioning it.

I got home to Dicey Avenue in a state of some confusion. So much had happened in the last few hours, I'd all but forgotten about George and Robert Stephenson. I called Ian in Los Angeles to see if he had any ideas and if he'd take pity on a poor bullshitter. He was away working in Italy but would be passing through London on his way home to LA: we could meet up and discuss my situation over dinner.

A few weeks later, I was waiting to meet Ian in Le Caprice restaurant in Mayfair on a balmy spring evening. He arrived, we had a hug and then a meal. After I'd filled him in on my cop show half-idea, he laughed. It turned out he'd always fancied writing a cop show set in the North East but Dick hadn't. He and Ian were a script-writing team, working only with each other, so the idea had never gone any further. I hadn't realized he'd be breaking with tradition when I asked him if he'd be up for writing a series. If he'd said, 'no,' or that he was contractually tied to someone or something else, I'd have understood. But he was keen. He said he'd talk to Dick about it. He didn't have the time to devote to a whole new series as he was writing all sorts of other stuff, but he'd work with me on the pilot episode. I'd won the lottery again.

My pal Colin Rogers sorted out the contractual side of things with the BBC relating to Ian's writing services, while Ian and I began to dream up characters, storylines and, most difficult of all, a name for the embryonic show. The done thing genre-wise was a generic title – *Hazell*, *Inspector Morse*, *Dixon of Dock Green*, that kind of thing – and we had to come up with a name that both we and the BBC were happy with.

Titles are very important. Don't let anyone tell you otherwise. They have to make an immediate impression. Try *Winterbottom of Dock Green*. Not nearly as good, is it? We kicked all sorts of ideas back and forth with nothing really taking our fancy. Then, I had a thought. Years before I'd read of an American blues musician called Freddie Fender. I liked the ring of the name, but we couldn't just lift it, lock, stock and barrel – anyway, he was still alive. After a lot of brainstorming and heated debate, Freddie Fender became Freddie Spender and we had our name. I can't remember which of us suggested 'Spender' but it was probably Ian. When I said I'd like Spender to be called Freddie, Ian was aghast. 'You can't call anyone Freddie!' he said.

'That's my son's name,' I reminded him. We went with it.

I never imagined people saying the name, writing it down, talking about the character. It seemed to be tempting fate. Mind you, I'd been convinced that no one would ever pick up on a show with a name as long-winded, unmemorable and plain awful as *Auf Wiedersehen, Pet*.

After a couple of months of long-distance phone calls Ian delivered the first draft of episode one, the pilot. I was less thrilled about it than Colin, but only because, having worked with Ian on all the scenes, plotlines and dialogue, I pretty much knew what was going to be in there. All the same, it was a knockout. As I'd wished, the character was a moody bastard, grumpy, surly, insubordinate and smartass. It would be a major stretch for me to play someone like him. There were other characters in there, too: Dan Boyd, the steady, dependable, desk-bound detective sergeant, Yelland, the boss, and Frances, Spender's ex-wife. But the most memorable of all was Stick, petty criminal and best buddy. Spender and Stick were different facets of the same person, and that person was me.

The script was submitted, and Colin Rogers loved it. The BBC wanted more of the same. But that was a problem: at that time, Ian was not available to write any more episodes. We started the long, difficult process of finding suitable writers. I sat in on many meetings between Colin and the various candidates. Some were well-known and lots were very good, but none, we both felt, was right. Things sat for a while with the project stalled until Colin came up with a suggestion that threw me. Why didn't I write an episode? Well, I'd never written anything.

'Doesn't matter,' said Colin.

'But what if it's shit?' I asked.

'Not the end of the world,' said Colin. The BBC would lose an episode fee, but it would survive.

I went home, thought about it, counted the pages in Ian's pilot and set to work. It was a big step: I had no idea whether or not I could do it. If it turned out I couldn't, then that would be yet more time wasted and maybe the BBC would go off the boil about the whole thing.

With Miriam offering firm but subtle encouragement, I visited the stationer, got stocked up with paper, pencils and erasers, set up a desk, sat down and began. What a pantomime. I started off working on a traditional typewriter, but it took an age, and I was no typist then. The result was paper everywhere, half a rainforest strewn around the floor.

The next stop was the computer shop. It was a quantum leap for me. I knew nothing about, and had no interest in, anything electronic, so I jumped in blind and bought what the shop assistant recommended. Back home, I spent the best part of a frustrating day surrounded by big brown cardboard boxes, plugging in all kinds of leads and cables. Finally I flicked on the power switch and, amazingly, my Amstrad was working. It soon became apparent that the machine had limitations with regard to scriptwriting, and it was at this point that I made a decision that had a lasting effect on my life. I defected to Mac. It was 1989, and my lasting love affair with the Apple brand had begun.

Back then, desktop Macs were in their infancy and anyone looking at the old models today would laugh, but they were funky, a design classic, and so much fun to use. It's hard to explain why. I had to squint to see everything on the screen, but every time I switched that machine on, heard the warm 'WAHH' tone and clocked the little smiling face, I got a thrill. I still do. Sad, eh?

Six weeks and a lot of worrying later, I finished my first commissioned script – that means someone is paying you to write rather than you doing it off your own bat, which is known as writing a 'spec' script. I've never been interested in doing it that way: I like to think I respond positively and productively to financial commitment. Entitled *Half a Ton of Heartache*, my script told the supposedly fictitious story of oil-riggers who regularly pooled their earnings to buy hard drugs in the south, brought them north and sold them on at vast profit. Ian helped a lot, with advice and encouragement, on the phone – I didn't have a fax machine back then. I'd do a bit, print out the pages, ask Miriam to have a look at them, then carry on. She was absolutely invaluable, almost a co-writer at times. It had been a mistake, though, to count the pages in Ian's pilot script before I began my own: he had over-written by about a third, so I did the same. I handed in my humble effort, all neatly formatted and well presented. Charlie Ollie, one of the glaziers at Watson's and a star turn in his own right, had impressed upon me the importance of always presenting a job the best way you could – even if it was badly done. Then I sat back and waited. A couple of days later Colin called to say he loved the script and would I be up for writing some more?

I was ecstatic – for all of two minutes. Then the holy terrors set in. What if I'd just got lucky with my first effort? It happens. What if that was the only story I had in me? What if, what if . . . so many what-ifs. Never mind, I'd have a go. Of course, Colin was just being a really good producer: the draft I'd written wasn't great but it had potential, and Colin made me believe I could pull it off again. Back to the most important thing throughout my life: encouragement. It worked a treat.

But I knew I'd need help. I was taking on something very big indeed, and I had no real grounding in the script-writer's craft. In fact, I had no literary or grammatical grounding. I discussed it at length with Ian, who very kindly suggested that I go over to Los Angeles and stay at his place where I could write under his supervision. This was turning into an adventure, and no mistake. What an offer! Hollywood!

In all the excitement I made an error so fundamental that, in retrospect, I find it almost impossible to believe, but I made it. I did not fully discuss my plans with Miriam. Instead I announced one day that I'd soon be off to LA for the year. I'd be over there doing my thing while she would stay at home and look after the kids. I thought I was doing the right thing but I couldn't see the other side – Miriam's side.

12

I'd been to Los Angeles before, but this would be different. This time I'd have a legitimate reason for being out there in all that lovely sunshine: I'd be working. Even better, I'd be working at my own pace — which would, of course, be ferocious, as I knew no other — on my own project. I'd not be at the mercy of some studio bully. So off I went to get stuck in.

I'd been concentrating so hard on the Spender project, and the more general issue of making a living, that I hadn't considered the impact my leaving might have on myself, Miriam or the bairns. Too late I grasped what a traumatic experience it was going to be and my leaving was horrible. I'd booked a chauffeur-driven car to take me to Heathrow airport. Unfortunately, a Mercedes stretch limousine arrived, an awful, ostentatious thing, but there wasn't time to send for a different car. And things were about to get worse.

Miriam and the kids were at the front door, waving. As the car pulled away from the kerb Tom, aged four, shouted, 'Daddy, I don't want you to go!' and started to cry. I can still remember how awful I felt as I watched my little boy crying because he wanted me to stay. I so wanted to cancel the trip but of course I couldn't: everything was booked and paid for. It was a terrible time to decide to be sensible, but Miriam had done a good job in encouraging me over the past decade. Now I felt almost obliged to be successful, and that feeling overrode just about everything else. I had to prove her right, show there was more to me than just playing Oz. The mistake I made was in not understanding how important it was that we did it together, as a couple and as a family. I would have liked that, but it didn't seem possible: there were domestic practicalities to take into account. Maybe I could have stayed put and made it work, but the end result would certainly not have been the same and it would have taken two or three times as long. My stay in LA entailed a great deal of sacrifice on Miriam's part and, of course, we should have discussed it in more detail, but we didn't and I was on my own.

Loneliness and longing apart, the year I spent in Los Angeles with Ian La Frenais and his family was productive and I'll never forget it. Ian's wife, Doris, their son, Michael, Doris's mum and brother Sam all accepted me into their Hollywood Hills home with much better grace than I could have mustered had the circumstances been reversed. Ian's house was a rustic pile nestled in a lovely part of the hills, high above Sunset Boulevard. Possums ran around on the roof. Ian's pal, musician Jeff Lynne, of ELO and Traveling Wilburys' fame, lived about a mile up the road, and Dick Clement lived about the same distance in the other direction with his wife, Nancy, and their young daughter, Annie. From the moment I arrived I loved the place. The idea of living out there, even temporarily, was beyond fantasy. All those films I'd watched as a kid had been made right there. It was where the best movie talent was billeted, and, because of Ian's social contacts, I'd soon meet a good portion of it. No lolling around by the swimming-pool, though. First, Ian didn't have one, and second, my work ethic wouldn't have allowed it.

I've always used work as a means of relieving pressure, and the only way I could justify being there was to work, so

Ian soon had me hard at it. Each evening on his return from his day job at the Warner Bros studio on the Burbank back lot, we'd have dinner then go over what I'd written that day and add to it. As a way of learning how to write for television, those evening sessions were hugely enjoyable, with Ian at one end of his long dining-table, his five-dollar gas-station reading-glasses hanging off the end of his nose, bashing away on an ancient typewriter, and me at the other end, doing my thing with my Apple Mac. We'd ask each other questions, laugh regularly and occasionally argue, but what a blast it was. To have someone like Ian, who was just about the most gifted television comedy writer of his generation, guiding, advising and encouraging me was invaluable. That stuff just can't be bought. He was never judgemental, always clear with his advice, and on the few occasions we disagreed big-time he defused the tension with wicked humour. He kept re-minding me to write about what I knew. One evening while we were discussing something to do with a middle-class character, he said, 'You do the housing estates, kid, and I'll look after the shires.' I was miffed, but he was right. I accepted it and learned from it. Many creative types don't feel comfortable with letting others get too up-close and personal: I reckon most of them don't like close scrutiny because they don't want to be rumbled for the chancers and literary pilferers they are. Not Ian: he is a man not afraid to share his gift with others so that they may benefit from his experience. In terms of learning how to do it, I cherish those days as among the most valuable of my life.

In LA, I'd be up early, around six thirty, without the need for an alarm call. Before I did anything else, I'd go into the en-suite bathroom and clean my teeth. Then I'd pop down the corridor to the kitchen, on tiptoe so as not to wake the rest of the household, and put the kettle on to boil while I took an invigorating power-shower. Then I'd make a pint mug of tea – I still do – with fresh milk and an English tea-bag, Tetley's or Typhoo, and start work on my Mac in my bedroom, applying any notes and amendments from the night before and writing as much new stuff as I could. I've always been at my most creative, in terms of writing and dreaming up ideas, in the mornings, before the rest of the day's mess has got to me. Out there in the Hollywood Hills, with the sun bleaching in through tall windows, it was the perfect environment for dreaming and scribbling. At some point I'd bump into Ian before he went off to work but it wasn't unusual for me not to see anyone all day. I'd work till about midday, getting through three or four mugs of tea, by which time I'd be ready for a break and a stretch.

Although I always had my hired Jeep sitting outside the house – you had to have a motor over there – I'd walk the few miles up the winding road, which eventually leads out on to Mulholland Drive, along a few hundred yards and then left, down to Beverly Glen Boulevard and the little cluster of shops that included the Glen Deli, my favourite diner. Along with a stupendous cooked breakfast, it sold the finest cakes, pastries and savouries. Choosing from the multi-page menu was always difficult and I had to exercise real restraint. I steered clear of heart-attack fodder, such as waffles with maple syrup, ordered a pot of English breakfast tea with a blueberry muffin, all very sensible, all very English, and sat watching the world go by.

I loved being an Englishman surrounded by Yanks. I longed for someone to ask me what I was doing there so I could tell them I was one of them, a player, but no one ever did. Many a well-known face would arrive in an immaculate chrome-plated vehicle, both two- and four-wheeled, to buy their sticky buns. The actor James Caan often appeared on a Sunday morning astride a gleaming Harley-Davidson, along with a bunch of executive would-be outlaws. They'd have a decaf, do a bit of posing, then split. Bruce Willis was an irregular. If folk think I'm surly and standoffish, he could have written the book. I was behind him at the check-out one day as he was grumping his way through paying the grocery bill. After he walked out, the young guy behind the till said, to no one in particular, 'Where does he get off, acting like that? It's not as though he's done much, one hit movie and a bunch of flops.' It's a tough town.

My daily walks to and from the Glen Deli caused some consternation at the La Frenais residence. Ian would often tell me nobody, other than those sad, haunted folk with their headbands and Walkmans, ever walked anywhere in Los Angeles. Indeed, where he lived there were no pavements by the roadside, just black Tarmac and kerb. He made walking sound quite uncivilized, but coming from a place where it was always raining, I wanted to walk everywhere. I loved walking – I still do. Ian was convinced I'd be mistaken for a robber casing the ultra-expensive joints on my way to the café. I think he was more concerned about his own embarrassment than my possible incarceration.

It wasn't long before he was proved right, and in pretty spectacular fashion. One bright morning, as I was wandering past a gated mansion, the owner took one look at me, decided he didn't care for what he saw, opened the big gates and let loose his guard dogs, two rather frisky Alsatians. They'd been barking and howling for some time and now they were upon me. I'd got into the habit of taking a copy of *Daily Variety*, the trade magazine, to the deli, and that day I had it rolled up in my right hand. I smacked the first dog to arrive as hard as I could on top of its head. Luckily for me it was a puppy.

It yelped, as much in shock as in pain, then scuttled off. Encouraged, I snarled at the second dog and, thankfully, it too turned tail. Seething, I went over to the guy's gates, intending to give him a piece of my mind, but he also ran off, into the big house. Just another day in LA, I guess.

On arriving back at the house after my daily tea-and-cake break, I'd look over that morning's work, do a bit of editing, then maybe have a snooze or go shopping until early evening when the house would come alive and we'd all have a catch-up. Dinner would be followed by the work session with Ian, then bed.

The writing process, the physical act of banging on those keyboard letters, is something I've loved from the off. I often sit for hours just typing or moving text around. I've spent days, literally, trying to decide whether to put a semi-colon or a colon somewhere, a question mark instead of an exclamation mark. Along with getting someone to commit millions of pounds to an idea or suggestion, creative writing has always been the most enjoyable part of the process. The rest, especially performing, is often an anti-climax. I often feel that, having shot it already in my head, when I act it I'm doing it all for a second time.

Ian's Sunday evening at-home get-togethers were popular and always well attended. Lots of exiled Brits would converge, swap stories and trade tea-bags. I once spent a lovely evening in the company of the late Maureen Starkey, Ringo's ex-missus. In the course of our conversation I happened to mention I was desperate to get my hands on some decent English tea-bags, preferably the proper northern stewing variety, not those wishy-washy minuscule things they sell in LA. Maureen sympathized. As a northern lass, she understood my craving. At around nine thirty the next morning, there was a ring on the doorbell. When I answered it I was greeted by a capped chauffeur standing in front of a black stretch limo, holding a box of proper, industrial-strength English tea-bags. 'Mr Nail?' I nodded. He handed me the tea-bags. 'From Maureen,' he said.

I spent a bizarre evening in the company of free-love trip-drug guru Dr Timothy Leary. Though blunted by decades of self-inflicted psychedelic abuse, he was nevertheless a pretty sharp cookie and fascinating to talk to, although his doctrine didn't appeal to me. After all the years I'd spent in an alcoholic stupor, I now wanted to be as 'there' as I could be, bright, focused, sharp and aware. I didn't want to miss a trick. I also needed to have my wits about me to avoid Mrs Leary, a rather fiery New York redhead some thirty years her husband's junior. I got out of the shower one evening to find her half sitting, half lying on my bed. I got really angry, which seemed to give her quite a shock. That room was the only privacy I had, the only place in the house that was mine. Ian and Doris understood that and respected it, but not Mrs Leary. Out she went, in short order.

I was lonely, though. I was over there and Miriam was in England with the kids. Things began to get a little fractious. Miriam and I did our best to stay in touch with each other and what was happening on the telephone, but neither of us loves the blower and there was the eight-hour time difference. When one of us had something important to share, the other was usually out of the house or fast asleep. Pretty soon keeping in touch became a bit of a struggle and I avoided the telephone. Blips occur in any long-running relationship and ours was no different.

But despite all the personal upheaval and missing my family, I was getting a lot of work done. Guilt can be a powerful spur. Things were going well enough for me to suggest to Miriam that she and the kids might come out and spend the summer months with me in sunny LA. We might never get another opportunity to do something like this and we agreed it would be worth the considerable expense the trip would involve. Also, we'd be together for Miriam's impending thirtieth birthday. By then we had employed a nanny, Sharon, and Miriam persuaded her to come along for the ride.

I couldn't impose such numbers and noise-levels on Ian and Doris, so I had to rent a place – no easy task when it has to be furnished and you need it for just three months. Enjoyable as it was, the time I spent looking at big posh houses ate into my work schedule and in no time I was falling behind. Cue major stress and anxiety. Eventually I narrowed down the choice to a house in Santa Monica, half an hour down the road from Ian, or a place in Westwood, home to UCLA, the city's university, and a large student community. The sprawling multi-acre UCLA campus included the frat houses – student digs – wonderful shopping facilities in Westwood Village, a state-of-the-art medical centre and sports facilities that would put most Olympic villages to shame. There was a great vibe about the district but the clincher, to my surprise, was that the Westwood house did not have a swimming-pool. Of course I'd wanted something Olympic-sized but Miriam put me straight: with the kids at the ages they were, four and nearly two, it would have been no fun patrolling the garden all the time, a duty that would, no doubt, have fallen to her. Never mind, it had a lovely spa pool.

Miriam arrived with the boys and Sharon on 28 June 1989, her thirtieth birthday. I had been eagerly awaiting their arrival and planning things for ages. Doris had volunteered to take care of a birthday cake, so I felt I had all bases covered. I went out to the airport and waited. It's always very busy with English folk meeting relatives and friends, so I kept my head down at the edge of the terminal until the Tannoy announcement telling me the flight had landed safely. My family were just beyond the arrivals gate. I was thrilled and dying to see the kids: they would have changed since I'd seen them last. Would my little soldiers even remember me?

At last, they were making their way up the ramp that leads into the arrivals area. Miriam and I clocked each other, made for the middle ground and I gave her a hug. Then, before she could do or say anything else, I got down on one knee and said, 'Happy birthday, darling,' pulled out a big diamond ring and asked her to marry me. I'd been thinking about it for a long time and figured this would be a romantic birthday surprise. I should have balanced that with Miriam having just finished an eleven-hour flight with two small kids. I've always been one for the big gesture, but I got this one well wrong. Miriam cast her bleary eyes around and told me to get up. Everyone was staring and I was embarrassing her, she told me. Somewhat subdued, we made our way outside, climbed into a stretch limo and headed for Ian's place.

I should have thought about Miriam being tired from the flight but I had no idea that this particular birthday had upset her. On reaching thirty she had wobbled and was having a tough time dealing with it. The last ten years had been demanding for us both. She had come to Newcastle from her home in Caerphilly, near Cardiff, to study for a degree and had been awarded a two:one. When she met me, her own plans and dreams had been sidelined. At thirty she had two young children, and she had felt for a long time that her identity was being subsumed into mine. She didn't want to be seen simply as the partner of a famous guy. We knew quite a few couples where the non-famous partner was basically ignored by all but close friends. All of this was going around in her head, so my proposal must have been like a red rag to a bull. In LA, I had been unaware of the struggle she was having.

We got to Ian and Doris and out came the cake. A multi-coloured marzipan hooker in crotchless knickers stood on the top cracking a bullwhip, beside Miriam's name and a single phallic candle. We all stared at it, speechless. Doris asked what we thought of it. I didn't know whether to laugh or cry, so I laughed. Miriam was too jet-lagged to respond. We have a photograph of that cake in one of our family albums.

The owner of the rental property, a dour doctor of metallurgy, was an eastern European *émigré* and a right fusspot, always at the house on some false premise, sniffing around, making sure we hadn't broken or stolen any of his tasteless goods and chattels. He checked the copper chandelier in the hallway one day, maybe thought I'd been swinging on it like Errol Flynn, my hero. A pain in the bum, he was, but never mind: the house was huge, on a lovely large corner plot with plenty of parking and lots of beautiful songbirds in the back garden.

Oh, what a glorious summer. Those balmy days, driving out of and back into Westwood, cool, cool Westwood. Guaranteed sunshine, picnics on the beach at Santa Monica, the kids running around in shorts and vests plus lots and lots of factor 100 goose-lard. The most magical part of each day, though, was the time just before sunset, when the garden would be visited by half a dozen hummingbirds. We'd watch in silent wonder as these tiny colourful creatures, with their long slender beaks, would hover, then dart head-first into the open bud of a flower, sneak a bit of nectar, then fly backwards in an almost mechanical motion. With their wings giving off a kind of über-bumble buzz, these incredible little contradictors of the laws of physics would entertain us for a few minutes and then be gone, like will-o'-the-wisps. The kids can't remember any of it, of course, but I treasure the memory. Ian's wife Doris is a dab hand with a stills camera, and she took some incredible shots of the kids in that garden. I have them on my desk. She'd do this thing with Polaroids where, after taking a shot, she'd mess with the picture as it was developing, rub it on her clothing until it was hot and blurred in places, kind of interfere with it. The results were often remarkable.

I was so happy to be with the family that the work was a doddle. I'd work on scripts in the morning, then go out with Miriam and the kids in the afternoon. We'd go to the beach at Santa Monica, build super sandcastles and bury Dad up to his neck, or drive across the city and watch the natural bubbling, glugging tar-pits in downtown Los Angeles. Parks, walks, beaches, movies, museums and flea-markets. Best of all was the LA weather: you could plan a trip in the morning and actually be able to enjoy it in the afternoon, instead of it being rained off as it is usually in England. The kids were happy, we were happy, and Sharon the nanny was happy, too.

One Monday morning I started working on a *Spender* idea that had popped into my head the previous day, the story of an ex-professional boxer who'd been reduced to participating in illegal back-street bare-knuckle contests to pay the bills and keep the already-fragile family unit from fragmenting. Maybe the story sprang from my own sub-conscious guilt, I don't know. A tale of pride and misplaced trust, of deception, betrayal and heartbreak, it would feature the Scottish actor

Maurice Roeves as the boxer; he turned in an outstanding performance. Our Tom, at five, was press-ganged into playing his young son. As I sat in my chair in Westwood, it all seemed to work pretty well in my mind's eye, so I wrote it down exactly as I pictured, imagined and heard it. No notes, no prep work, nothing. I just wrote it as I envisaged it on the screen. By Saturday I'd finished it. Fifty-odd pages. Six mornings' work. I called it *Tough*, and gave it to Ian to read. He was happy, and didn't have any notes. I sent it over to Colin Rogers at the BBC in London. It was accepted, again without notes. In the end it was shot exactly as it was written and turned out to be a terrific episode. How did I manage it? I'd just got lucky. Try as I might to pull it off again, it hasn't happened since.

September was upon us all too soon. Miriam and Sharon packed and went home with the boys. I wanted to go with them. I'd experienced proper family life for a while, with everyone playing a part and doing their share, and I'd loved it. I'd also become aware of just how much work was involved in looking after the boys. Miriam was at it all hours of the day and worn out by the evening. My family needed their dad. But I had a bit more work to do with Ian before I could go home. I set to with a vengeance, and not long after, I was on my way to Dicey Avenue, job done.

13

In the autumn of 1989, I was back home, and the *Spender* project was about to become reality. The thrill of going on a journey with an idea, pitching it, selling it, seeing it through to development and making a television series was incredible. And it was more than a creative thrill: it was a major vote of confidence from the drama executives at the BBC who would put millions of pounds into its production. I had never done anything like this before and I liked the satisfaction it brought. It had happened incredibly quickly – I would only come to realize just how quickly a few years later when I embarked on the same journey with other projects.

We had a producer in Martin McKeand, who'd produced *Auf Wiedersehen, Pet*. That was a big plus for me – I knew Martin and liked his easy-going style. A funny thing happened while we were discussing his possible involvement over lunch in Charlotte Street. In mid-sentence I spotted the great Mark Tully, the BBC's renowned and revered India correspondent, at an adjacent table. I wanted to go over straight away, but having been on the receiving end of that type of thing, I made myself wait until he'd finished his meal. When at last he had, I excused myself to Martin, went over, introduced myself, assured him I wouldn't keep him long, and congratulated him on a lifetime of outstanding broadcasts from all corners of the Indian sub-continent. He obviously didn't know who I was – why should he? – and when he asked, I told him I was just one of his many fans.

We had a director on board too, Mary McMurray. (As a

rule I prefer working with women: they seem far less intent on proving something that usually has nothing to do with the job in hand – maybe it's a guy thing, a macho thing, I don't know.) We had our scripts, and they were good. Now we needed to find and secure the special people who might, with a little luck, bring the thing to life. We were about to begin casting.

The audition process isn't easy for anyone. If you're the actor you want to give a good account of yourself, shine in the part. If you're the writer you're desperate to have someone glean the best from the words you've toiled over. If you're the director or producer you have to get the choice right. It's make or break time. Many projects falter at this stage. And you have maybe twenty minutes to work it all out and carry it off. It was even more complicated for me as, at various times in the process, I was all of the above. Sometimes I was asked to read my part, Spender, with other actors, and sometimes not. The actors we met were all bravehearts and it was tough knowing they wouldn't all land a part. I'm glad the final choices weren't mine to make.

Early on, Berwick Kaler came in and was dead right for Dan Boyd, the stoical desk sergeant. Berwick had been in *Auf Wiedersehen, Pet* and had been up for the part of Oz, so immediately we had a little common ground. Berwick and I became friends; my family and I look forward to making the annual pilgrimage to York to see him in pantomime. It's one of the year's highlights for us. He's been in residence at the city's Theatre Royal for twenty-five years, writing, producing and starring in panto, and is a much-valued member of the community – he was made an honorary freeman of York in 2003. Now he can graze one or both ends of the pantomime cow on Acomb Common, should he so desire. Paul Greenwood, an experienced Shakespearian actor with the RSC, was cast to play DCI Yelland, my immediate boss. Denise Welch, wife of Tim Healy, was cast to play my ex-wife, Frances, the mother of our two daughters. As a maverick cop, Spender had to have an ex-wife and a personal life in turmoil. Denise bemoaned the fact that her character always seemed to be in the kitchen making tea – I'm afraid I took that as an opportunity to see how often I could imprison her there. There was also the part of musician Keith Nichol, who was suffering from MS: we managed to persuade the BBC to agree to our casting my old musician buddy Tony McAnaney. He was already on board to compose and supply the show's incidental music and had come up with a memorable whistled melody for the titles and credits. He had never acted, though, so it was a punt that, thankfully, came off well. Almost bald, pony-tail, nursing a guitar on his lap, Tony looked dead right.

Hardest of all to cast was Stick because it was the plum part, even better than mine. Stick was the classic dodgy buddy, the 'Ratso', the villain with all the best pay-off lines. It was essential to get it right. Mary McMurray narrowed the field down to two, both from the North East, both vastly experienced: Dave Whittaker and Sammy Johnson. I read scenes with them and it was a real blast – they were both terrific in their different ways. We would have been in safe hands with either of them. Mary went with Sammy. She said there was a glint in his eye.

I was over the moon about the series going into production, but what I hadn't thought about was the schedule: I'd be away from London for the best part of eight months. I'd only just got back from having been away for the best part of a year. But I had no choice: after all this work I couldn't just not go. Miriam and I decided it would be better to buy a house in Newcastle rather than throw away the

BBC's money by bunking down in an hotel for all that time. If things went well with the series, there was a chance I'd be up there for a few seasons. It turned out to be a good move.

Production began in the spring of 1990 with Mary McMurray at the helm, and me with a PA and a driver. Corinna Bonicelli was a local lass with an Italian dad, very handy for pasta tips. I'd avoided it for as long as I could, as I thought it might look a bit poncy and big-headed, but in the end I had to have help. There was just too much for me to do on my own, too many questions, and not enough hours in the day to answer them all. Geoff Knox – no relation to Big Peter – was a buddy from my schooldays, although we'd never attended the same school. A fellow music-nut, he came on board as my driver and worked for me for over a decade, looking after me and even accompanying Miriam and the kids on holiday when it was impossible for me to be with them. He talked me into letting him play a blagger in one of the *Spender* episodes and he was very good – he stole the show, which was appropriate.

I was proud to take the production home, to where I'd started off with all my daft ideas. Not so daft now. The first day's filming was an absolute thrill: I stood behind the camera to watch and listen as the actors delivered lines I'd written. They worked. It was odd filming on the streets I'd grown up in. *Auf Wiedersehen, Pet* had only been up there occasionally, but this shoot would be there six days a week for the next eight months. We had a truly marvellous crew, all up for it, all giving it their best shot, particularly Mary, and Nigel Walters, the director of production, for the programme's outstanding visual grit. Film director Ridley Scott – himself a Geordie – complimented me on the look of the show. High praise indeed.

While I was filming the new series, my father, whose health had been deteriorating badly, was taken into the Freeman Hospital. He had suffered from emphysema for decades, and it was made clear to us by the hospital staff that there was no chance of him recovering. He should have died before he did but, typically, he fought on for weeks. I visited him whenever I had an hour free or during my lunch breaks. At least I was in Newcastle when he was taken ill. Had I been filming something on the other side of the world, I'd have been unable to get there at all. The time I spent with him at the hospital was important for us both, our conversations dictated by clarity, urgency and honesty.

One weekend Miriam brought the kids up from London so we could have a few days away as a family in a hired camper van. Before we left Newcastle we called in at the hospital so the boys could see their granddad. We all sat on the bed, my dad, the boys and me, three generations together.

We had reached Alnwick, some sixty miles north of Newcastle, when we received a phone call to say he had passed away. I like to think he waited to see the kids before he clocked off. Once they were asleep we parked the camper outside a pub. I nipped inside, raised a glass and sank a single pint to his memory. Just the one. It tasted absolutely wonderful. No time to grieve, though. The schedule didn't allow for that. I envy anyone who has a strong religious faith – I could have done with one just then. As it was, I felt as though I'd run into a brick wall.

A couple of weeks later, while I was going through my father's few bits and bobs, I came across his old brown leather wallet. Inside, among his CIU (Working Men's Clubs) membership cards and some other inconsequential stuff was a worn, faded piece of cardboard. On closer inspection I was surprised to see it was a security pass for entry into Staten

Island Dockyards, New York, during the Second World War. I'd doubted all those stories he had told me as a kid, considered them to be no more than a father's tall tales. Now I had to believe, although what on earth my dad was doing in the US Navy for eighteen months remains a mystery.

It was a long time before I could dispose of my dad's ashes. I had them in the back of my car for over a year, used to talk to them, which may seem macabre, but it wasn't – I'd know when it was the right time to say goodbye. In the end I chartered a trawler and scattered his ashes at sea off the Northumbrian coast. He got me one last time, though. I was careful about my position on the boat, standing downwind at the stern, but a gust blew some of the ashes back into my face. As awful as it was, I had to laugh.

The first episode of *Spender* was broadcast at nine twenty-five p.m. on BBC1 on Tuesday 8 January 1991. By and large, the press previews had been encouraging, and the BBC were so happy about what we'd delivered they'd already commissioned the next series of scripts; that meant I was guaranteed my writing fees before I started work. It's common within the television industry not to be paid for ages after you've finished a job, but I won't do any work until I know when I'm going to get paid. This is to do with fears of being ripped off, but to me the idea of spending weeks or months working on something for nothing in terms of financial reward is inconceivable. And it's not simply a mercenary thing. Receiving payment is about more than just money: it's validation, vindication and encouragement.

Not only was the character brand new: so was the actor. How would viewers receive the all-new, slimline, long-haired Nail? Would they hate the idea of Jimmy as a cop? You never can tell. It had been a long, hard road getting thus far and I had had a long wait for this particular day. Now here it was.

Transmission time. Stonker or stinker? I'd soon know one way or the other. But I wasn't in London – or even England. I was back in Los Angeles working on the next scripts at Ian's place. At least if it went down like a lead balloon I wouldn't be there to suffer the indignity in person.

Come the time, I was sprawled out in the den watching a daytime ballgame on television, trying not to think about the programme I'd been living and breathing for the last year or so, when Ian arrived home from the Burbank lot clutching a wad of faxes. 'As if your head's not fucking big enough!' he said. 'Here, wank over that lot!' The reviews had been faxed to him by the BBC.

I read them, then re-read them. I couldn't believe what was in front of me. They were far and away better than I'd dared hope. They described the show as a visceral, vital slice of *urban noir* television and the eponymous character as an important addition to the cadre of television cops the viewing nation thrived on. They called me a sex symbol, for goodness' sake! It was all a bit much to take in, but Ian put it into perspective: 'We've pulled it off, kid. The show's a hit.'

I wanted to speak to everyone. My first call was to Miriam, who was as happy for me as I was for myself. She told me she was so proud of what I'd achieved, which made me feel ten feet tall, and that there had been lots of congratulatory calls from pals. Then I called my mam – thankfully, she wasn't aware of all the hullabaloo surrounding the show's success: she would have been frightened by it. I wished my dad had lived long enough to see it.

After all the work we'd put into the show, it was a satisfying outcome for Colin Rogers, Ian La Frenais and me. The sweetest part was that I'd proved wrong the nay-sayers who'd had me down as just a lucky beggar who'd landed, in Oz, a great part. Maybe I was lucky, but this show had my name down as writer, creator and producer, as well as actor. Its success said, loud and clear, that I wasn't just a hired hand: there was a bit more to me than that.

It was around this time that I met a truly magical, special man. By most people's standards I'd had some extraordinary and memorable encounters with all kinds of folk, famous, infamous, talented and rich. But all before, and since, were eclipsed by a chance meeting that led quickly to friendship. And it was all down to a ukelele.

At one of Ian La Frenais's regular Sunday evening get-togethers, the house was filled with the usual mix of showbiz people, actors, models, producers, directors and musicians. To this council-house kid from Benton it was always an interesting crowd to watch, listen and sometimes talk to. Liberating, too, as accents were no big deal like they are in Britain where you're immediately placed in a social and intelligence grouping the moment you open your gob. As far as the Yanks were concerned, we all sounded weird.

This particular evening most of the Traveling Wilburys had turned up and were mooching around the house. Great for me, the music fan. Suddenly there was a big exodus into the kitchen, where I was. Everyone seemed to be trying to get away from the noise next door. I stuck my head in the den – and there was George Harrison strumming away on a ukelele. I asked him if he'd mind me joining him and he told me to come on in and sit down. Jesus, I was on the settee next to a Beatle! An awful urge to call someone, anyone, came over me, but I couldn't move. Instead I just sat there until George asked me if I played. I told him I could strum a guitar in a basic way. Did I want a bash on his ukelele? All right, I said. What a nerve I must have had. I picked up the uke and managed a few rough chords, the first few of the Beatles' song 'Something', which George had written. He was so knocked out to find someone else who played the ukelele that he asked if I'd like to get together with him the next day at his bungalow in the grounds of the Bel Air Hotel. I wondered if that would be all right with his wife, my just calling in like that, but he said it would be fine, it was his job, it was what he did.

Not much sleep that night. The next day I drove down to the Bel Air and was led to George's bungalow. We sat all afternoon strumming on ukeleles. George always carried a spare in case he met a like-minded individual who might be up for a strum. From there, I got to know George Harrison. It was beyond my wildest dreams. I'd met plenty of famous people and it was no big deal, but this was George. THIS WAS GEORGE! FAB GEORGE, FROM THE BEATLES! I kept saying to myself, 'Is this really happening to me?' It was. George and his wife, Olivia, were the warmest of people. I've been told several times that he was careful about who he hung out with, and I can believe it. But here we were, George and me, and for a good few years we were pals.

When I got back to England George invited me to his place. Miriam and I went to visit him at Friar Park, his home in Henley-on-Thames. The house took my breath away. The idea of going to see a Beatle at home was almost unreal. I know this must read like the ramblings of a madman, but remember what that band meant to me and millions of others around the world. Never mind them being the soundtrack to a generation, the Beatles were a big part of almost every facet of my life. If I looked closely at an idea, a dream or an ambition, the Beatles weren't very far away. The thought of hanging out with George Harrison made me catch my breath.

Meanwhile, Ian and I were on a roll. In *Spender* we had a bona-fide hit, and I'd co-written it. It was the first filmed television drama series to be shot entirely on locations in

Newcastle and the North East, and I'd fought hard for that. Newcastle was struggling economically, with most of its heavy industries either already gone or on their last legs, and there were high levels of unemployment. We had over a hundred people on the cast and crew, and those who weren't local stayed in hotels or rented houses and spent their leisure money in the area. The pubs and nightclubs benefited. There were more practical, cost-effective options, like filming the recurring interiors in London, but I wasn't having that: I owed it to Newcastle to show the rest of the country what it was really like in Geordieland. Sure, it was rough, tough and eastern-bloc bleak in places, the dialect was pea-soup thick and near-impossible to decipher, even for me at times, but it was so much more: it was rich in character and steeped in tradition. Its inhabitants were warm-hearted, resilient folk. Its Georgian architecture and city-centre buildings, its wild countryside and windswept coastline were magnificent. I wanted the show to look, feel, taste and smell like the Newcastle I knew and loved. Most of all, I wanted Geordies to be proud of it: 'Aye, that's about right, that's how it is – that's how we are.' I hope we managed that.

With the success of *Spender* I thought it might be a good time to return to my music career. It had been dormant since the expiry of the one-album Virgin deal some years previously, and I wanted to record some songs and maybe make another album. Although I'd done all right last time money-wise, I'd learned a lot from the Virgin experience and was determined not to make certain mistakes again. If I got lucky, I'd try to make sure I was available for promotion this time round!

First I approached Danny Schogger, whom I'd met while I was working at Dave McKay's studios on my album *Take It Or Leave It*. He and I had hit it off straight away, and he agreed to work on some new songs with me. He suggested bringing in a third writing partner. I'd met Guy Pratt briefly when we both appeared on *The Tube* in the late 1980s. At the time he was playing bass with the Womacks, who had invited me on stage to sing with them on their final number, 'It's All Over Now', and subsequently invited me to do the same at their Albert Hall gig a week or so later. I declined their offer but remembered their masterful bass player. Now it was 1991. Guy had played bass with Pink Floyd, Madonna and Michael Jackson among others. It turned out his dad was the late Mike Pratt, an actor probably best remembered for appearing in the 1960s cult television series *Randall & Hopkirk (Deceased)*. Mike had played private detective Geoff Randall alongside Kenneth Cope's ghostly white-suited Marty Hopkirk. Like me, Guy was a big Tony Hancock fan, and his raw sense of humour was similar to Danny's and mine. He agreed to come aboard and we started kicking ideas around in Danny's studio up in Totteridge.

Pretty much straight away we were knocking out tunes. One particular melody was impossibly infectious. Charlie Dore, another colleague of Danny's, helped us with the lyrics, and once Guy's signature bass-playing had been added to the rough mix it was so catchy it drove you bonkers. It was called 'Ain't No Doubt'.

At the time I had no music management, but it was obvious I was going to need some if I was to take all this to a recording deal. Danny told me about a guy he knew who'd been asking what we were doing and had offices on West End Lane, not far from where I was living. Laurie Jay had been a drummer in the sixties, had gone on to run London clubs and was now involved in personal management, looking after Billy Ocean among others. I liked Laurie immediately. He was a lot of fun.

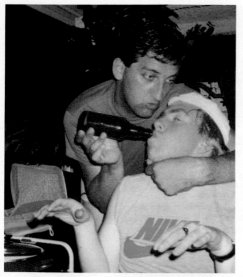

46. The things you'll do for a mate! Me feeding Tim Spall a beer

47. Tony Mac (left) and Rob Lockhart, Dicey Avenue, London, *c.* 1986. Look at all that lovely long hair!

48. My in-laws, Jean and Jack Williams, Llanddonna, Anglesey, North Wales

49. Me and the missus take baby Tom to Paris, 1986

50. Two of our dearest friends from Newcastle upon Tyne, the late 'Big' Peter Knox (left) and John Gordon. Toon army!

51. With Tim Spall and Peter McDougal, New York, 1986

52. My dear friend Chad Shepherd, helping us
ut, plumbing us in, Dicey Avenue, London, 1987

53. Probably my last glass of beer in a bar:
Auckland, New Zealand, 1987

54. I'm leaning on a lamp-post … Auckland, New Zealand, 1987

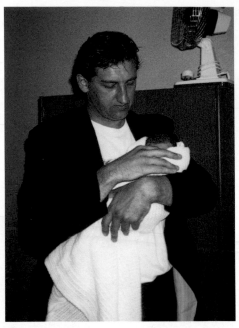

55. Father and son 2: me and baby Freddie, London, October, 1987

56. The blind leading the blind? Geoff Knox with the bairns, Dicey Avenue, London, 1988

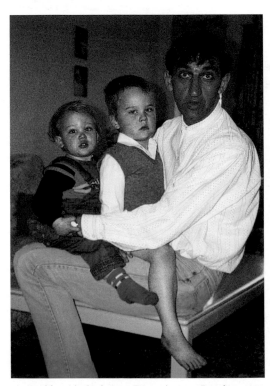

57. Daddy with the bairns: Dicey Avenue, London, 1988

58. A very rare glimpse of my friend and business partner Ray Black as he wrestles with crab's leg, West Hollywood, 1990

59. Miriam, me and that cake! Hollywood Hills, June 1989

60. Ian La Frenais, Miriam and me, Hollywood Hills, June 1989

61. Behind the camera at last! On the *Spender* set, Newcastle upon Tyne, 1990

62. That's me holding Freddie while director Mary McMurray shows Tom what to look for. *Spender* set, 1990

63. Mr Moody, eh? *Spender*, river Tyne, 1990

64. Denise Welch, my 'wife', rehearsing, *Spender*, Newcastle upon Tyne, 1991

65. Geoff Knox on location with the *Spender* series, Newcastle upon Tyne, 1992

66. Taking a break from filming at Lake Powell, Arizona, 1992

67. *(Left)* Me climbing into the basket of a hot-air balloon, as Ian La Frenais (in white top) frets. Newcastle upon Tyne, 1992

68. *(Below)* How was I to know he suffered from vertigo!

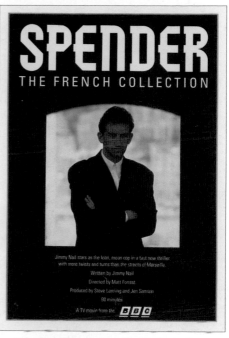

69. With the boys on the promenade,
Santa Monica, 1992

70. Publicity flier for the *Spender* single film we
shot in Marseille, France, 1993

71. This one always makes me smile: my mam, reading, Newcastle upon Tyne, 1993

72. The photograph I
didn't know existed:
George Harrison and
me jamming,
Blackpool, *c.* 1994

73. Me and the boys,
Lake Windemere,
Cumbria, 1994

74. Me and the missus
with Sting, 1994

75. *(Left)* Modelling
Comme des Garçons
in London, 1994

76. *(Below)* Signed by
the master: portrait by
David Bailey, *c.* 1995

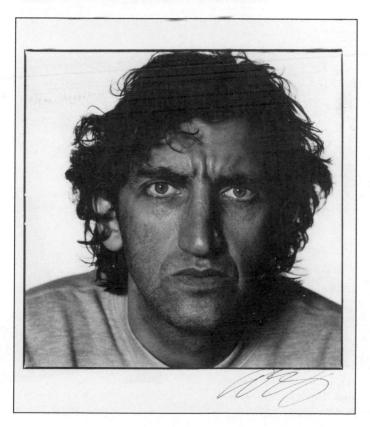

77. My favourite photograph of Miriam,
St Bart's, 1995

78. *Crocodile Shoes*, 1995

79. Me with my mam and sister Val at the
Dorchester, 1996. They'd come down to see
Pavarotti at the Royal Albert Hall

80. Me and my mam, St John's Wood,
London, 1996

81. *(Above)* As Agustín
Magaldi, *Evita*, 1996

82. *(Left)* The *Evita*
première, London, 1996

83. *(Below)* As Agustín
Magaldi, *Evita*, 1996

84. Tarquin Gotch, me and Emma Kamen, St John's Wood, London, 1996

85. *(Left)* Freddie playing Geoff Dugmore's drums, Wembley Arena, London, 1996

86. *(Above)* Miriam, Fred and Tom, Florida, 1997

87. Comeback kids: *Auf Wiedersehen, Pet,*
Arizona, 2001

88. Cuba 2002: Dick Clement, Ian La
Frenais, Franc Roddam and me. Taken by a
man using a cardboard box as a camera!

89. The one free weekend we had: Tim Healy,
Tim Spall, me, Kevin Whately, Chris Fairbank,
Punta Cana, Dominican Republic, 2003

90. Rehearsing a scene with director David
Innes-Edwards (on left, wearing straw hat),
Auf Wiedersehen, Pet, Dominican Republic, 2003

91. 'Kind of' Cuba:
Auf Wiedersehen, Pet,
Dominican
Republic, 2003

92. Me and the missus, Thailand, 2004

We played him some of the songs we'd recorded, and he reacted positively. He suggested we continue working on stuff at Danny's, then bring the tapes down to his place for a professional polish. In the meantime he'd put out some feelers, see if there was an album deal out there with my name on it.

As it turned out there was plenty of interest, and we eventually decided to go with Sony Records. A deal was drawn up, but Sony pulled out at the last moment: Laurie and I were sitting in Sony's opulent Soho Square offices, the contracts having been brought in for my signature, when the Sony finance director said something to the head honcho and the deal was off, just like that. We left the building and stumbled into a café to try to figure out what had just happened. To this day I still don't know. But as one door closes, another opens, they say, and we were offered a deal by EMI. Just before we committed, Laurie played me a message on his answerphone from Max Hole, the MD of east-west Records, a Warner's subsidiary. Mark Fox, a pal of Danny's and a percussionist, then moving into A&R, had played him a tape of our songs and he had liked what he had heard. He begged Laurie not to sign with anyone other than east-west. He was convinced that one of the songs, which none of us could stop humming, was 'an out-of-the-box smash'.

The next day we met up with him at his palatial offices in the Electric Light Building just off Kensington High Street and accepted his substantial five-album offer. The track he'd raved about was 'Ain't No Doubt'.

With the east-west advance we were able to move into more spacious and luxurious recording facilities and we took one of the big rooms in Livingston Studios in north London and got stuck in. I recruited a lot of help and called in a lot of favours. The guest guitarists included Dave Gilmore (Pink Floyd), Elliot Randall (Steely Dan), Gary Moore and George Harrison – George, playing on one of my little songs! As far as I'm concerned it gets no better. It had taken me a long time to work up the nerve to ask him. It seemed a liberty, but as Laurie said, 'If you don't ask him he might be miffed.' So I sat in my car outside Laurie's office one wet morning and called him up on my Motorola 8800 housebrick-sized mobile. I'd only got as far as, 'George . . .' when he said, 'Of course I will.'

'What?' I asked, thrown.

'Aren't you gonna ask me to play on your record?' he asked. He made it really easy for me.

George rang Danny Schogger to arrange for the multi-track tapes to be sent over to his place where he'd put some guitars on. I took them over to Friar Park myself and was in for a surprise. George listened to a few tracks and suggested he play on 'Real Love'. He also suggested getting Gary Moore over to play on a ballad called 'Absent Friends'. Gary kindly agreed and contributed some blistering guitar-work. George's solo is perfection, beautiful, sweet and lovely. I don't usually listen to any of my own music but I sometimes play that track to remind myself that it really happened.

The album, *Growing Up In Public*, was released in 1992 on the back of the successful first single, 'Ain't No Doubt', and immediately went gold, moving over a hundred thousand copies in a couple of weeks. Max had been right about 'Ain't No Doubt'; it went through the roof, selling over six hundred thousand, and seemed to be just about everywhere, on the radio, on TV, on jukeboxes, on supermarket Tannoys, in lifts. Jen Samson, who was then working as a script editor on *Spender*, complained of getting to the top of a Tibetan mountain in an attempt to escape all things Nail, only to hear that song coming out of a radio in a rickety wooden shack. It entered the UK chart at number five, went to number two the following week, then to the top spot.

We were all over at the Spalls' house having Sunday lunch, with my mam, who was visiting for a few days, when I got a call from the management to say I was at number one. I was ecstatic and danced around the kitchen with my mam in my arms. Everyone was happy for me that day but it's the memory of my mam, as pleased as punch with her Jimmy, that I'll treasure the most. Ever since I was a kid, she'd had to listen to all my half-baked ideas in the quest for musical success, and she'd never dismissed my dreams. Against all the odds, it had happened, and I'm thankful we could savour that moment together.

14

By now the fame thing was as potty as it gets. Miriam and I decided we wanted to get away from London so we moved out of Dicey Avenue and rented a place in North Wales, where the kids could continue their Welsh-language education. In retrospect the move wasn't a good idea. North Wales was just too far for me to go from Newcastle, and I was there only a few times in the year we had the place. In the end Miriam declared it too isolated so we returned to London, and rented a huge place in St John's Wood.

I had to write a *Spender* script set in Marseille, so I took myself to Toulon for four months. This self-imposed exile may seem crazy in view of what had gone before, but it worked because Miriam wasn't isolated: she was in London with her friends nearby. And in our case absence really does make the heart grow fonder. Sometimes less is more.

While I was in Toulon I found out that Sting was to play the local arena, so I called Pippa Markham, my former agent who looked after him, and asked where he'd be staying. It turned out he was in an hotel just down the road from where I was billeted, so I left a message inviting him for a cuppa. I'd watched him playing with his band, Last Exit, at the Newton Park pub in Newcastle, but our paths had never crossed and I guess I was half expecting to meet a big-head. No way, José. He turned out to be a humble soul, and funny. I wasn't expecting that. We spent the next few days hanging out together, recalling times past, and parted friends. Don't believe the derogatory stuff you read about Sting: I'm telling you, he's not what they'd have you believe.

Spender ran for three seasons. By 1993, we'd made twenty episodes as well as a two-hour film. I'd taken the series outside the BBC and into the independent sector, primarily because the financial rewards were better: Duncan, who pioneered talent packaging in the UK, stepped in and swung a deal that allowed me to make the show myself for a per-episode fee. As a result, Miriam and I were able to buy a big, dilapidated four-storey house in Alma Square, St John's Wood, from a merchant bank for a knock-down price. We were on holiday at the Forte Village in Sardinia when I spotted it in an advert in the *Sunday Times*. We'd always fancied St John's Wood as a permanent base: it was handy for the West End and had a villagy feel. I flew back to London, viewed the house and by the week's end we'd bought it.

I'd also fallen victim to my personal curse and become bored. Success can be a dangerous thing, and in my experience it's never quite what you expect it to be. After all that work getting *Spender* up and running, I decided to pack it in. It wasn't a popular decision: the BBC had spent a lot of money on it, they had a hit and would have been happy for it to go on. I would have made a lot more money, but I was bored and no amount of money compensated for that. I'd been away for long periods and I wanted to be at home more. With *Spender* I'd proved to the world I could do it from scratch, and it no longer challenged me.

Crocodile Shoes, the script that Ian La Frenais hadn't liked all those years ago, was the project for 1994. But I'd had time now to work on it. It revolved around songwriter Jed Shepperd, the lead character, and his journey from Newcastle to Nashville and all the way back. Jed was based on the younger brother of my old pal Chad Shepherd. Chad! How cool was that for a council-estate boy? Steve McQueen had a son called Chad. And Jed? There was Jed Clampett, from *The Beverly Hillbillies*, but no one had names like those back then, at least not in our neck of the woods. It would more likely be Alan, Peter, Paul, Michael, David, Brian or John. There weren't many Jimmys, even, just me and my dad, as I recall. When the time came and I needed names for my leading characters, it wasn't a struggle to find them. I'd waited years for an opportunity to use those monikers.

In the UK television market there was a great deal of money to be made from owning and producing your own television programmes and records, but there were big costs that had always to be recouped before you earned a penny. Advertising was one, production another. It seemed to me that if I could make television drama featuring music as an inherent element, we could pool the advertising spend and save a lot of money. My new music management team agreed.

I had parted amicably from Laurie Jay, and hooked up with Tarquin Gotch, whom I'd met, once again, through Ian La Frenais. Tarquin and Emma Kamen agreed to look after my music affairs and it proved a fruitful relationship, both creatively and financially. I now had agents and music management and I needed them both. There was an awful lot going on.

Around this time something else happened, which had a profound effect on how I viewed life. Ever since I was a kid, I'd dreamed of becoming a millionaire. In the 1950s and 1960s it had been a magical, unattainable number, but over the previous two years, mainly because of Duncan's shrewd deal-making, a great deal of money had come my way. I asked my accountants to call me when the great day arrived – not on paper or in the value of my house, I wanted to be told when I had cash running to seven figures in the bank. I'd worried about balancing the books, having enough to get by, for as long as I could recall and I thought I'd be off the hook at last. Come the day, I answered the phone and was told I was there. What an anti-climax. I felt empty and stupid. Worst of all, it made not a jot of difference. Like a lot of folk who've started with nothing and done all right, I still worried about money. That's never changed. I don't suppose it ever will. It sometimes doesn't do to realize your dreams.

Cut to 1993 and the end of *Spender*. Duncan and I met Alan Yentob at BBC Television Centre to discuss my idea for a new series. I wanted to get away from stuff I'd be doing year after year. I also wanted to do a little project about music. Whether Alan liked it or not I don't know, but I was hot property so we were given the green light to make seven hours with my own company. The condition was that we had to make the series in partnership with a more established independent, as a safeguard against anything going wrong. We trawled around and finally did a co-production deal with Red Rooster, a company based in Floral Street, Covent Garden, owned and run by Linda James and her husband, the director Stephen Bayley. It seemed like a good idea at the time, but sadly proved a match not made in heaven.

We needed some songs, and they had to be exceptional. As far as possible I wanted to retain a kind of organic north-eastern connection to the creative side of the Jed Shepperd character so I approached Paddy McAloon, a Geordie, whose band Prefab Sprout was on hold. I met up with him in Newcastle, explained the project to him, and he agreed to give it a go. This was quite a coup as I had been expecting a knock-back, but Paddy was lovely from the off. A few weeks later the first of his efforts arrived in the post. As I listened to beautiful ballads like 'Cowboy Dreams' and 'Love

Will Find Someone For You' in the kitchen at Alma Square with Miriam, I knew we'd hit the jackpot. These weren't just songs, they were gems. Paddy's compositions went a long way to making the project a success and I'm in his debt. What a gift, to be able to come up with magnificent songs on a regular basis. Don't stop, mate. The world needs groovy songs.

Around this time we received some dreadful news. Miriam had been having problems with her joints ever since Tom's birth ten years earlier. A visit to Professor Black at the Royal Free Hospital in Hampstead revealed that she was suffering from rheumatoid arthritis. It's one of the more common types of arthritis and causes immense pain. It also triggers related conditions, like Reynaud's Syndrome, which causes the extremities to go white and numb. Although the news was crushing, it explained a lot. No wonder she was unhappy after a long flight. It must have been agony for her.

Rheumatoid arthritis is a viral condition: it can go away for years then be back in an instant. Stress can trigger an attack – or a flare-up, as they're called – so, plenty of guilt for me. I wish I could buy her a cure – I'd give everything I have in a heartbeat, the lot, were that possible. But it's not. Some things can't be mended with money.

It was also around this time that I decided to consult a therapist. I had to sort out the muddle I felt over my identity. I'd considered it before but had dismissed it as too 'Californian'. Avoiding the issue, I guess. I had occasional sessions over the next couple of years, mostly alone but sometimes with Miriam. Contrary to what I'd expected, there was no specific advice, only questions left hanging in the air to resonate at the end of a session. It wasn't an easy journey but I learned a lot about myself and hopefully am a better person for it.

The shoot was not a happy one. I had taken on far too

much responsibility, and the conduct of some left a lot to be desired. I remember one day on Regent's Canal having to placate an angry man who wouldn't let us get on with filming because his girlfriend, a low-ranking member of the crew, had apparently left him to carry on an affair she was having with another person on the production staff. I knew nothing about any of this until I turned up on the set. I sympathized with the man but explained that it was neither my doing nor my problem, we had a hundred-strong crew standing around sucking their thumbs and we had to get on or fuck off. He accepted my point, but we had lost precious time. Chaos followed as the weeks went by, until we brought in the steadying hands of producer Peter Richardson. Things settled down after his arrival but making *Crocodile Shoes* was an unenjoyable experience, which was frustrating, considering it was my idea, my company – and my ass on the screen.

We filmed in Newcastle, London and Nashville, using a lot of the actors I'd come to know so well from *Spender*. Sammy Johnson and Berwick Kaler were prominent members of the cast. David Richards was the lead director and did a good, solid job. Against everyone's wishes I insisted we cast James Wilby, not known for his light comedic touch, to play the gritty part of ravaged A&R veteran Ade Lynn. He turned out to be less than ideal. Another lesson learned: let others make those decisions.

We had a second director, Malcolm Mowbray, best known for *A Private Function*, written by Alan Bennett and made by George Harrison's HandMade Films. He seemed to me to be a terrible procrastinator, and seemed quite incapable of explaining what it was he wanted. I felt he was the wrong man for the job. It happens. He refused numerous requests to give the first assistant director any kind of shot list, saying that such a request compromised his creative integrity. But it's industry standard, how everybody works and we couldn't continue as we were, losing time every day. A few weeks into shooting Malcolm Mowbray left. The last thing anyone wants to happen is to lose a director: it causes chaos and usually costs a fortune to remedy. I was lumbered with directing duties until Rob Knight came on board. I hated it but it was either that or close down the shoot, which would have meant losing the transmission and album-release dates. However, James Wilby then appeared to get the notion that I was taking over the show – which was my show anyway – and our relationship became very strained. There was a mad period of about five days when I got no sleep whatsoever.

The whole thing came to a head when I was discovered sitting on my trailer floor, confused and delirious. Tony Antoniou, my doctor, appeared and drove me away. He told me I was suffering from mental and physical exhaustion and wanted to have me hospitalized, sedated and drip-fed for the next few days. I didn't fancy that and pleaded with him to allow me to go home. He relented, but only if I agreed to do absolutely nothing. It wasn't hard to comply. I lay on the settee for days, unable to even think. When Miriam asked if I'd like a cup of tea, I found myself incapable of replying.

A few days later I arranged to meet with Wilby at my office in Regent's Park. This was strange as he and I shared the same acting agent, Paul Lyon-Maris, but Paul was, as always, totally professional about the whole thing. Over tea I informed Wilby I'd decided to pull the plug on the show. This would mean a great deal of grief for me personally but no amount of money was worth killing myself for, and I was fed up to the back teeth with how difficult things had become. He seemed genuinely surprised. What about all the work we'd done? he wanted to know. What about all that footage already in the can, footage of him? I explained that I'd gone out on a limb for him in getting him his part, and thought that it would count for something. I was worn down with all the grief.

After a while, mulling it over, he said that if I would continue and finish the show, he'd get on with it. I asked why I should believe him. He gave me his word. I thought about it for a while, then I agreed. Make the best of a bad job, I thought. As he left he turned and said to me, 'I'm so glad that's sorted. I couldn't have kept it up for another day.' I wanted to knock him out there and then, but he was on his way down my spiral staircase and it would have been difficult to land a decent punch on his jaw.

We finished the series and I've not seen or heard from him since.

For all the trauma of making it, *Crocodile Shoes* was a success with the punters and that, ultimately, is what counts. In terms of ratings it pulled in between eight and nine million viewers during its seven-week run, at that time perfectly acceptable for a non-formulaic one-off serial and these days more than enough to qualify as a hit. The music was a thundering success: it spawned three top-twenty singles, the first selling half a million copies, and the album went on to sell over a million, a thrilling figure.

The series also prompted my first national music tour. After the success of 'Love Don't Live Here Anymore', I'd been approached over the years by promoters eager to cash in on my fame and popularity but I'd either not had the time or just not fancied it. A million album sales alters your thinking. This time, when the call came, I was up for it. Tarquin spoke to various promoters and we signed up with Tim Parsons at MCP, who suggested we put four dates on sale to test the water, see if anyone would pay to watch me play and sing. The dates sold out quickly so Tim booked a couple more, with the same result. In the end we sold out twenty-two dates. I was thrilled, but also a little apprehensive. The voice is a fickle thing, and everything would be resting on mine. Still, it was the next challenge, and what had begun as a tentative look-see experiment turned into a bona-fide occupation.

People often ask me which I like more, singing or acting. It's not a question I can answer with a simple 'this' or 'that', because it's unrealistic to compare the two. Although both come under the category of creative arts, they are, in my case, so different as to be almost unrelated. I don't do theatre so my acting is confined to occasional in-front-of-the-camera stints. I'm never offered theatre work. Duncan thinks I'd go bonkers with its repetitive nature, but I'm not so sure. I'd like to have a crack at it, and certainly musical theatre would seem to make sense. I think I'd be able to make a decent fist of it if the piece and the director were right for me.

As a musician with thirty-five years' experience, however, I feel at home on a live stage fronting a band. I've never had stage-fright before a gig. Most performers will tell you that if a person says they're not nervous before a performance they're lying, but I've rarely felt uncomfortable. Just the opposite, in fact: usually I can't wait to get out there. The reason's simple: if you know all the words to the songs, your voice is in good nick, your band is well rehearsed and you've sold all the tickets, what on earth is there to be nervous about? Messing up? Making a mistake? It happens – but so what? In a live situation it doesn't really matter. I've dropped some right old clangers over the years but most times you get away with it, and if the audience should happen to notice you've dropped a bollock, or you bring it to their attention, as I do, they usually respond positively. It shows them you're human.

The Crocodile Shoes tour would be different from the old

days with the King Crabs, when we charged around the North East from pub gig to pub gig in our tatty old pink Transit van. Tarquin and Emma assembled a band and crew who were veterans of the road and of the highest calibre. So, ladies and gentlemen, a big hand for the band: on electric guitar and harmonica, Chester Kamen; on keyboards and squeezebox, Guy Fletcher; on pedal steel and Dobro guitars, Melvin Duffy; on bass guitar and mandolin, Finn O'Laughlan; on drums and all things percussive, Geoff Dugmore. What a line-up. After the first day of rehearsals I realized I was a lucky boy to be in such company. They are all talented musicians with CVs to prove it. They took a flyer in agreeing to go out on the road with someone like me, someone off the telly, unproven on a big stage, and I thank them for their faith and all their encouragement. They were great.

And they were a lot of fun. We all worked hard but, boy, we had a laugh. After all the television-based politics and nonsense I'd been involved with over the previous few years, it was a breath of fresh air. Our tour manager was Dee McGlaughlan, a Dubliner who'd been around the block and the world many times, seen it all, done it all. Robbie McGrath, another Dubliner, late of the Boomtown Rats and Simply Red, was in charge of front-of-house sound. On the monitors, the worst job on the tour in my book, we had Flakey, late of Elvis Costello. The guitar technician was Phil Docherty, a Scotsman who now looks after Dominic Miller, Sting's long-time guitarist. Don't let anyone tell you rock 'n' roll is a lazy man's alternative to the day job. It's incredibly demanding, but compared to making a television show, it was a joy. No politics: just people who love the life working their nuts off to help you shine for a couple of hours every evening. I was the headline act, the star turn. It was my name alone on the posters and tickets, not the band's. The whole thing would stand or fall on what I came up with and how I sounded. There was no one else to shoulder the weight or to whom I could pass the buck.

I knew that if the dates were to be a success I'd have to get my voice in shape so a few weeks before the start of the tour, I sought the advice of Tona de Brette, famed vocal coach. Based in Muswell Hill, she had worked with people like George Michael, Phil Collins and, famously, John Lydon. I went along to see if I could strengthen my vocal cords, but I got much more than that out of the process. People would probably describe Tona as eccentric, but I recognized her as a really committed teacher. She asked me what I needed to achieve and I explained that I wanted to be able to hit the high notes every night. She asked me to play her the tracks, which I did, and I pointed out the notes I was concerned about as they came along. Tona soon had me singing scales and doing various other exercises. Tuition in breathing, and its beneficial effect, came as a shock. I improved almost immediately – it's amazing how the voice responds to being worked correctly. After a few weeks, Tona asked me to hit a note she played on the piano and hold it, which I did. Then she played a lower note, maybe a tone down from where I'd just been, and explained to me that this second note was in fact the highest note on my album. The psychological effect was immediate: I felt as if I was capable of singing anything.

As I'd realized with *Auf Wiedersehen, Pet*, you're only new once, and as much as you might try you can't replicate that first experience. It's over all too soon and it's easy to miss the sheer joy that is part of the experience. I was lucky. Because I'd already been there with *Auf Wiedersehen, Pet* I knew how quickly the tour would pass and I was determined to step back and savour it as best I could. I felt at ease with my surroundings: the acting was something I'd had to master quickly as I went along, but music was my forte, something I'd been doing since I was a teenager. And from the moment I stepped on to the rehearsal stage I felt as if I'd come home, to use Tim Spall's phrase. That first tour was such a buzz, with audiences singing along to the songs from the album. They knew every word. It was nothing short of thrilling to stand there singing along with them all. It was also a revelation in as much as it confirmed something I'd not dared think about: people were willing to pay good money to see me perform live.

One of the things I had to get accustomed to was using in-ear monitors. You often see singers wearing them onstage, with curled cables disappearing down the back of a collar to a battery-driven belt-pack receiver. They're fiddly to put on, and it was the last thing I wanted to be bothered with moments before the start of a performance. In the end I was swayed by the pitching advantages. If you take enough time with the sound balance you can get an absolutely wonderful mix, which then gives you the best shot at being in tune. They are a modern alternative to the more traditional and much less accurate stage-mounted wedge monitors and fills. You're in your own zone, cut off from the atmosphere of the room, and often can't hear people's shouts. All went well until a gig at the NEC in Birmingham. Suddenly, mid-way through a song, my earpiece exploded with noise from a passing mini-cab radio. There was a volume dial on the belt-pack but for some reason it wouldn't turn off. It was excruciating. In front of ten thousand punters I had no option but to rip out the earpiece and throw it on to the deck. My head was reeling but the sound boys switched me over to the wedge monitors on the floor in front of me and we kept going. It didn't do much for my mood, though.

The concert we played at the Newcastle City Hall on that

first tour was cathartic. We'd all been looking forward to and dreading it in equal measure. Robbie McGrath told me afterwards that the crew had been desperate for this to be a successful gig because they'd all known how I felt about coming home. Playing your home town or city is always nerve-racking. You never know what sort of reaction you're going to elicit from the audience or what sort of evening you're in for. I'd thought about it a lot and tried to dismiss it as just another gig, but it was a monumental occasion for me. During my time making television I'd been insulated, protected, kept away from contact with real people and their opinions. Now, one way or another, I'd get to know how my fellow Geordies felt.

It was a long day. We'd travelled down from Glasgow, where we'd played the night before and had a grand old evening, and followed what was now our daily routine. There was a sound-check at four thirty. They usually ran until about six but this one went over. Then a meal for band and crew. I could never eat before a gig – the last thing an audience needs is a great big belch when you're belting out a ballad. So:

Doors open at seven p.m.

Support act, Deana Carter, on from seven forty-five till eight thirty.

Intermission.

Eight fifty: ten-minute warning from tour-manager Dee.

Nine p.m.: showtime!

Onstage until ten thirty p.m., then finish. A minute longer, and you incur financial penalties imposed by the local council. If you decide to do an encore, it costs you.

That wait backstage was a long one. I'd been wondering about a night like this for over a decade, and now it was upon me. What would it feel like? Who'd be out there?

Someone with a grudge or a score to settle? I half expected someone to take a pop at me as I stood up there, alone in the follow-spot's bright light. But enough of all that dithering: it was eight thirty and I had to prepare. The place was jam-packed with people who'd paid their money and they were expecting to be entertained.

I followed the established routines. First the bathroom routine, then dressing routine, then the breathing routine, then vocal routine, then the bathroom routine once more. After that I dawdled in the wings.

The lights went down and it was time to hit the stage. The band struck up, and a moment later I walked out into the semi-darkness from stage left. A follow-spot picked me up and . . .

The audience gave me a five-minute standing ovation. I'd come home, all right. I'll never forget that feeling and that evening as long as I live. That night the Geordies were good to me.

Although everything, to the last detail, had been pre-planned with military precision and ran like a Swiss clock for most of the time, there were one or two unfortunate moments. Having played a gig in the city the night before, we left Birmingham at lunch-time on our way to Brighton for the show that evening. I was looking for some sweets on the tour bus – there were always plenty on board, thoughtfully supplied by Brum Dougie, our redoubtable driver who also happened to co-own the company, Phoenix, but that day all I could find were some fruit pastilles in a big bag. Whose were they? It was just gone one o'clock and the boys in the band had gone to bed in their bunks, so I couldn't ask. I tucked in as I read my *Daily Telegraph*. Very tasty, they were. So tasty, in fact, that before I knew it I'd polished off the whole packet.

A little later on, Kellie Gordon, my PA, appeared from her cubicle-cum-office near the front of the bus. I hadn't seen a packet of sweets lying around, had I? Pastilles, big bag. Embarrassed, I admitted the greedy deed and apologized for not leaving her a single one. We'd pull into the next service station and replenish our depleted stocks. Kellie looked more upset than she should have done. Worried, even. Hadn't I read the wording on the packet?

I shook my head.

They were laxative lozenges. Superstrength. No more than two to be taken at once. And I had eaten a bagful.

By the time I took the stage that evening my stomach was burbling and gurgling like a cannibal's crockpot. With cheeks nipped together I made for the microphone. The opening number was 'Crocodile Shoes'. I got as far as the first line, and then – agh! A semi-solid disaster nestled in the backside of my trousers. Could people see? Nah, it was dark and I was dressed in black. But they'd smell it soon enough. Knees pressed together to prevent my crocodile shoes getting covered with untreated sewage, I waddled backwards to where Geoff Dugmore was parked on the drum rostrum. He was smiling, having a ball as usual while keeping perfect time. Once we were face to face, he said, 'How is it?'

'I've shat meself!' I replied, loud enough that he could hear me above the clatter of the band but not so loud that the mics picked it up and broadcast it to the audience. Geoff's face was a picture – he didn't know what to say. In the end he shrugged. I had no choice but to get on with it. The evening was long and uncomfortable.

Sadly, there was tragedy too. After I had played two sold-out nights at the Hammersmith Apollo I was informed that a member of the audience, a lady in her late thirties, had gone to the loo, suffered a heart-attack and died. I was floored and quickly became angry that I hadn't been told sooner. Tarquin explained that he'd feared I'd go to pieces if I was told at the time, and the gig might have descended into pandemonium, with the possibility of more casualties. He was probably right, but I was still in bits. This was someone's life and death. It made what we were doing seem so pointless. We contacted the lady's husband: she had been married with a couple of kids, like me, and he told me she was a big fan of mine. She'd been looking forward to the concert for months. She would have been enjoying herself, he said, having a good time, and happy. They were kind words but I couldn't help feeling that it was somehow my fault. If I'd not done that tour, if I'd not played that gig, she might still have been alive. It took away any pleasure I'd felt about successfully completing the tour and makes me sad to this day.

15

That incident was an inauspicious start to what would soon turn out to be a big adventure, one of my biggest and most eventful yet. That, for me, is the second most wonderful thing about working in the entertainment business: you never know what's round the corner. Sometimes it's bad, but for me it's been mostly good, and once or twice it's been unbelievable.

The grey stone façades that make up Hanover Square in the West End of London looked damp and drab that wet Wednesday afternoon. Duncan Heath and I were travelling down in the lift from the fourth floor of my then lawyers' offices. As the doors opened Duncan turned to me and said, 'Oh, we must speak about this movie thing.'

'What movie thing?' I asked.

'*Evita*,' he replied, as he dashed towards the door. *Evita*? 'Didn't I mention the telephone call?'

I didn't know about any telephone call, I said, at once excited and pissed off. Hang on! What telephone call?

'From Alan Parker.'

The internationally renowned movie director? What did he want? 'To find out whether you'd be up for going to see them to talk about a part in his upcoming movie, *Evita*.'

My mind raced and spun as it tends to do at such times. Proper movies, the real deal, the silver screen? Limos, red carpets, flashbulbs? Steady, James!

I'd met Alan Parker only once before and very briefly, up at – where else? – Ian La Frenais's house in the Hollywood

Hills during one of his Sunday evening get-togethers. Alan and I were introduced and had a friendly chat over drinks in Ian's kitchen. We'd yakked about the film he'd just finished shooting, *Come See the Paradise*, starring Dennis Quaid, which told of the rough treatment many Japanese-American internees had to endure during the Second World War. Then, the American movie-going public, made up predominantly of single white males aged between thirteen and twenty-five, were not much interested in that type of story (are they ever?) and the movie stiffed at the box-office, but Alan was upbeat that night and great company. I was a big fan of his and it was great to meet him. We discussed the kind of things ex-pats tend to discuss in such circumstances: how you miss your HP sauce, how you can never get a decent cup of tea in the States, the usual stuff. He struck me as a sound guy and his beginnings had been similar to mine – i.e., humble. There was no bullshit about him, no side, and he was very funny. I liked him straight away and we seemed to get along, but there was no more to it than that, no talk of my playing parts or anything remotely promising.

Actually, that's not strictly true: there was just a little thing, but any actor reading this will know what I mean. Every once in a while I'd clocked Alan clocking me in the same way others had done, people like Roger Bamford and Ian La Frenais: as if he were logging details into a memory bank to be stored for retrieval some time later on. At least, that was what I'd assumed they were doing. They might just have been having a good squint at the configuration of my boat race. Who knows? Anyway I'd seen and heard nothing from Alan since then so this was an exciting surprise development.

By the time we left the lift I knew a little more, but Duncan didn't have time to explain in detail. As he ran out to a waiting cab he shouted over his shoulder that he'd call and fill me in. I hardly slept a wink.

The next day brought exciting news: *Evita* was to be a full-scale film production of the stage musical, a massive enterprise with a budget of $70 million. It would be filmed in Argentina, Hungary and the United Kingdom. Hardly able to contain my excitement, I asked if anyone else had been cast. 'Madonna is to play Evita, Antonio Banderas is to play Che, and Jonathan Pryce is cast as Juan Perón.' Would I be up for a meeting with Alan Parker to talk about the project over a cup of coffee? They were interested in me for Agustín Magaldi, an Argentine tenor who had apparently befriended and seduced the young Eva Perón on her way to Buenos Aires and immortality. *Would I!* When? Where? What would I have to do? Paul Lyon-Maris, who handles my acting affairs at ICM, suggested I should familiarize myself with the soundtrack/score of the *Evita* musical.

At this time I was working on what was to be the follow-up album to *Crocodile Shoes*. A while earlier I'd started writing a song at the rickety old piano we had in the drawing room at Alma Square. It had a strong feel to it and I was rather pleased. The chorus was all about the Tyne so I called it 'Big River'. I eventually completed it one day on the tour bus. We recorded the album at Mickey Most's Rak Studios in St John's Wood, just a short walk from our house. While I was at Sir George Martin's Air Lyndhurst Studios in Hampstead one day I happened to bump into Mark Knopfler who asked me what I was up to. I played him 'Big River' and he offered to put a bit of guitar on to it. That was a thrill. Mark was from Newcastle too, and I'd always been a fan of his. As well as playing guitar, he also lent a helping hand with one of the verse lines I was struggling with. 'Big River' was the best thing I'd ever written and by far the most popular with live audiences. I wish I could have come up with more songs like it, but I fear it was the only one of its kind I had in me. Never mind. I'm proud to have written just one.

I was in the middle of mixing the *Big River* album and happened to mention to my co-producer Danny Schogger that I'd have to take a morning off to audition for Alan Parker. Danny asked me what I was up for and when I told him he laughed. 'You'll never believe it,' he said, 'but I played in the original West End production of *Evita* in the 1970s!' While he was studying at the Royal College of Music, Danny used to dash off after his classes to play in the pit on the show. This was not only a coincidence, it was a major stroke of good fortune. Danny would take me through the score, help me prepare for my audition and accompany me on the day.

It had been a long time since I'd been to any kind of an audition, not since *Auf Wiedersehen, Pet*, in fact. I'd had things comparatively cushy and didn't see any need to put myself through the kind of nonsense auditions often entail. Some of the things you're asked to do at these get-togethers can be nothing short of degrading, so it's better all round for me not to put myself in those situations. I've probably missed out on many an opportunity but never mind. *C'est la vie.*

I had to go to meet Alan Parker and Ros Hubbard, the movie's casting director, at a primary school somewhere in central London, then run through some songs from the show. Come the morning, I had listened to the *Evita* soundtrack a hundred times, and at ten a.m. Alan, Ros and I, with Danny at the piano and a young lad who operated the video camera, were in this big bare first-floor classroom. As we lined up the picture frame and checked the sound, the lad looked half-asleep. Bless him, I thought. All dishevelled and dreamy, he could have been one of my sons. We shot the breeze for a while, skirted around things, then Alan suggested we run through one of the songs. The one I'd routined was 'On This Night Of A Thousand Stars', a big showy number that Magaldi had made his own. I'd rejigged the end of the song with Danny so I would hold the final high note for seven bars, quite a lungful and quite a challenge at ten in the morning. I'd practised it, though, and was confident.

I stood in the middle of the room and Danny gave me the intro with a flourish that set me up perfectly. A deep breath, a quick prayer and I was off. It must have been my lucky day – either that or the prayer had worked wonders – because the rendition went marvellously. I hit every note on the button and finished with the seven-bar finale, on and on and on, and then . . . out! It elicited a round of applause from Alan and Ros Hubbard and even from my man Danny, who's not one for insincere flattery. Even I was pleased with my performance that day: I'm no great fan of my own endeavours but I knew I'd nailed it.

Alan said, 'Fuck me! That was amazing! Where did you learn to sing like that?' I couldn't answer properly: I'd only practised my breathing and those vocal exercises at Tona de Brette's piano some two or three years earlier. I'd just busked it as best I could, as per usual. I allowed myself the luxury of being hopeful.

Alan turned to the lad on the camera and said, 'Right, rewind it and let's have a look at the tape.'

The lad glanced at us all in turn, went even paler than he already was, then looked at Alan sheepishly. 'Did you want me to record that?'

Silence in the room. I knew, and so did everyone else, that I'd never pull it off again like that first time. I looked at the young lad. For a moment I wanted to choke him to death with my bare hands there and then. My pop at a Hollywood movie, gone, lost, out of the window, and all because of this light-headed, sleepy dimwit. Alan put an arm round my shoulders and said, 'Sorry about that. Shall we do another?' I agreed, and we did and it was fine, and I hit all the notes and held the long one at the end, but it was nothing like as magical as that first one. We watched it back and it was all right, but I was seething. Off it would go to Hollywood and someone there would say, 'Well, it's OK but it's nothing special,' which was true.

Alan walked me to the door. 'I don't think we'll be using him on the movie,' he said, nodding towards the now dejected-looking young lad.

'Right,' I said, and then I was outside in the fresh air. '*We* won't be using . . .' Did he mean 'we' as in he and the rest of them? Or could he have meant 'we' as in he and I? No, surely not. I couldn't let myself believe that. I went back to the studio to continue the mixing.

At the time I had an office in Portobello Road and about a week after the audition I was there discussing business matters relating to the musical side of things with Tarquin and Emma, the next album, which was to tie in with the second *Crocodile Shoes* series, when the phone rang. It was Paul Lyon-Maris to tell me Alan Parker wanted me to play Magaldi in his movie! Cue major celebrations and even a little bit of dancing around the coffee table.

Later I met up with Paul and Duncan at the ICM Oxford Street offices to discuss the project. It was an interesting day. I'd been offered a lot of money to do a commercial, almost seven figures over two years. As I sat studying the *Evita* script, Paul popped his head round the door. At that moment I was reading about how Magaldi seduces the young Eva

Perón then dumps her in the big city to fend for herself. Double-take. Mind-muddle. I read it again, disbelieving, but there they were, right there in front of me, those same words: I'd be in bed with Madonna! I laughed, hollered and whooped. What did I want to do about the commercial? Paul was asking. I asked Duncan what he thought. 'Do you need to do it?' he asked. No, I said. 'Do you want to particularly?' I didn't. 'Then don't,' he said.

Paul informed me that the *Evita* money was two thousand dollars a week. It was an indication of how far I'd come that I was just about to have a moan, when he added, '*Per diem.*' Two grand a week *per diem*! That meant the expenses an actor is paid by the film company to cover laundry and meals away from the set, et cetera, while they're on location. Two grand a week! On telly jobs it's normally a tenth of that figure. Never mind that it's only dollars. My actual fee was well into six figures, along with perks like two first-class round trip tickets to Buenos Aires, all courtesy of the Mouse – the Disney Corporation, who were financing the movie.

I raced back to Alma Square to share the news with Miriam and we celebrated with a meal. I wasn't sure that she would want to do the thirteen-hour overnight flight to Buenos Aires, but she was excited at the prospect, and keen to go if we could work out cover for the boys, who were now aged ten and eight. She had an Argentinian connection that made the whole thing even more appealing to her: her aunt Cathrin taught Welsh in Patagonia. Nannies permitting, we'd soon be Argentina-bound.

The first day of rehearsals was nerve-racking, to say the least. You make as though you're not too bothered and everything's cool but of course you are and it's not. Everyone is uptight and anxious. It has to be like that, really. Madonna alone would have been a daunting enough prospect but this was Madonna, Antonio Banderas, Jonathan Pryce, Alan Parker, David Caddick (Andrew Lloyd-Webber's and the movie's musical director), and little old me from Benton. I'd done as much preparatory work as I possibly could: as well as memorizing my own pieces, I'd listened to all Madonna's albums, read up on Antonio Banderas and Jonathan Pryce, and sung endless scales so that I'd be vocally prepared and, hopefully, able to cope with anything that might be thrown at me. Now the time had come. At the appointed hour a big posh car picked me up and I was whisked away, a bundle of back-seat nerves.

The rehearsal venue couldn't have been less auspicious: the first floor of an old warehouse in King's Cross. Grim, unglamorous, chosen, I'd guess, deliberately by Alan to let everyone know that he would be making all the decisions on this shoot. The room was cavernous, with a high vaulted ceiling, good for live vocals, and just a piano in the centre. David Wimbury, Alan's line producer, whom I knew from my first visit to LA, offered me coffee and generally exuded an air of calm. My nerve-ends felt like live wires.

Antonio was already there and was friendly from day one. He's a lovely man, totally committed to his work and family yet always up for a laugh and a joke. On top of that he's probably one of the best-looking blokes in the world. The lucky bastard had it all. I liked him from the off and that never changed. He called me Jimmy Nails and I called him Tony Flags – a translation of his name into English. He made a joke of his singing, saying he was dreadful and knew it, but his voice was fine with a rich husk to it, no doubt the result of all the Marlboros he got through. There was a good bit of coughing in those first few weeks as Antonio got used to the breathing required to hold those notes, but he was a willing pupil and his enthusiasm was infectious. There was no big-star bullshit about him. He knew, of course, as did the rest of us, that no one would have been in that room if they couldn't hack it, even Madonna. Alan Parker is not one for carrying passengers or suffering fools. Cap'n Al was master of the ship and I was glad to be a member of his crew. Because I'd spent several years on the road, singing with various bands, I felt a little more comfortable and confident than some in that room, but I wasn't about to take anything for granted. The Queen of Pop had yet to arrive.

All of a sudden she was there, making for Alan and big hugs. Bob, her Atlas-like bodyguard, was with her and never far away. I'd been told some of the people around her were authorized to carry guns, but Bob looked quite capable of murdering simply with a look. I waited my turn nervously in the introduction line and then there she was, and we were saying hello. I remember thinking how short she was in comparison to me and how fit she looked as we shook hands, all sinew and muscle, great definition. Madonna was gazing up at me and shaking my hand! I had to take a quick reality check. She said she'd been told I was a musician. I said that was right, although not on her scale, which was a stupid thing to say, as no one was on her scale at that time. I think, though, that this one thing we had in common: that we were two musos in a movie full of 'actors', made her feel a little more comfortable with me. It couldn't have been easy for her, as an American, a woman and a musician in control of her own universe, to come over to Britain and play the lead in a movie written by Brits, directed by a Brit and for the most part performed by Brits, to be sung in a style very different from her own.

Jonathan Pryce arrived, completing the main turns. He seemed a rather quiet type, with no sign of nerves. If he was bluffing he was convincing, but his track record in movies and musicals was impressive so maybe he wasn't fazed by it. After more introductions and a bit of laboured banter, we were at last standing around the piano. I felt I was on safe ground now and breathed a sigh of relief. As the music began I thought about how far I'd come from those long-ago days in Newcastle when I'd dreamed as a kid about days like this one.

We took our turns at singing, with David Caddick guiding us through the various passages. After a few verses it was clear that Madonna could sing really well. Her voice was clean, pure and impressively strong, even in the lower registers, and had such a comforting familiarity to it that I forgot about the circumstances and just enjoyed it. She had also done her homework thoroughly: she knew not only the piece but all about everyone else involved. I understood that total commitment to preparation and nobody worked harder than she did to make something special of that movie. She wasn't particularly fond of the music but she dished up some great vocal performances, particularly on 'Another Suitcase, Another Hall' – which was given to her character in the movie rather than to the young girl Juan Perón is seducing, as in the original musical – and, of course, 'Don't Cry For Me, Argentina'. For my money she bestowed upon those songs a quality and depth they'd never previously had.

I kept thinking it was beyond belief for me to be standing at the piano in such company. It was all I could do not to shout, I was so excited. At times like those you desperately want to call up a pal and say, 'Hey, you'll never believe what's happening here!' but of course you can't. Doesn't stop you thinking about it, though.

I felt great going home in the big posh car at the end of that first day, relieved I'd not let myself or anyone else down.

That's the worst nightmare, the idea of letting down folk who've shown faith in you, disappointing them. And my fellow cast members were now aware I wasn't there on looks alone.

On day two, it started hotting up. Madonna and I had a scene in which she had to belt me with a tatty old suitcase, then storm off. Now, there is no need whatsoever to lay into someone with a suitcase in rehearsal, but of course she did, harder and harder, time after time. I guessed she was waiting for me to complain, but I figured it was maybe nerves on her part so I kept it buttoned. At the week's end I had a blue bruise the length of my upper left arm. She told me later, with a giggle, it *had* been deliberate. I didn't mind but I was glad I hadn't made a fuss. Not in front of anyone, anyway.

The week's rehearsal had established a few important things as far as I was concerned. We'd broken the ice, the rest of the ensemble knew that I could hold my own on any level – other than, perhaps, in sparkling repartee – and, most importantly, Alan was happy with what I was offering up. A massive relief, that one. If the boss isn't happy you can still get the bullet a week into a job.

There would be a three-month pre-recording period, then about five months filming and post-production work to do. What made the job unusual was that, first, the entire piece was sung, there was no spoken dialogue, and, second, it would be pre-recorded and we would mime to it on set. Asking audiences to sit through a couple of hours of sung-through Rice/Lloyd-Webber was asking a lot, I thought, no matter who was directing, who was in the cast or who was playing the lead. A lot fell upon Madonna's shoulders, but she bore it like a trouper.

We embarked upon the recording sessions at the Sony/CBS studios in Whitfield Street in London's West End, the same studios I'd been working in when I'd gone for the audition. Straight away there were fireworks. Madonna had her own guy in from LA on the mixing desk, which I understood. It's difficult to record vocals properly and regularly. If you're the producer or the engineer, no two microphones, recording booths, or mixing desks are the same. It's a highly skilled job yet it's far from an exact science. If you're the vocalist, your head has to be in the right place, you need to feel comfortable, confident and at ease with yourself, your surroundings, the playback level and mix coming through your headphones, the microphone, the room temperature, the tape operator, the tea boy, the world. You need to be relaxed and happy; you need to feel everyone in the building is on your side. Then you begin wailing and yowling, purring and hollering in the hope that some part of what you're putting down will have a little bit of magic dust sprinkled on it.

That's not to say there's no help available: it's a sad fact that nowadays, with the aid of modern recording technology, you could sing a lyric in a monotone drone and in no time at all you'll be hitting any note the engineer programmes in. You can change the key of an entire vocal should you want to. State-of-the-art studio techno-toys make just about anything possible. Every producer and engineer in the game uses these tools at some point, sometimes to repair a single syllable, sometimes to make a decent fist of an entire song. Anyone who says otherwise is telling fibs. If you're stuck in a studio with a singer who can't hit the notes, or sings flat or sharp – quite a common occurrence – these tools can be a godsend. No need for them on this job, though.

The first vocal sessions were a laugh – or, at least, I can look back and laugh about them now. At the time it was stressful: I was required to do some two-handers with madam, or Mads as I used to call her sometimes. Not Madge, though. Never Madge. That particular moniker is more recent and she hates it. A week or so into the recording sessions, she and I had a bit of a disagreement about something or other, probably the incense candles she had smouldering away in the booth. In the middle of a take I noticed her giving me a single finger, which threw me. We exchanged some heated words and she told me to do something I wouldn't even repeat in print. Then, for no apparent reason, she decided she'd be better off lying on the studio floor. Nothing to do with me. By the time Alan Parker arrived, she was on her back and I was looking like the bad guy. Alan suggested that he and I retire to the pub for a drink. I agreed, at which point Mads said, from her berth on the deck, 'I thought I read you didn't drink.'

'That's right,' I replied, 'but I'm nearer to having a beer right now than I've been in the last ten years.' So off we went to the pub.

Booze was never an option – it would have been a disaster if I'd started back on the drink that day – so I gulped down non-alcoholic lager. 'You're going to have to help me, Jim,' Alan said. 'Madonna's got a lot on her plate with this and it's having an effect. One day she may be up, the next down. I need you to be nice to her, be supportive. Can you do that for me?'

I went from feeling furious and aggrieved to feeling an utter twat in about three seconds flat. I had nothing but the utmost respect and admiration for Alan, and he was asking me for help. I felt I'd let him down. I promised it wouldn't happen again. To the best of my knowledge, it never did.

We went back into the studio and while the engineers reset I took time out to have a natter with her nibs. I explained to her that it was my job to support her, just as foundations support a building. Alan was the builder, his script our blueprint, and she was its penthouse. If we all did our jobs well and the penthouse looked good, we'd successfully sell the building. She probably thought I was bonkers. I also told her I was there on merit and wouldn't be going away, so if she ended up liking me that would be lovely, but it wasn't essential. She could have insisted I be replaced, but to her credit she didn't, and I'd like to think we finished that movie as pals.

16

The recording sessions carried on up to Christmas 1995. As far as they were concerned, it was akin to a holiday for me. No, better than that, it was being paid to do something I would happily have done for free. It was only singing. The other stuff could sometimes be a little taxing, mind. On one occasion we had to do an orchestral session at CTS Studios in Wembley. The main room was massive, big enough to accommodate all the fiddlers, blowers and bangers.

As is my habit, I got there early. Never mind late, I can't even bear to be on time. It was an early one, nine thirty a.m., and the control-room staff were already buzzing with nervous anticipation as they awaited her ladyship's arrival. By this stage of the project I'd watched her routine played out many times and was never sure in my own mind whether I was impressed by it or considered it ridiculous. A bit of both, I suspect.

The security men's hip-radios would crackle into life with 'M due with you in twenty minutes.' Then it would be fifteen minutes. Then ten. Then five. From there it would be counted down in single digits. By the time she arrived, everyone's nerves were in shards. Steady men got the shakes, sensible pros stammered. You could smell the fear. It was no way to conduct a recording session. Not down to her either, I'd guess.

That morning I took myself off to the far end of the live room, opened up my *Telegraph* at the crossword page and waited for the fireworks. It wasn't long before she arrived. I watched through the big glass viewing panel as she said hello to the production team. Then she was asking something and an engineer was pointing towards me. Out she came, heels clip-clopping on the parquet as she made her way down the long room. I hid behind my broadsheet, waiting. The clip-clopping stopped and a hand came down, crumpling the pages. 'Good morning,' she said, in a way that left me in no doubt that she was pissed off with me for not being among the welcome committee.

'Morning.' I smiled.

'Shall we get on, then?' she asked imperiously.

'Ready when you are,' I answered.

I knew it would take a little while for her to get the recording booth just the way she liked it with the incense, lighting and vibe, so I wasn't really living dangerously, but it made for some spiky sessions. It wasn't contrariness on my part. I just couldn't bring myself to do that obsequious worship stuff. I've never liked it and have always felt embarrassed for those who chose or were forced to go along with it.

The times I spent in the vocal booth with Madonna were terrific and, once we were singing the material, we had a good laugh. She is an accomplished vocalist who knows how to use her vocal cords *and* the sound of her breathing; she knows the power of a word gently spoken, and as soon as she sings you know straight away that it's Madonna. Who else could it be?

One of the best things to come out of the time I spent on the *Evita* shoot was unexpected. Madonna had to wear caps on her front teeth to disguise that famous gap so a dental technician came up to sort her out. While he was there I took the opportunity to ask him about my own, rather more noticeable gap, the result of losing a front tooth in my teens. It had worked well for Oz, but I felt it wouldn't look right for this production: Magaldi was the type of bloke who'd spent a career smiling insincerely as he was ever-so-lightly showered with applause. I consulted Alan, as I had about anything and everything else. With or without? He felt with, and that was that. I was measured up and a few weeks later my gap had been filled. I'd tried a dental plate years earlier but had soon binned it as I couldn't stand the feel of it inside my mouth. This, though, was (still is) an incredible little number, fixed by fusion on to the tooth at either side by some kind of laser thing, and so good a match that it looks more real than the real one next to it. They warned me to take care when I bit into something hard like an apple or a French stick, but so far so good. It was awkward for a long while as I tended to lisp, but we'd already recorded the sound before we shot picture on *Evita* so it wasn't imperative for me to be speaking, or singing, crystal clearly. I might have sprayed one or two folk inadvertently, though.

When the recording sessions had been completed and the Burbank powers-that-be declared themselves happy with the results, I headed for Buenos Aires at the front end of a British Airways jumbo. Until 11 September 2001 I had travelled around the globe for the best part of twenty years, and in my experience there was nothing to compare with the service I received when flying first class with BA. Now everything has changed, and not necessarily for the better, as far as the passenger is concerned, but back then BA bossed the skies in terms of unadulterated luxury. Which was only right and proper, bearing in mind the astronomical prices they were charging. But on this trip I wasn't paying, Mickey was. The flight was an overnight one, with duvets and hot chocolate. It's the only way to travel but it does spoil you. I drifted off into dreamland, all snug and warm, far above the clouds, and slept like a log. In no time at all we were in Buenos Aires, Argentina.

Rude officials, surly security men and worried-looking travellers: everything seemed normal at the airport. But I was wary about landing in a country full of angry Argentinians, which had seen its share of military dictators over the previous few decades. Many people were still unaccounted for, their own people. You'd be a fool not to take things like that seriously. It's not a joke, or an on-screen scenario in which the good guys and the bad guys fire blanks at each other and explode in ketchup. I'd be an outsider, a visitor, a stranger in their manor. And we'd been at war with Argentina in 1982 over their illegal occupation of the Falkland Islands. Many lives had been lost on both sides, and I had no doubt that Argentinian feelings would still be raw. This was not a nation to be messed with.

There was also something else, something I remembered from my childhood. I'd seen their antics way back in 1966 when they had come to Britain to play in the World Cup – which we won, by the way. They had proceeded to kick, hack, punch and spit their way through some of the world's finest footballing talent, teams and individuals, including our own. As far as I'm concerned, anyone who's capable of doing things like that in front of impressionable children and the eyes of the world is to be treated with caution.

But how would they behave towards a sprawling, UK-staffed, US-financed film unit of some two hundred people? And it was not any old film. It would tell the story of Eva Perón, who appeared to be both loved and loathed in her home country in equal measure. Memories of her were still strong on the street and her presence was to be felt almost everywhere. Unless you've been to Argentina it's difficult to imagine how all-pervasive Eva Perón's spirit and legend are. She haunts the nation and everyone has an opinion.

As far as the government was concerned the script had been read at the highest levels and we were allowed to continue. In a situation like this, it's not unusual to hand in a different, less contentious draft, one that's been doctored to obtain the required permissions, but I don't think this had happened: the potential scale of it all going wrong would have been too heavy even for Hollywood to take the chance. A buck may be a buck and the dollar may be king, but a life is a life and not to be risked. Especially if you happen to be talking about the life of a megastar like Madonna. Just think of the insurance claim that would land on the corporate mat if she were to get whacked. What I do know is that, as in a great many Latin-American countries, corruption is endemic throughout every level of society in Argentina and the amount of palm-greasing that took place was enormous. Coming from a country and a society such as ours where all that stuff, though widespread, is much less blatant and (I think) on a much lesser scale, it came as quite a shock, but you just have to say, 'When in Rome . . .' and accept it.

Predictably, a right song and dance erupted about the production's supposedly negative reception on its official arrival in Buenos Aires. In fact, there was nothing more than a few daubed slogans on a flyover as we approached the city, and in all the time I was there I only ever encountered one uncomfortable incident. I'd taken my mountain bike with me, a US-made Scott, and I was in the habit of catching the train up-country to the town of Tigre, about an hour away, then cycling back to the city. It was fun for a while, especially as the Tigre delta is an incredible natural haven for wildlife and man. On little strips of land hemmed in by the numerous tributaries stand the holiday homes of wealthy city-dwellers. They are accessible only by boat, and to get there you have to pass the Argentine National Naval College. In the untended grounds at the front there was a pock-marked gun-turret, which, until 1981, had belonged to an Argentinian warship. A small plaque attached to it gave damning details: the damage had been inflicted by British warships, the shellholes made by British cannon. The sunshine forced an uneven glint from the numerous lumpy coats of paint on the heavy sheet metal, which reminded me of the great ships I'd witnessed being built on Tyneside. Many had been warships, destined for active service with the Royal Navy. Perhaps one had been responsible for that gun-turret ending up there on the scrub. I always felt sad and a little uncomfortable when I passed it, and stopped to ponder: had young Argentinian lads lost their lives in it? Probably. Had the British lads and lasses who'd fired the rounds made it home safely? Maybe, maybe not. Had heavy-calibre shells ricocheted around the inner walls of that gun-turret, causing injury and death? More than likely. I always fancied that someone in military uniform would come running out, rumble me as a Brit, point me out, then chase after me bent on vengeance, but it never happened.

The nearest I got to any bother was on the train coming back to Buenos Aires. For a change I'd cycled up to Tigre and my legs weren't up to the return journey. With my bike safely secured in the guard's van, I was sitting minding my own business when a dozen or so guys appeared at the far end of the carriage and made their way towards me. Unshaven, dressed in combat fatigues and boots, they were engaging the seated passengers in conversation. Then I noticed the fliers they were handing out: one word stood out prominently, MALVINAS. I guessed these guys were ex-conscripts carrying a grudge. They weren't tooled up, as far as I could see, but they might have been packing something under the cloth. People tended to do that over there.

As the rag-tag bunch shuffled and grumbled their way nearer, handing out their fliers, attempting to engage the recipients in conversation, I could see that some of them looked a little crazed. I hoped we'd arrive at one of the many stops along the route but we didn't. Where the hell had all those little stations gone? No time for any more weighing-up, though, they were almost upon me. I had to make a decision. Should I get up and move back through the carriages towards the guard? Or sit still, say nothing, and front it out? I was getting a bit sweaty. As I was considering the options I happened to notice that most of the passengers in the carriage were either giving the fliers back to the guys or ignoring them. One elderly woman scolded them, gave them a wag of her finger and a piece of her mind. They seemed bemused by that and stared at her.

At the last moment I decided to take the say-nowt course. A guy thrust a flier into my hand. Trying to look as hardboiled as I could, I shook my head, turned and gazed out of the window. The guy asked me something. I looked at him a second time, this time more intensely. He was young and in need of a good meal. Haunted eyes. I so wanted to say all kinds of things to him but it was neither the time nor the place; I knew if I opened my mouth there would be trouble. So, again, I shook my head and turned away. He gave up on me and moved on.

My hotel was not far from La Recoleta, a district consisting entirely of a sprawling cemetery filled with mausoleums so large it looked from a distance like one of the city's affluent residential areas. With their doors, windows and grey stone façades these multi-floored monuments to the departed were like mini-mansions. When I entered through one of the many iron gates, though, the place's true nature became evident: coffins sat behind broken glass panels. Strolling around this extraordinary place is a popular pastime for locals and tourists alike, and the Duarte family mausoleum is one of the most-visited sites of all. The embalmed remains of Eva Perón, née Duarte, are supposedly bolted securely down underneath a thick concrete slab: the kidnapping of the dead for political gain is not uncommon in many South American countries. I say 'supposedly' because the story of what happened to Eva Perón's body after her death is so outlandish. I suspect only God knows who or what, if anything, lies beneath that concrete duvet. It's a tale of bodysnatching, necrophilia, and corpses resembling Eva's (there were six, apparently) being buried in different parts of the world, including a plot in Italy provided by the Vatican, of her remains being dug up and driven at dead of night along the Riviera to Spain, there to be reunited with her exiled husband and sisters, then being brought back to Buenos Aires and finally laid to rest under that bolted-down concrete. And we sometimes think we're an uncivilized bunch!

A favourite pastime of mine, wherever I happen to be, is to seek out the cafés and bars where ordinary working people take their breaks. I found just such a place half-way up the Plaza de Mayo, Buenos Aires' main square, and just down from the obelisk monument. It was a low-ceilinged, strip-lit, Formica-clad *cantina* filled with chatty customers and served up meat, chicken, pasta and rice dishes from big stainless-steel containers. My favourites were the *empanadas*, mini-pasties filled with meat, chicken or veggie things like cheese and spinach. Over the years I've gone right off eating the red meat on offer in Britain mainly because it doesn't taste of anything, but in Argentina it's so great that I soon reverted to my former carnivorous ways. In no time at all I was tucking into steaks galore.

Argentinian cattle roam the vast areas of grassland known as the pampas. The Atlantic to the east and the Andes to the west form its natural borders, and cattle and sheep munch away, untroubled by the farming methods that have brought the UK meat industry to the brink of ruin. Argentinian farmers believe that the relatively stress-free existence their livestock enjoy is the reason their meat tastes so good.

The first scenes we shot were those that told how a teenaged Eva Duarte made her way by steam locomotive from the backwoods to the big city, accompanied by love-rat Magaldi. Everyone was a little uptight but once we were shooting, people's nerves settled down. Alan was great: he knew exactly what he was after, which put everyone at their ease. He told us in clear, unequivocal terms what he wanted. Madonna and I were shot clambering on to carriages, waving, winking and worrying. Then came the wonderful wide shots of the train travelling across the pampas, its chimney-stack belching black smoke into the blue sky. Between us and the camera, gauchos were at the gallop, their horses raising a great cloud of dust. A huge swathe of orchestral score would go under these images. It was an astonishing sight to behold and I was thrilled to be in the middle of it, albeit in a fairly minor part. My mega-star companion felt differently: 'I'm bored. Who do I have to fuck to get off this picture?' She was only joking, of course, but I was so incensed at what I perceived as her ingratitude that I called her an ungrateful little . . . well, something. At this point the makeup and hair staff ran off to the end of the carriage and left us to it. We sat there in silence for a while, then just got on with it.

Shooting those big scenes on the pampas meant we had

to bunk down in the wilds once or twice, away from the super-luxurious pampering of the Hyatt Regency in Buenos Aires. On one memorable occasion I stayed with Alan Parker and a few others on a working *hacienda* in the middle of nowhere, miles from the nearest town. After a wonderful dinner and, at Alan's insistence, a ropy rendition of 'Crocodile Shoes', strummed on an out-of-tune guitar taken down from its mount on a wall, we all went outside to look at the night sky. It was breath taking. It looked like a great black canvas covering the earth, with just the light from long-dead stars to illuminate the heavens. We all just stood there lost for words, staring up at the majestic beginnings of infinity.

The Hyatt Regency was a wonderful place with outstanding facilities. Their tenth-floor business centre, where Jonathan Pryce and I made the most of the complimentary food and drinks, offered stunning views across the city and was never busy. Prycey often landed there early on and got stuck into whatever there was before he went on to dinner somewhere else. Goodness knows where he put it all! I spent a lot of time in the fitness rooms and gym, which were tip-top. I weighed around 185 pounds and made sure I stayed at that. There's nothing worse than feeling your costumes getting tighter. My routine was always the same: some stretches on a mat, then a brisk walk of maybe three or four miles on the treadmill, some free weights and bench-work, then a run on the treadmill of a few miles, some more stretches, then a steam or a sauna to finish. It usually ate up four or five hours so I'd look to start at around nine a.m. and be done for lunch, which would be a chicken sandwich and a pint of fresh orange juice by the pool. This was happening every other day so I was in pretty good shape. Madonna had her own work-out gear set up in her suite and worked out there with her personal trainer. Common sense, really: had she used the gym it would have turned into a zoo. There were always dozens of fans outside her rooms, both day and night, begging for a glimpse of their idol. She'd often nip out on to the balcony and wave to them. Although she sometimes bemoaned the lack of privacy her megastardom brought, she was never condescending towards her fans and I never once heard her speak disparagingly of them.

She sometimes invited me over for dinner or a drink, which was always interesting, if somewhat nerve-racking – the walk across the first-floor lobby past the gaze of the armed security men, then up in the lift to her quarters. Sushi was favourite, but I used to laugh when I opened the fridge: it was always chock-a-block with chocolate. There'd always be bits of dogshit on the floor from the little mutt she had with her, a tiny thing, it was, with great big eyes. I'm not the world's biggest dog fan so that was a real turn-off before a nibble. She kept a record of her thoughts and events, which was later published to coincide with the movie's release, and would sit at her laptop typing away. Woe betide anyone who got near enough to glimpse what she was writing. I once made the mistake of looking over her shoulder and was immediately told to fuck off. 'Fuck off' and 'fuck you' were regular refrains but I didn't mind – it made me laugh. I wouldn't like to have been on the wrong end of a roasting from her, mind. Just witnessing her dish out a bollocking was enough to chill the bones. Whatever else was going on, though, and it was a constant circus with all the petty political manoeuvrings inherent in a big shoot, you always knew exactly where you stood with Madonna. We shared a lot of laughs during those long months and I don't have a bad word to say about her.

A sequence between the young Eva Duarte and Agustín

Magaldi, as they made their way across 1930s Buenos Aires by bus, followed our jaunt across the pampas. Come the day of shooting the city's officials had allowed the production to cordon off a dozen city-centre blocks – the equivalent of closing the western section of Oxford Street, from Oxford Circus to Marble Arch and half-way down Park Lane through to Regent Street. Goodness knows what it cost in back-handers but the effect was incredible: all the buildings had been dressed with huge pro-Perón banners and the people were wearing period clothing. I felt as though I'd stepped back in time. Moments like that give me the same kind of thrill as when I see articulated trucks carting rock 'n' roll equipment across the UK. The scale and clout of the music industry always makes me smile: it's as though we've won the battle against the conformists, the nine-till-fivers, the straights.

Off to Costume, Makeup and Hair, then into your air-conditioned trailer to wait for your call. All of my spare moments were gobbled up in trying to finish the six scripts for the second *Crocodile Shoes* series, which was due to start filming in mid-May, just a few days after I was scheduled to finish on *Evita*. I had also to complete the songs and incidental music that were to underscore and accompany the episodes. I tried not to dwell on the schedule as the reality was scary. I had all these production dates in front of me and no finished scripts. Somehow I got through all the work but I was neither happy with nor proud of the end-result.

When we started filming that day, things went a little crazy. The period bus we were travelling on was pursued by about two dozen paparazzi riding pillion on motorbikes piloted by local kamikazes. I was sitting next to Madonna and they were attempting to get right beside the window to take their photographs. In the midst of all this mayhem we were supposed to be turning in a performance for the film cameras mounted on the bus. It's one thing someone taking a photo of you outside a restaurant or club, you learn to live with that, but these twats were making difficult work even more so. They were like flies around shit. I wanted to reach out of the window and smack them, knock them off their bikes, but I'd been warned not to do anything like that. I could only shake my head at the madness of it all.

Of all the little treats our hotel used to provide us with, my favourite was the tango dancing, not my own clodhopping efforts but those of the immaculately turned-out couples who, on alternate evenings, glided effortlessly through the foyer. No big deal, no fanfare, just the sublime beauty of the dance. Not long before I had spent a couple of months in a room at the Vanderbilt Racquet Club, in Shepherds Bush, trying to learn the basics of this complex dance to cope with a two-step in the grip of her nibs. As I kicked the shit out of my instructor's shins, I appreciated all the moves the pros made to look so easy. The tango is a dance that developed out of moves and steps performed between prostitutes and their pimps, and finally evolved into the complex routines of today; consequently it's very tactile and sexy. My attempts to master the basics were a waste of effort as the dance sequence we shot, a fantasy where the dying Evita imagines herself waltzing with each of the men from her past, was cut from the final film. Alan reckoned it wasn't needed, and he was the boss, but I was gutted. Still, Geordies should know better than to try to dance the tango.

I had been receiving faxes from home, pictures the kids had drawn for me, which made me homesick. At last, it was time for Miriam to come out and visit. I met her at the airport and this time I didn't propose. She was going to be in the country for ten days, and as I had a bit of time off, it was perfect. We did the city from end to end, the tango clubs, the museums, the works. One day, on the spur of the moment, we decided to pay a flying visit to her aunt Cathrin in Patagonia.

Two hundred years ago, the Argentinian governors in Patagonia, descendants of the Spanish conquistadors, were desperate to make sure that all the land was settled by white Europeans, rather than the indigenous people, so they offered to anyone willing to make the long journey great swathes of land as an inducement to do so. Michael D. Jones, a nonconformist Welsh minister and the victim of religious persecution, set sail with his congregation in 1865, bound for South America. They reasoned, correctly as it turned out, that they'd have more chance of preserving their native tongue than if they'd headed to English-speaking North America, like most other *émigrés* of the day. After a sea voyage lasting some two months, they landed, set up camp and stuck it out. Nowadays, the indigenous community in Patagonia, a squat, dark-haired, brown-eyed people, are fluent Welsh-speakers. Cathrin spent six months of each year in Trelaw teaching Welsh there. Her digs were basic. She didn't have a telephone so we couldn't let her know we were coming or even check that she'd be in when we got there, but off we went. I was dressed from head to foot in black leather, jacket, trousers, boots, completely inappropriate even for the weather in Buenos Aires, never mind the semi-desert conditions that awaited us in Trelaw. The flight, due south, took four hours. As we got off the plane the heat was almost overwhelming, up in the nineties. We managed to get into the centre of town and it was apparent the place was dirt-poor – no displays in the shop windows, nothing in the shops at all, in fact, just dusty shelves.

After an hour or so we found Cathrin's rented house, a

tiny, whitewashed, single-storey place situated just off a main street. I knocked on the door and waited. No answer. I knocked again, this time a little harder. Still no answer. We were just about to give up and walk away when the door opened and there was Cathrin. She just stood there staring at us, as though we were back from the dead. It wasn't shock, more disbelief. She simply couldn't accept what she was seeing. I ended the silence by asking if we could come in. Cathrin made us a cup of tea and we brought her up to speed on things. It was an odd day, meeting the Welsh-speaking locals, visiting the Welsh Hall, where the original deeds to the tracts of land given to those first settlers were displayed on a wall, and taking afternoon tea in town. I'd love to have travelled on down to Tierra del Fuego, a magical place-name that has intrigued me since childhood, but we didn't have time.

Not long after Miriam went home, our time in Argentina was up. Two months had flown by. Then it was off to Budapest for the next leg of the adventure, but not before a spot of rest and recreation. It was mid-March and my birth-day was just a few days away, so Miriam and the boys flew to St Bart's, where we all met up. We had a lovely time in a rented villa, complete with infinity pool. Tom and I walked the whole island, and it's a beautiful place. The wildlife on our doorstep was incredible: it was a live nature class for us all, with brightly coloured parrots, hummingbirds and tortoises tootling about. Also, rather scarily, there were one or two tarantulas. You really don't want a nip off one of those buggers. One day we spotted a big one by the pool and made a right old noise. The maid appeared, clocked the reason for our panic and was just about to wallop it with a broom when we stopped her. We didn't wish it dead. But she reasoned that if it was left to scuttle away it might make its way into the house and, possibly, one of the bedrooms. The prospect of that overrode our compassion, I'm afraid, and we gave her the go-ahead to flatten the poor thing.

At that point most of the cast and crew made for Hungary, but I returned to London to mix some songs and music for the *Crocodile Shoes II* album and series. One track was a beautiful ballad, 'Blue Roses', written by Paddy McAloon. Paddy is one of our finest songsmiths and through the mass-exposure of television I hoped to bring his work to the attention of a wider audience. His compositions, among them the sublime 'Cowboy Dreams', had helped the first-series soundtrack rack up sales of well over a million copies. That's an enormous number for domestic UK sales, seldom reached by anyone. We hoped to do half as well the second time round.

On arrival at the location in Budapest's old quarter, I headed to the set to say hello and see how it was all going. I made my way to the Makeup trailer to find Madonna already in the chair. She demanded to know what I'd been doing in London, so I told her. She inquired if I had a copy of the finished mix with me, and when I said I had, she told me to whack it on the beatbox. Everyone else was asked to leave so that she could give it her undivided attention. I hit the play button and on came 'Blue Roses'. It moved her to tears. Of all the reactions I might have expected from her, that wasn't one and it touched me. Now whenever I bump into her, she sings the opening lines by way of hello.

There was another reason Madonna might have felt even more emotional than normal around that time. I'd not been in my hotel room five minutes when the phone rang. It was her nibs, asking if I'd join her in her suite. I cleaned my teeth, then headed up to the top floor, past the security men, and knocked on the door. A moment later it opened and

Madonna was there, wrapped in a big white towelling robe. She ushered me in and closed the door. 'How are you?' I asked.

'I'm pregnant,' she replied.

I confess that my first thought was, How will we get through the filming without it showing? but I offered congratulations and asked how she felt. She said she was frightened: she'd have to have an amniocentesis test, no pleasant thing, because of her age – she was thirty-six. I felt so sorry for her: she was one of the most famous and powerful women on the planet, but now she was alone and scared, just like millions of ordinary women all over the world when they learn such tumultuous news. I asked her if she'd told anyone else. 'Just Alan,' she said. How had he reacted to the news? 'Great,' she said. He'd been really cool about it. I doubted that was his immediate reaction, but admired him for keeping it from her. It could have left him in a right pickle. But nature doesn't recognize schedules.

The unit was in Budapest for a month, with me flying back and forth, working on both projects. Once it had wrapped, it was back to rainy old England. Six weeks at Shepperton Studios were scheduled to finish off *Evita* but things didn't go to plan. Madonna's unexpected pregnancy had a disruptive effect on the schedule: scenes had to be rejigged and moved around. The result was that we overran: it meant I would finish filming on *Evita* on a Thursday, then begin work on *Crocodile Shoes II* the next day, Friday. Other than passing messages and instructions to them through Kellie, my PA, I'd not had a chance to sit down with any of the heads of department to discuss ideas, aims and needs for the shoot. It had been impossible to organize a single meeting because I had been unavailable.

I was less than thrilled at the prospect of starting without any preparation or proper rest, but contracts had been signed, advertising slots booked, and as my company, Big Boy Productions, had been commissioned to make the series, we'd be liable for millions of pounds' worth of cancellation costs should we fail to meet the agreed dates. I'd been lucky enough to secure the services of producer Peter Richardson and I was mightily pleased about that. Peter, a warm, friendly northerner, possessed as safe a pair of hands as was available out there, and he was interested only in making the best of the job. He had no hidden agendas or ulterior motives and, other than his all-embracing passion for Manchester United, we agreed on most things, had a laugh and got on well. I'm just glad we weren't working together in 1999 when Man U won the Champions' League final. I'd never have heard the end of it.

17

As tumultuous as the year had already been, it had another surprise in store – a dreadful one. One Monday evening in May I was at home in St John's Wood with Miriam watching *Coronation Street*. We're both big fans and everything at home tends to stop at seven twenty-nine so that we can get ready for the latest instalment. Immediately an episode was over Shane Spall, Tim's wife, would call Miriam, or vice versa, to discuss all the latest developments. All of our friends knew not to disturb us while the show was on, so when the telephone rang we were less than pleased. Who'd be calling at this time? To my eternal regret, I answered the phone rather brusquely, only to hear a hysterical Shane at the other end, sobbing and spluttering, 'Timmy's got leukaemia.'

A few weeks earlier Tim had been to see Dr John Gaynor about a medical for a movie. For insurance purposes, actors have to be passed fit enough not to take a bad turn or die during the period they're contracted to work on a shoot. This is standard practice across the entertainment industry. There is no choice in the matter; we all accept it. While Tim was in with Dr Gaynor he mentioned he'd been feeling run down. He was also nursing some bruising on his arm. Dr Gaynor had taken some blood samples and off Tim went to await the results. This was on Thursday. The following Monday he was shooting a commercial when Dr Gaynor telephoned with the shocking news. He told Tim to drop everything and go immediately to University College Hospital in central London where they'd be expecting him. Tim had always been prone to hypochondria. A headache would be certain indication of a brain tumour. We'd always pulled his leg about it, told him not to be so bloody daft. Now it was horribly real. Goodness knows what went through his mind. It was made even worse, if that was possible, by the timing: he was due to go to the Cannes Film Festival the next day for the screening of his latest Mike Leigh movie *Secrets and Lies*. (It went on to win the Palme d'Or.)

I was straight out of the house and on the way into the West End. I could hardly bring myself to believe what I'd just heard: Tim was my closest buddy. I shot a few red lights on the journey to the hospital and I tried to think of what I might be able to do when I got there. When I arrived at UCH and signed in, Tim was on a bed in a private room on the sixth floor. He looked remarkably normal. I wanted to give him a hug but was nervous in case it hurt him, so I left it. I asked him how he felt. He said great, that he wanted to go for a pint round the corner but the doctors wouldn't allow it. They planned to start administering a course of chemotherapy in the morning. I asked if there was anything I could do and he shook his head. That frightened me. I went home and cried.

Instead of basking in sunshine and well-deserved praise at Cannes, Tim was laid up on a hospital bed having a chemical cocktail pumped into him via a Hickman line, a clear plastic tube that wouldn't have looked out of place under a car bonnet. It was inserted first into his chest, then, when that became infected, into his groin. The nurses who attended to it had to wear thick rubber gloves for protection, such was the drugs' toxicity. Tim was massively pissed off at having missed such a golden window, but it soon became clear just what a close call it had been. According to Dr Gaynor, the pressure inside the cabin on the flight to France would probably have brought on fatal internal bleeding. Tim has always had a wonderful sense of gallows humour. Just as well: he had plenty of opportunity to use it in the weeks and months that followed.

No two ways about it, they were dark days. According to Dr Panos, Tim's specialist, his chances of making it through weren't great. It was all to do with the bone marrow and its ability to produce healthy platelets, or white blood cells. Tim's platelet count should have been near to 140. At that early point it was six. If the chemotherapy didn't do the trick there would be radiotherapy. A bone-marrow transplant was a last resort but they got on with checking Tim's family for a possible tissue match. His brother Richard was found to be a suitable donor. In a time of unknowns, it was something.

When Tim fell ill I was still working on *Evita* and just about to kick off *Crocodile Shoes II*, so those last few weeks on the movie were difficult. I'd lie in bed going over all the different permutations. Maybe there'd be another specialist somewhere – an even more specialist specialist who maybe knew something or could do something special. I trawled the Internet and read medical magazines, but soon realized Tim was already in the best hands. Miriam made sure Shane knew we were there for her but I felt useless. I couldn't chin this thing, much as I wanted to. It was in the hands of the doctors and the lap of the gods.

In no time at all I'd started filming in Newcastle. I travelled down to see Tim as often as I could. All of his pals did the same, and Shane was his rock throughout. Talk about defining moments. I took time off when I should have been on set and the TV show might have suffered as a result, but I'm glad I did things the way I did. Fuck it! It was only a television programme. Tim was fighting for his life. I'd fly from Newcastle to Heathrow or get the train to King's Cross. From there I'd go straight to UCH, with all those artificial strip-lights that seemed to blur day and night into a constant greyish twilight. Into the toilets, scrub hands and face, put on the regulation mask, gloves and slippers, just in case I took any dangerous germs in with me. Tim's immune system was so low that any microbe might have been fatal to him. We all took the greatest care. This was not television drama, it was all too horribly real. My best pal's life was on the line and there was nothing substantial I could do to help him. I could only hang around and yak, keep him company, try to make him laugh, offer support. Poor Tim, I probably bored him to tears. I prayed, too, like I had when I learned of Miriam's illness. I'd prayed then for her to get better but this was different. This was asking that Tim be allowed to live. It was selfish in a way. If Tim left us, all our lives would be diminished. In fact, I did a fair old bit of praying, as we tend to do when all else seems to be failing. It was dumb, really. Why should my prayers be heeded ahead of all the others from around the world? Daft, desperate, clueless, useless. I was trying to cover all the bases.

Something I could do was organize a little film filled with get-well messages from Tim's friends and family, many of whom he hadn't seen for years. I thought it might make him realize how many people loved him and needed him to get better. My buddy Matt Forrest shot it, travelling far and wide. Everyone we asked wanted to be in it. No one said no. People rearranged their schedules and went out of their way to help. We gave the finished film to Shane. It ran about thirty minutes and was very moving. She played it for Tim when just the two of them were together in his hospital room. Later Tim told me it had been a real fillip, just what he needed at that point.

We all did what we could in whichever way we thought

best. Where I went for the big gesture, Miriam lent quiet but rock-solid support to Shane. No mawkishness, just clear common sense. Resolute, unquestioning compassion, tenderness and love. Great friends already, they're now even closer.

Sometimes I'd get to the hospital only to find Tim wasn't up to having visitors and I'd go home, but it was always worth the traipse. I learned more about the important things then than I had at any other time in my life. And I learned most of all about Tim. For some reason I'd always thought of him as a bit soft, a bit weak, I guess because he's not a very physical guy, not interested in exercise. I couldn't have been more wrong. He was much braver than I would have been in the circumstances. I know that for a fact. We had some laughs but they were always clouded by the bigger, darker picture. Tim had to face some long nights alone. Anyone in his position would have been forgiven for freaking out, screaming and crying, but Tim was a real man. For everyone else's sake, for Shane, and the kids, and all the rest of us, he kept on smiling, kept on shining, kept on being the person we all loved and needed. And he made it. He got through all the pain, grief, fear and months of treatment, and came out the other end intact. He didn't need the transplant. Nowadays he's a different person, not better or worse, just different. Who wouldn't be? He has a much more laid-back take on things that once seemed important – work, for instance – and that's a good thing.

Strangely enough, I think we're less close now than we were before he was ill, but that's right in a funny way. If you've been through something that intense with someone, you don't want or need to be seeing them and chewing it over all the time. I tend to remind Tim of how lucky I feel we are that he made it, I can't help it, but I'm sure he gets sick of hearing it. Quite rightly, Tim wants to look forward now. His career's gone from strength to strength. I look at what he's doing, working in Hollywood with the likes of Tom Cruise and Jim Carrey, and I'm just proud to be able to say, 'He's my friend.'

I'm different for the experience, too. You couldn't not be changed by it. I'd like to think I'm a better person because I watched Tim deal with his illness in such a dignified and courageous manner. I'm also sixteen years into my life of sobriety. I miss the mad times he and I had when we were both a bit more barmy, but we're older and wiser now. Great to have done all that stuff but a relief to have left it behind. Most importantly he's alive, and I thank God for sparing him.

The *Crocodile Shoes II* shoot ground towards its conclusion, with me not fully focused on the job in hand. There was too much other stuff going on, and dropping back to domestic television after the excitement of Hollywood was an anti-climax. And I was producer, writer and lead actor. I was completely exhausted, and things came to a head on the penultimate day. I was required to be on board a trawler moored in the harbour at Alnmouth, one of the many pretty villages to be found on the Northumbrian coast. The scene called for my character, Jed Shepperd, to take a tumble over the side and disappear into the sea. We should have used a stunt double but we didn't – another bad call I made through tiredness.

Action! I went over the side and under the water. So far so good. Then the current dragged me under the trawler. I was upside down and confused. I managed to right myself and looked up to what I took to be the surface of the water. In fact it was the trawler's hull. I kicked out hard and smashed my head into it. When I made it to the surface, the director asked if I'd mind going down again as I'd not been fully in the frame when I came up. They were still filming. I'd forgotten what we were doing and why we were there. Dazed, I went under a second time. This time, though, I started to lose consciousness. I signalled to the divers – in the water with me in case of just such a mishap – that I was in trouble and was quickly pulled out of the water and into the boat. I was very cold and feeling sick.

I have no recollection of the next few hours but I was taken quickly to Newcastle's Royal Victoria Infirmary, scene of many a previous patch-up, where I underwent a scan. Throughout the rest of the day and all through that night I was woken regularly by nurses asking me how many of their fingers I could see.

The next morning a specialist arrived at the foot of my bed and informed me he couldn't be sure but he thought I'd suffered a depressed fracture to the skull. He'd like to do another set of scans. I asked when I could leave and he told me I could go home later on that day but should do nothing except sit in a dark room for at least a week. I told him that was impossible. There were people waiting for me across the city, a film crew and actors, and all kinds of problems would ensue if I wasn't there. He laughed and said that I couldn't do anything.

His advice was sound but he wasn't the one looking at a cancellation bill in six figures. Insurance cover? Yes, I could have claimed an extra day, but it would have meant reassembling the cast and crew, most of whom were booked to start their next jobs in a couple of days' time. Time was so tight we would have been looking at missed transmission dates. Advertising slots for the series and the album had been booked months in advance – there was going to be a massive push and we couldn't have changed it. If I didn't get it finished we'd have to cancel the whole thing. And I was due to fly out to LA, where Miriam was waiting for me with the kids.

An hour later I checked myself out and left. What with the bump on my head, I didn't think to call Miriam, but she didn't really need to know about it at that point. Why worry her? That last day was long and very difficult. Despite the super-strength painkillers I swallowed by the handful, my head pounded and throbbed. I was plonked in a canvas director's chair near to the camera and, once everything was ready, lifted into position. I said my lines as best I could, then collapsed back into my chair.

Somehow I got through that final day of shooting and we wrapped with everything in the can, but it was a messy, unsatisfactory end to a difficult and, for me, unhappy shoot. What with Tim being ill and my recent prolonged absences on *Evita*, I'd not wanted to be away from home again. I was angry with the production – and now my head was broken. But at the root of my unhappiness was my conviction that I'd not given the project enough care, attention and time. Unforgivable. On top of that, I wasn't thinking straight. It was, I felt, the end of my love affair with television.

There was a little bit of light in all this darkness in that the finished soundtrack album for the new series sounded great. I'd co-produced it with Steve Robson, who'd worked with Tony McAnaney on the first *Crocodile Shoes* album, and he'd done a terrific job. Jon Kelly mixed it for us and Anne Dudley did the arrangements – thank goodness, we'd secured her services just before she won an Oscar. After that her fee would probably have quadrupled. Paddy McAloon supplied some gorgeous songs: 'Blue Roses' and '(I'm A) Troubled Man' were both pearls. You couldn't not be moved by them, no matter whose rendition you listened to. We also cut a version of Brian Wilson's 'Still I Dream', which I was pleased with, but for me the highlight was a little song called 'I Will Fear No Evil'. By now my mam had returned to the Church of England and, because of its biblical theme, she loved that song, which made it all the more important to me. She'd played it to her cousin Irene and all her friends at the church hall, and was dead proud.

When I told Miriam about my head, she didn't want me to fly out to LA. She wanted to come home, but I wouldn't hear of it. Once something like that's been arranged, paid for and people have travelled, I'm not going to be the let-down. I'd got holiday into my head and holiday it was going to be. After I'd checked with BA that it would be safe for me to fly, I boarded Concorde to New York. I was given a pillow and the cabin pressure gave me no problems. The next leg of the journey, from New York to Los Angeles with American Airlines, was a nightmare. Almost from the off my head felt as though it was going to explode. The flight, some six hours, seemed to last for days. I consoled myself with the thought of lying peacefully on a recliner in the rental-house garden.

Miriam was waiting at the airport to whisk me off to our posh holiday digs. I was expecting posh because it had cost an arm and a leg but Rustic Canyon was just that: rustic. The house itself was lovely but there was no garden furniture, not a stick. Call me spoilt, but was I expecting too much? I think not. Off we went to the nearest Home Depot and bought some recliners. I settled down in the garden and lay there for two weeks with Miriam looking after me and the kids entertaining each other. Some holiday! The break we'd all been so looking forward to was cattle-trucked. If nothing else, though, the bang on the head had forced me to stop chasing about like a madman and do nowt. Afterwards I was better rested than I'd been for a long while.

All too quickly it was time to go home and face the rigours and long hours of post-production on *Crocodile Shoes*. I was due to travel a day later than Miriam and the boys so, as I was feeling a little better, I decided to drive to the airport with them then go back to the house. I could dump the car at the airport the next day. On the way to LAX we passed the Santa Monica pier with its massive ferris wheel. The boys asked if we could stop. We had time to spare so we parked the car, always so easy in the States, and wandered around the amusement arcades and rides. At the entrance to the ferris wheel the kids said they wanted a ride. Miriam was about to take them on it when I decided to join them. She asked me if I was sure I wanted to, what with my head, but as I felt better I thought it would be fine. We paid our dollars and were bolted into the bench seat, the happy holiday family.

The moment the wheel moved I knew I was in big trouble. My balance went and I felt very sick, but we couldn't stop the ride. Round and round it went, with me feeling like I was going to die, but staying quiet so as not to freak out the kids. I'd hoped it would be like the rides in England – over in moments – but this was America where the customer expected, and almost always got, value for money. On and on and on it went. I wanted to vomit but was afraid to in case I showered someone underneath, so I held it back. I've not bothered with fairground rides since.

Nineteen ninety-six ended with a trip back to Los Angeles for the US première of *Evita* on Saturday, 14 December. The movie was given a limited release in a few theatres just before the year's end so that it was eligible for Oscar nominations the following month. I'd been to a few pre-mières over the years but, in terms of scale and expense, this was like nothing I'd seen or experienced before. Miriam broke the bank on a lovely dress and then we were off to Los Angeles, first class on BA, then to the Four Seasons Hotel to await a call from some over-energetic soul in Press and Publicity at Disney Corp. Because of the amount of money at stake, these things are usually organized and executed with military precision, but we threw a spanner into the works. It wasn't our fault: the limo driver was late and didn't know where to go, so we ended up jumping out of the motor a few blocks from the Shrine Auditorium and legging it in blind panic.

Once there, we were confronted not only by huge crowds of people but also ultra-heavy-duty security. I tried to explain to the beefcake that I was in the movie and really needed to be on their side of the cordon, but they weren't having any of it. So, our worst nightmare: all this time spent on the project to get to the launch, in front of banks of the world's press corps and more photographers than you could shake a stick at, and where was I? On the wrong side of the cordon!

And now . . . here they come! I could see Antonio in the distance with Melanie Griffiths, his wife. I was watching from the crowd, hemmed in, couldn't move even to get my invitation out of my pocket. Then, at last, a break. David Wimbury, the movie's line producer, was strolling down the red carpet, being photographed by the snappers in case he was someone mega-famous they didn't know. I shouted his name: 'David!' About as undignified as it gets, but I had no choice. The people around me gave me the best of dirty looks, no doubt figuring I was just another chancer trying to gatecrash the do. I couldn't have cared less what they thought. David ignored me. I tried again. 'David! It's me, Jimmy!'

At last he turned and clocked me. What was I doing in the crowd? he wanted to know. The movie was due to begin in ten minutes. At his behest a beefcake lowered the cordon and Miriam and I clambered over it on to the red carpet – just in the nick of time. Right then Madonna glided round the corner. The light from the flashbulbs was blinding. It was an odd place to say hello to her. Just a wave, and then in. Let her get on with being the movie star. And no one could have done a better job of it. Talk about born to it.

Inside the theatre I could relax a little. We were ushered up grand stairs to our allocated seats in the dress circle by one of a legion of half-starved, beaming, Chanel-suited Disney girls and settled in. No popcorn. After a brief introductory natter by Alan it was down with the house lights and at last the movie played. I have to say I found it exciting. Whatever your opinion of Lloyd-Webber's music, the effect of hearing the fully orchestrated soundtrack coming through big banks of top-end speakers was overwhelming. Alan's pictures were a treat on the eye. He'd pulled it off and made the whole thing work, no mean achievement for a sung-through project.

Yet for me there was something unreal about it all, something daft, which left me feeling detached and unconcerned as to the outcome. Maybe it's different when you're playing the lead, or doing this kind of thing all the time, I don't know. The movie was well received, but what could you make of that? The theatre was full of invited guests, folks flown in from all corners of the world at great expense: they couldn't really sit there and boo, could they?

The after-film party was a hoot. Tim Allen, star of US television show *Home Improvement*, turned up seemingly so off his face he literally couldn't speak. Madonna introduced us. I thought about telling him that, not long before, I'd been up for a part in his upcoming movie but it would have been pointless. I didn't get the gig anyway.

Evita's London première, on the following Thursday, 19 December, was, if anything, even more spectacular – a party like I've never seen or been to either before or since. The movie was screened at the Odeon, Leicester Square, with all the hullabaloo that a Brit-written, Brit-helmed blockbuster merited, and then some. It's a strange feeling to walk through a throng of snappers and punters, shouting your name and barking requests. I've never felt I've done enough to earn that kind of reception and, of course, on this job I hadn't. Everyone was there to catch a glimpse of, and maybe eye-contact with, Madonna and Antonio. I like to walk the last few paces to the red carpet instead of sitting in a limousine as you tend to be stuck there like a goldfish in a bowl for ages while folk peer through the tinted windows and put their greasy fingers all over the glass.

The entire cast were to be trotted out and introduced to the audience, a bit of an ordeal. I stood in an aisle, dressed in expensive Comme des Garçons, talking to the actor Laurence Fishburne, a mean-looking, grumble-voiced dude, then it was lights dimmed, applause and out on to the floor. It felt a bit like an identity parade, and I think that's at the root of my discomfort in such situations: they're too reminiscent of bad times past. There was an awful lot happening that evening with many a well-known face saying hello and well done, but the one thing I remember more clearly than anything was Madonna telling me I had the most wonderful eyes on the screen, a lovely thing to hear.

After that it was off to W12, where a whole commercial building had been rented in Shepherds Bush and dressed to look like a Buenos Aires brothel, with entertainment on all floors. Robert Stigwood, owner of the *Evita* movie rights, had worked hard for many years to bring it to the screen. Big-name players like Oliver Stone had been attached to the project at various times, only for it to fizzle out. Just when things were shaping up, looking good, something went wrong and the thing would falter once more. Stiggy had waited a long time for his moment and had pushed the boat out.

The party was a hoot, with hundreds of people eating, drinking, dancing and generally making a hell of a racket. Miriam and I were seated in a cordoned-off VIP area along with large helpings of posh nosh and bubbly. I never feel comfortable in those situations either, knowing people are looking at us enviously. Richard E. Grant was trying to get over the cordon and I was glad he made it in the end. At one point the Duchess of York ended up on my lap and she was a bigger girl then than she is today. She was being given an awful time by the press and I could empathize with her on that.

I always like to share these events with old pals and I'd invited Geoff Knox, the broadest of Geordies, to come to the do. He must have spent a good half-hour chatting to the Duchess. He was made up – couldn't get over the fact that she'd given him a bit of her time. At times it's a struggle for me to understand Geoff so I'd love to have been a fly on the wall, privy to their conversation. Goodness knows what they talked about.

I managed to make a dream come true for my mam. During the last twenty years of her life she wasn't able to travel very much as, due to lower-back problems, she found it too painful to sit for more than five or ten minutes. Planes and trains were out of the question, so we didn't see much of her in London. I noticed in the papers that her hero, Luciano Pavarotti, was scheduled to play at the Royal Albert Hall, so I called her up. As much as she'd love to see him, she told me, there was no way she could get to London.

I had a thought. What if I booked my tour coach, the one I used when I travelled around the UK doing concerts? In terms of sheer comfort and luxury these coaches are beyond most people's imaginings: lounge areas with luxurious settees and reclining chairs, fridge-freezers, halogen cooking hobs, beds. Most importantly, my mam would be able to get up and walk about. I put it to her and she agreed to give it a go. Up went Dougie, the coach firm's boss, and collected my mam, my sister and my great-aunt. We kept in touch via mobile phone and a few hours later they were in suites at the Dorchester Hotel on Park Lane. My mam couldn't get over the bell on the wall that summoned a man carrying a tray with tea and biscuits. And the curtains! She was very taken by all the fol-de-rols round the edges. I'd booked a box near to the stage at the Royal Albert Hall so on the night she was close to Pavarotti. I spent the evening watching her watching him. She was so gloriously happy she forgot her pain for a couple of hours.

Around this time I was able to do something else for my mam. I met Pavarotti's flautist, an Italian guy called Andrea, at Sting's place in Wiltshire and happened to mention to him, over a plate of spaghetti, my mam's utter adoration of his guv'nor. He asked me if she would like a signed photo of the big man. I told him that such a gesture would make her year. A few weeks later it arrived, with a personal message, written in Italian, to Laura from Luciano. We had it framed and put up on her bedroom wall, and whenever I visited her in Newcastle, she'd look at that signed photo of big Pav, her other hero, smiling down on her, and beam with happiness.

18

Around this time, in 1997, I had an exciting call. A few months previously I'd travelled down to the wilds of Wiltshire and recorded a beautiful old Northumbrian ballad, 'The Waters of Tyne', in a duet with Sting, accompanied by Catherine Tickell, the renowned Northumbrian piper, and pianist Dave Hartley, to go on a compilation album Sting was putting together to raise awareness and money for his Rainforest Foundation. The media tend to rip the piss out of him over this, writing of 'pet projects' and 'Indians with saucers in their lips', but isn't what he does worthwhile and necessary? If he didn't put himself out and do it, who else would? It's the planet we're talking about here. He doesn't need to do it but he does, and he puts up with all that shit because he cares about the future for all our children. Good on him.

It was an easy session as our voices worked well together. Maybe it's something they put in the water up the road. There is a pitching similarity between Sting, AC/DC's Brian Johnson and myself, in as much as we're all comfortable singing in a high register. I reckon it's down to all the shrieking Geordies tend to do in conversation. That and the diphthongs. The theme of the album was to be favourite childhood songs, and all sorts of people, including Luciano Pavarotti, James Taylor, Annie Lennox, Shawn Colvin and Bobby McFerrin, had come up with tracks. The end result, entitled *Carnival!*, was a very listenable collection.

Now Sting wanted to know whether I'd be up for singing

'The Waters of Tyne' with Catherine and him at a benefit concert that his wife, Trudie, was organizing at New York's Carnegie Hall. *Would I!* Yes, please.

Carnegie Hall. Wow! It has a lot of history. Everyone who's anyone has played there. I'd played the Royal Albert Hall a couple of times, kind of its London equivalent, but I'd never performed on a stage in New York. There'd be nowhere to hide. This would be just the three of us in front of a room filled with movers and shakers. The ticket price, a thousand dollars, would see to that. So, no pressure there, then. Child-minders safely in place and cupboards stocked with treats for the boys, Miriam and I flew to New York. Our pals Matt Forrest and Sarah Wadey came, too.

We arrived two days prior to the gig and checked into the Plaza Hotel, right on Central Park. It desperately needed refurbishment but had a cosy, traditional feel and was well placed for all the shops, which would be handy for Miriam.

The rehearsal, in a large recording complex somewhere in mid-town, was something else. In different parts of the room, Elton John, James Taylor, Annie Lennox, Sting, Bobby McFerrin, Lyle Lovett, Bonnie Raitt, Shawn Colvin, Garry Shandling and others did their best to run their songs with the house band; on guitar and MD duties, Nile Rodgers; on bass Nathan East, who also happens to be an accomplished magician; and on drums, Narada Michael Walden. Add to that a red-hot brass section and backing vocalists and you have a bit of a band. On top of all this there were film crews from CNN, NBC, ABC, CBS and the BBC among others, trying to get an exclusive with someone. It was absolute pandemonium, but I didn't care – I would have paid to stand in that room and just watch what was going down.

Then a door opened and everything went quiet. Stevie Wonder had arrived. All the clowning died away. We knew we were in the presence of someone special, even by those stellar standards. Contrary to what a lot of people assume, 'Little' Stevie is in fact a big guy, at least six foot two, and heavily built. We'd met a couple of years earlier, introduced by Laurie Jay after an amazing gig he'd performed at Wembley Arena. It was interesting to watch the reactions of the other superstars present: they all seemed readily to accept and acknowledge that he was on another level. I witnessed a similar thing in an hotel in Kensington straight after a Bob Dylan gig in London, when a group of heavyweight musicians, including George Harrison and Van Morrison, seemed in awe of the great man. On Dylan's arrival, everything had gone quiet. I guess it just shows that everyone's a fan of someone, everyone has their own personal hero and is liable to be struck dumb in their presence.

Stevie was led across the room by a couple of young, punky black kids, who looked out of place in that room. He sat down at a Fender Rhodes keyboard and started to play. Music flowed out of him, as though the keyboard were an extension of his body. He was just messing around, singing and laughing, but you could have heard a pin drop in the room. Suddenly he needed a chromatic harmonica. A stretch limo was despatched and in no time the instrument was in his hands and at his lips. He went into 'Overjoyed', a beautiful, complex ballad. I was with Sting and we looked at one another – 'There isn't anything to say, is there?' It was a privilege to be in the same room.

At the gig the next day, time was tight and so were people's nerves. A rehearsal schedule was drawn up to within the minute. Sting's wife Trudie was in charge. She does that stuff very well. It can't be easy, harnessing all that talent then having to stroke all those egos. I was sharing a dressing room with Sting. I have to say the bastard has a great body. All that yoga, no doubt. Worth it, though. I don't know what pushes Sting. He'll drag his arse out of bed and drive a hundred or so miles to do a guest slot on breakfast telly or a Saturday morning kids' show. He certainly doesn't need to. In answer to that question, put to him recently by a journalist, he said something like, 'If I didn't go out there and do it, what would I be? Just a rich bloke who sits in his garden at home counting his money and reading the papers.' I remember reading that and thinking, That's my life's ambition!

Back on the stage and, time-wise, things had taken a turn for the worse. Stevie was at the keyboard and he was singing a melody for someone's kid. It was lovely listening to him sing a little lullaby for the bairn, but there was no time for it. But what do you do? Answer: nowt. He was the only person on the bill Trudie wouldn't tell to hurry up. On the night he was going to do 'Overjoyed' and an encore with 'Living For The City', one of my all-time favourite songs. Once again, the rehearsals were moving. I was standing to one side of Stevie's keyboard, next to Elton John, while Stevie performed his ballad. At the end I was in tears. I'm not one for gushing, not in public, but this just did me in, and Elton, too. When it was over, we stood silently for a moment, then I shook my head and said, 'I'm going for a lie-down,' to which Elton replied, 'I'm off for a wank.' Kind of broke the spell.

Before I could leave, though, one more thing had to be sorted out. Sting informed me that a volunteer was needed to accompany Stevie on the harmonies in 'Living For The City'. 'It's only you and me can get up there to those notes, and I've already got plenty to do. Would you mind?' I ran the song with the band. There's a descending vocal passage at the end of each chorus, the bit where Stevie sings, 'Na na na naa, naya na naa, na na na na naa na naa, naa naa naa naa,

318

na na na na naaa!', which is tricky to pull off but truly magical once you're on top of it, and after a little while I had it.

Come the evening, I was in the dressing room getting ready when Sting said to me, 'Thanks for doing this.' I told him it was not only my pleasure but also an honour. 'No,' he said, 'it means a lot that you're here. We're both from Newcastle. You understand?' I did. I do.

The gig was sensational, and also very funny in an unexpected way. All the performers were on stage throughout, seated in a big semi-circle. When it was your turn, you just stood up and walked forward to the microphones. I was sitting next to Elton for a good bit of the evening and the stuff he kept coming out with, in loud stage whispers, was hilariously outrageous, but impossible to repeat here. I was praying that no one in the front rows, within sight of us, could lip-read what he was saying.

To say it was an honour to stand out there and perform is an understatement. We were giving the cream of New York society a Northumbrian anthem, and they loved it. It went down a storm, and Miriam was out there in the audience. I've never felt so proud to be a Geordie, before or since.

At the show's finale, I stood next to Stevie Wonder and, lungs filled to bursting, belted out one of his greatest songs. That was the best it's ever been. It seemed like a dream – so I'm glad Miriam was there with Matt and Sarah to confirm it was real.

Afterwards there was all the inevitable but justifiable gladhanding and back-slapping. Lots of famous folk gushing congratulations. Lyle Lovett, a real gentleman, introduced Miriam and me to his ex-wife Julia Roberts, who is surprisingly tall. They seemed to be on good terms.

Then there was a wonderful party with an auction in an

hotel, which raised even more money for the Rainforest Foundation. We shared a stretch limo with Peter Asher and James Taylor. There was a funny moment when the Italian singer Zucchero, who'd bid a ridiculous amount for a Mercedes convertible, was handed a pen and a slip of paper by a young black girl. With a shrug and a smile, he asked her to whom he should address the autograph. The girl put him straight: it was the receipt for the Merc. That was followed by a lavish do at Sting and Trudie's Central Park duplex, where we met, among others, Gianni Versace and Paul Simon. Miriam recognized neither of them, of course. She's hopeless like that – it's rather endearing. I have to say I struggled with Paul Simon, who was dressed in a kind of formally cut denim jacket with matching peaked cap. He looked as though his mam had dressed him. Maybe she had. Soon afterwards, Versace was tragically shot dead in Miami.

By 1998 we'd moved – again – from leafy Alma Square to a house nearer the kids' school in Hampstead. Moving has never bothered me – I tend to balance leaving a place full of family memories with the profit we've made on a place – but Miriam dislikes all the upheaval and disruption intensely. Rented properties included, this would be our eleventh home. The four flights of stairs in the Alma Square house had become too much for Miriam with her arthritis. We'd bought it in 1994 for a relatively knock-down price and made a handsome profit on it, selling it for more than twice what we'd laid out. We bought a place over two floors only, as estate agents tend to say, with parking for six cars and backing on to the Heath extension. The kids could walk to school in six minutes – that had to be better for them than sitting for forty-five minutes in the car every morning and afternoon.

I was offered a part in what turned out to be a lovely little feature film. *Still Crazy*, scripted by my old pals Dick Clement and Ian La Frenais, told the tale of a dysfunctional gang of dodgepot musicians collectively known as Strange Fruit, whose warring members temporarily bury the hatchet and re-form for one last shot at the big-time, only for the old problems and animosities to resurface and remind them why they'd packed it in the first time around. I played Les Wickes, the band's surly bass-player, and the rest of the cast was a dream-team: my mate Tim Spall played the drummer, Hans Mathesen was the good-looking young guitarist, Stephen Rea was perfectly cast as a prickly, sourpuss keyboard player, Billy Connolly was the roadie, Juliet Aubrey our manager, and, in a star turn that blew everyone else clean out of the water, Bill Nighy played the neurotic, messed-up lead singer. If you like your movies with lots of laughs, see this film for Bill's barnstorming performance. It has everything: pathos, bathos, ups and downs, perfect timing and execution, poignancy, sensitivity, subtlety, sarcasm, warmth, wit and a good dollop of physical magic. Bill also did all his own vocals, something he'd never done previously. Performances just don't come any better than that and Bill rightly won a clutch of awards. As I write this, he's recently won a Bafta and lots of other awards for his star turn in *Love Actually*, again as a dodgy old rocker. (Why wasn't there any punctuation in that movie's title? Surely there should've either been a comma or a colon? When I asked Richard Curtis, the movie's writer and director, he told me not to ask!) The music producers were Clive Langer and Alan Winstanley, two easy-going guys known and respected for their magnificent work with the likes of Madness, Elvis Costello and Bush. I had a great time recording with them at their base, Westside Studios in London's Holland Park, which I'd used many times before and in which I felt comfortable. A tip-top team. The late Brian Gibson directed us all and came up with a movie of real warmth and wry observation. On its UK release it did nowt and after a couple of weeks in cinemas it disappeared. It did, however, make an impression on the foreign film critics based in America and, much to my surprise, a song I'd performed in it, 'The Flame Still Burns', was nominated the following January for a Golden Globe award. Off I went to Hollywood once more.

When you're lodged in the Four Seasons Hotel and everything is on the film company's tab, it's a treat. When you open the door to that sumptuous suite . . . oh, what a life! Believe it or not I still do the obligatory jump on the bed. How sad is that? Back to the excitement of being a kid, I guess. In a way it's a pity I don't drink any more: I could have slaughtered their impressive wine list. As it was, I spent a wonderful week in the company of all the British nominees who were billeted alongside me. I seemed to see Robert Carlyle and Emily Watson every time I went down to the hotel lobby.

Early one morning I received a call from David Foster, an LA-based Canadian music producer I'd worked with a few years earlier on some songs. David is not only great company, he's also a major player in that town, so when he asked if I could do brunch with him and a friend later on that morning, I said, sure, no problem. Where should we meet? They'd come over to me, he said. Great. Who was the friend? I asked. Anyone I might know? Quincy Jones, said David. I certainly knew the name.

In terms of his CV and the length of time he's been at the pinnacle, Quincy Jones is probably the biggest living name in American music. From his scores for movies such as *In the Heat of the Night*, to his work with such recording artists as Sinatra and Michael Jackson – for whom he produced *Thriller* among other things – Quincy Jones, or Q, as he kept telling me to call him, has been at the top for over five decades. If you're someone like me, you accord him the utmost respect. In the flesh he was the epitome of cool, real cool, with his husky voice, sparkling eyes and memories to beat them all. When you're where he is there's no need to talk about your success. It's global, all-encompassing.

What was all this about, though? Such people don't call you out of the blue to share a joke and an egg-white omelette – or at least they don't call me. A few hours later I went down to the restaurant and there waiting for me was Foz, along with the legendary Mr Jones and another guy. On the table lay a plain white test-pressing CD marked 'Quincy Jones: Compilation'. The name against track one was Frank Sinatra. I didn't bother reading any further. After introductions the third guy left us to our brunch. I was desperate to know why I had been invited to sit at this power-table but I knew better than to ask. Just sit tight, keep your gob shut, listen to all that's being said, and sooner or later it'll become obvious.

After a wonderful half-hour mostly made up of Michael Jackson and Will Smith anecdotes, the conversation turned to movie musicals. David and Quincy both professed a desire to crack this difficult but enormously lucrative area of the market. Quincy explained their quest thus: they wanted to come up with a movie musical format that was classy enough to deliver great music, yet hip enough to appeal to the young. They felt it both unrealistic and unacceptable to have performers just burst into song, and were searching for the holy grail: a method of transition from speech to song and vice versa. Bearing in mind his track-record, Quincy's drive was impressive and infectious. After all he'd seen and done he still had a kid's enthusiasm. As I'd done quite a number of music-to-film projects they wanted my take on it. So there it was, the reason for my invitation. I so wanted to tell them I had some cool magic formula that would knock their socks off, but I couldn't 'cos I didn't. Still don't, although after a great deal of thought I have come to the following conclusion, for what it's worth: as long as your film has wonderful music, compositions like those of Paddy McAloon, for instance, it'll work. It'll move people. Whether it goes ballistic and earns you squillions of dollars is another matter.

On the night before the Golden Globes, a Saturday, the city and the Four Seasons were buzzing with excitement. As a guest of Ian La Frenais, I'd had a stupendous al-fresco dinner under the Beverly Hills stars along with a bunch of people that included Gregory Peck, a dignified, well-mannered man. I remember thinking, I can't wait to tell Mam — she'll be knocked out. I was back at the hotel and in my room around midnight, getting ready to turn in, when the phone rang. It was Miriam.

Unknown to me, my mam had fallen ill and been taken to hospital the previous Tuesday. My sister hadn't told me previously because everyone had assumed that Mam would be home again after a couple of days on medication. That was what usually happened, but not this time. She'd had a stroke, then passed away in the early hours of Sunday morning. I know my sister decided not to tell me with the best of intentions, and Mam would have felt terrible if I had missed the big night for a false alarm, but how I wish I'd known.

Instead of making my way by limousine to the Golden Globes, I headed for the airport and the sad journey home. As it was a Sunday, LAX was quiet, and the British Airways first-class lounge was empty, save for one couple: Alan Parker and his partner Lisa Moran were travelling to London that evening. I was glad to see such familiar friendly faces. Alan asked me why I wasn't at the Globes and I explained. After offering their condolences, Alan asked my mam's age. I told him she would have been eighty-four in a couple of weeks' time, on 14 February, Valentine's Day. Alan shook his head. 'That's my birthday, too,' he said. For some reason that coincidence made me feel a little better; as if there was a connection with my mam on that aeroplane other than me. Having said that, it was, inevitably, a long and difficult journey that finally ended in Newcastle upon Tyne.

I visited the hospital's chapel of rest and sat with my mam for a long time, remembering everything she'd done for me throughout my rollercoaster life, all the good, kind things, her help, encouragement and love. I tried to make my peace with her and myself but that wasn't possible and I found myself apologizing again and again for not having been there when she'd most needed me. How could I not have been there? I was sure I could have done something for her. When it came to my mam's health I had always overreacted, fearing the worst and throwing money at the problem. This time it wouldn't have been an overreaction: it would have been justified. After all she'd done for me, how could I have let her down so badly? I sat there, disgusted by my own shortcomings. My mam, the great encourager, would no longer be there to encourage me.

Jet-lag had begun to kick in. The room and everything in it seemed to be black and white or shades thereof. It seemed as though the clock had stopped for us both. I said goodbye to my beloved mam for the last time. Before I left her I asked the staff if I could take with me a lock of her hair.

I walked out into the grey Newcastle daylight, an orphan. For a long time I'd pictured life and death as a cliff, with my parents ahead of me, all of us shuffling nearer and nearer to the edge. There was always a feeling of comfort and security as long as they were ahead of me, but now they were gone and I was next in line, with my boys behind me.

The funeral was as difficult and sad as funerals are, but there were a couple of sunny moments. It was a High Church Anglican service and the priest, Father Peter, spoke with real warmth about a person he'd come to know well; about how she'd arrived at a carol service one Christmas to find the church full. She'd loved singing hymns and was so disappointed that he'd sneaked her in through a side door and given her a seat in the front row. From his vantage-point in the pulpit he'd watched as my mam beamed and sang her way through the carols. He said that he couldn't remember her ever having a bad word for anyone. Above all, he would remember her smile, he told us. We appreciated his words, and I thank him for his kindness towards my mam throughout the time they knew one another.

At the final parting, one of Luciano Pavarotti's recordings of 'Nessun Dorma' was played. It's a stirring piece at the best of times, but in those circumstances I found it impossible to remain composed. My mam had loved big Pav, as she called him – she even forgave him for running off with his young secretary, although she didn't approve. I've never felt happy about what little I was able to give back to my parents, and especially my mother, but I thought of when I'd made her dream come true with that box at the Royal Albert Hall. She'd been truly happy that day, so this was a fitting way to say goodbye. Now, that piece takes me straight back to the pain of that day and I can't bear to hear it.

After the funeral, we were preparing to leave the hotel when I bumped into Alan Shearer in the car park. I'd met him a few times at functions and had presented him with an award a couple of years earlier. He asked if I'd be at the match the following day for the home game against Aston Villa. I explained the situation and said Miriam and I wanted to get our sons home after such an emotionally charged and difficult day. Then Alan very kindly asked if the boys would like to come along to the game as his personal guests. I was about to say, 'Thanks, but no thanks,' when I caught sight of their faces. They were so excited and up for it that I couldn't refuse. We postponed our departure and the next day we all went along to the game and Newcastle won, thank goodness. Afterwards we had a drink and a natter with Alan and the other players in the players' lounge.

My mam was in the care of the Royal Victoria Infirmary from Tuesday afternoon until the early hours of Sunday morning, when she'd died. If the shock of losing her like that was bad, it was as nothing compared to what slowly unfolded over the next fifteen or so months.

After a lengthy and protracted investigation, carried out by the local health authority, into the circumstances surrounding my mother's death, dreadful instances of neglect and improper practice were acknowledged. I discovered all this by accident when I asked to meet the doctors and nurses who'd looked after her during her final hours. During that meeting it soon became obvious that all had been far from right. In fact, it added up to a terrifying catalogue of ineptitude. Because of the way in which food was served then to the patients, the only thing the hospital could say with any certainty that my mother had eaten in the five days from Tuesday to Sunday was half a tub of yoghurt. My sister, visiting on the Thursday, had found her to be near-starving and had gone straight out to M&S and bought some chicken sandwiches. She had returned to the ward and fed Mam the chicken from between the slices of bread.

Worse, it came to light that even though she'd been prescribed morphine on Tuesday to alleviate her excruciating bowel pain, she hadn't received any. It was later discovered that three different batches had been despatched during that week from the pharmacy but not one had reached her ward – or, if it had, no one knew, or was saying, where it had gone. Where could it have gone? I asked. The hospital could not say. Apparently at that time no one had to sign for anything or account for it.

It became obvious at this point that we were dealing with criminal acts, so on the advice of my lawyers I went to the local police to ask for their help and advice. In the end I had to decide whether I wanted to bring charges against the local health authority. Part of me was hell-bent on vengeance. I wanted justice – I wanted all those responsible to be brought to book for what they'd allowed to happen to my mam. But what then? Wouldn't that just frighten other elderly patients, and undermine their confidence in the local health service that had served my mam well in the decades before this tragic catastrophe? And, of course, a case involving someone like me would be all over both the local and national press, with the accompanying slurry such coverage brings. There would be no winners.

After much soul-searching I decided against it. I felt that my mam wouldn't have wanted me to go after people. She was too good-hearted to do something like that so I decided that, as much as it grieved me, I would do as she would have done. The local health authority gave me written assurances that protocols would be implemented so that nothing like this would befall another patient. Did I make the right call? I don't know. What I do know is that to this day I'm tormented by the memory of those dreadful events, and no matter what I say or think or do, and no matter what kind words people offer me, they trouble my conscious thoughts and haunt my dreams. I feel a terrible sense of failure.

We didn't win the Globe either.

During the summer of 1999 I set about recording what I feel to have been my best effort, the album *Tadpoles In A Jar*. Although everything I did around that time was over-shadowed by my mam's death, it's a fine collection of songs, if I say so myself. Jeff Lynne played on and produced the single, 'Blue Beyond The Grey'. *Q* magazine gave it four stars, and they don't dish 'em out to the likes of me unless they're merited. I was thrilled with the results but, as is often the case in the music business, politics took a hand in things. Rob Dickens, the Warner Brothers Records chairman who had personally championed the album, left the company, and suddenly all interest in it cooled. We'd spent over £300,000 recording it, yet it was released without any push or fanfare, and soon died. After everything else had gone either platinum or, in the case of *Crocodile Shoes*, triple platinum, it was frustrating and disappointing. I don't think I'll ever do better.

19

Towards the turn of the millennium I was on my way to buy some new mugs from Ceramica. I couldn't park anywhere near where I wanted to go – what's new? – and ended up having to leave the car on the more dodgy east side of Portobello Road, outside a bathroom showroom. The fittings in the window looked really posh so I stuck my head in and had a look round. Indeed it was posh, with a one-off Philippe Starck free-standing circular shower a giveaway at only £3,500. Despite the best efforts of an attractive redhead, I decided to pass and head off in search of my mugs. Miriam would have been proud of my resolve.

A successful, albeit expensive hour later, I had them. As I passed the bathroom-shop window on the way back to my car I couldn't help noticing a bum, wrapped in expensively faded denim, stuck in the air as its owner bent double over some expensive bogware. The body straightened up and I saw it was Franc Roddam. We hugged and exchanged hellos; it had been years since we'd seen each other and although I didn't know him well, I liked Franc, not least because he had come up with the original idea for *Auf Wiedersehen, Pet*. Franc's mate Mick, a bricklaying buddy from his growing-up years in Middlesbrough, had happened one day to tell him how and why he and thousands of other building workers had had to go to Germany at the end of the seventies to find work and wages, and about the adventures they'd had in the process. Franc had recognized the situation's dramatic/ comedic potential, and had written a screenplay based on

Mick's stories, but it wasn't made until Dick and Ian had read the script and suggested turning it into a television series.

While they were writing the first *Auf Wiedersehen, Pet* series, Dick and Ian had asked Franc if he could put them in touch with Mick for research purposes. He gave them a phone number with strict instructions about the time they should call. Dick and Ian would dial at the appointed hour from leafy Benedict Canyon, and moments later a phone would ring in a phone box on a Middlesbrough council housing estate. Mick would be waiting to pick it up.

After we'd shot the breeze outside for a while, dodging the dog-poo on the pavement, Franc told me that ownership of the format rights to *Auf Wiedersehen, Pet* had reverted to him. Alan Yentob, Franc's near neighbour, was doing something with it for the BBC, and would I be interested?

Until Sunday, 8 February that year I would have had no hesitation in saying no. The idea of revisiting any previously worked on project has never much appealed to me, for all the obvious reasons, and this one would be uniquely hazardous, loaded with potential down-sides: the nation's former favourite, very hard to walk away with your reputation intact, retain any credibility etc. It was best left as a wonderful memory. But on 8 February we'd organized a bash at the Newcastle City Hall in memory of Ronnie Johnson, known professionally as Sammy Johnson, to raise money for a charitable trust fund we'd set up in his name. For all three seasons, along with a Christmas special set in Marseille, Ronnie had played Stick, the villain you couldn't help but like, in *Spender*. When he wasn't working in Britain he'd lived in Spain, and was out running one evening when he suffered a massive heart-attack and died. We were all stunned at the suddenness of his passing, and no one more so than Tim

Healy: he and Ronnie had been the closest of friends. All things must pass, I know, but it was hard. Ronnie had seemed so alive, invincible. I guess that's another lesson learned right there.

Among the things we hoped to include on the all-singing, all-dancing *Sunday Night For Sammy* was a short scripted scene involving the three Geordie characters from *Auf Wiedersehen, Pet*: Tim Healy's Dennis, Kevin Whately's Neville, and my Oz. On hearing about the gig, Ian La Frenais had promised three or four pages in plenty of time. I was aware that he and Dick were very busy so I wasn't holding my breath. There was a Plan B, in case the pages never came through, but don't ask me what it was.

Dick and Ian faxed me the pages a week before the gig – only there weren't three, there were seventeen. They were very funny, and I called the guys to thank them. They told me it had been immensely enjoyable to write dialogue for those long-lost, oft-remembered friends. But how were we ever going to get it together? Three scenes rather than the requested, and only half expected, one? Seventeen pages. Props, lights, extras. Kevin, Tim and I all working on other jobs. And one week until the show.

Kevin and Tim came over to our place on the Thursday before the show and we ran the lines. As we scratched away at the surface layers, looking for the gems hidden in the subtext, I was mindful of what Kevin had said to me all those years ago, when I was trying to decide whether or not to do the second *Auf Wiedersehen, Pet* series. 'Scripts like these don't come along very often, once in a lifetime, if you're lucky.' The years had proved him right. And they were still great, but it was peculiar for all three of us to read those scenes and try to crawl inside those once-familiar skins and inhabit those personas one more time. In truth it was not very enjoyable: I was distinctly uncomfortable. It felt as though I was playing a dead man, to whom I'd long since said goodbye, didn't particularly wish to meet again, and who had muddled my recognition of my own identity. Tim and Kevin, the professionals, shamed me, having already memorized their lines while I had to read mine. I used lack of time as an excuse. Feeble: I hate being the last one off the page. I don't mind not being first at anything – in fact, I don't care at all – but I do mind about being last. It takes me back to my schooldays and I won't let it happen – at least, not without a battle. After a couple of hours we had convinced ourselves it would be all right on the night, which of course it always is. Funny, that.

Sunday Night For Sammy was a resounding success on every level: all the tickets sold out long before the gig, and by general consensus a great time was had by all, performers and audience alike. I felt a real sense of Geordie pride in the whole thing: the way people pulled together, and got on with it – for Ronnie. I had a lot to do, singing a couple of songs on top of doing the *Auf Wiedersehen, Pet* scenes with Tim and Kevin, which necessitated two elaborate, speedy costume changes – and this for someone who'd never done theatre before. No time, or room, for personal assistants. I was running around like a blue-arsed fly trying to get costume, kit and props ready, apply inch-deep Panstik I'd scrounged from Tim's wife, actress Denise Welch, to conceal my goatee, then run through my lines in my head. And then, oh, my goodness, we were on.

Tim and Kevin took the stage first, in darkness, to silence. The PA played the *Auf Wiedersehen, Pet* signature tune, the lights went up and . . . Dear me! They were given such a thundering, awesome reception that I was quite miffed I wasn't out there with them. I'd soon get my moment, though.

They went into the dialogue – or, rather, attempted to – and every line was greeted with raucous whooping and cheering. Now it was time for me to deliver my first line, via a microphone, from the wings. I took a breath and then I was him again, Oz. It was spooky. I was unsure how I sounded: like me or like him? Then all doubts vanished as the place went potty – and I hadn't even walked on to the stage. At this point I was caught: on the one hand I wanted just to stand there, let the cheering go on and on, and on the other I was desperate to get out into all that adulation, bathe in it, gulp it down, get drunk on it. I waited as long as I dared and then I made my entrance.

Popular character, popular television show, home crowd, you choose; the reaction as I walked out on to the stage was nothing short of frightening, the sheer raw emotion in the room totally overwhelming. Two thousand plus people, most of them adults, were going bananas. The balconies were visibly moving as people jumped up and down. The sound and lighting rigs were wobbling. The whole building seemed to be shaking. I just stood there for a while, gazing out dumbly into the cacophony, enjoying the moment. Newcastle United winning the FA Cup couldn't feel any better than this, could it? The cheering and screaming went on for what seemed like an eternity, but in reality was probably no more than a few minutes. Kevin, Tim and I could only look at each other, speechless. Then we smiled, big daft smiles. After a while I put up my hand to try to stop the racket so I could deliver my next line. Otherwise we would have been there all night. It worked. I said my next line, and – *boom*! Pandemonium again.

Strange indeed. I was up there in front of all those people playing a character I'd brought to life almost twenty years earlier and it was more than a little unnerving. I'd glibly assumed that I would slip straight back into him as a foot does into a well-worn shoe. I didn't. And I was nowhere near word perfect, which really pissed me off. Always has. Only when you're completely familiar with the text can you begin to look for ways to explore and expand within a scene's given parameters. Never mind. We got through it, and I had the big punch-line, which, almost literally, brought the building down.

Later on, sitting alone in my big posh suite at the Malmaison hotel, I was still not sure whether I'd enjoyed myself. Just like other truly memorable moments I've enjoyed as a performer, and there have been a good many, this one seemed to have been over so quickly. But it had been different, this night, different from singing with Stevie Wonder and Sting at New York's Carnegie Hall, from headlining at Wembley Arena and the Royal Albert Hall, from dancing with Madonna, from playing the ukelele with George Harrison, from meeting the royals. Tonight had been a profound experience, disturbing, almost, the kind that moves you to think, examine and question. I sat alone for a long while just thinking. Lots of mixed emotions on an emotional night. I tried to put the evening into perspective, tried to draw some meaningful conclusion from it all, but I couldn't, other than knowing that Ronnie would have been as pleased as punch about it and as proud as a peacock. Right then, that single certainty was enough. 'Champion, kidder!' he would likely have said.

So when Franc asked, I said, 'Well, let me think about it.' It would still be a hell of a decision: did I want to go back to a character who had almost unhinged me? It had taken me a long time to establish myself as something more than Oz. Did I want to be stared at and have all that fuss everywhere I went? Did I want to dip my toe into those murky waters once again? The answer was no, but . . .

Fast forward to April in Los Angeles. I had called in there

on my way back from a family holiday in Australia to see Tim Spall, by then four years in remission and in rude health. He was working on a movie, and I was sitting with Dick and Ian in some swank Beverly Hills eaterie having lunch. The boys had just returned from a trip to Hawaii where they'd been doing some script doctoring on *Pearl Harbor* for Jerry Bruckheimer. During a suitable lull in the lettuce-munching I mentioned that the *Auf Wiedersehen, Pet* format rights had reverted to Franc. We all agreed it had been a blast working on the scenes for Ronnie's benefit night and, there and then, began to kick around various storylines. It was exciting, as it always is with Dick and Ian, but before we all got carried away, there was the little matter of getting the rest of the cast to agree to it.

Although we'd all kept in touch and, to the best of my knowledge, got along, the six surviving members of the main *Auf Wiedersehen, Pet* cast, Tim Healy (Dennis), Kevin Whately (Neville), Tim Spall (Barry), Chris Fairbank (Moxey), Pat Roach (Bomber) and yours truly (Oz), all very different individuals, had gone their separate ways and were busy boys. Busy dads, too. Rafe and Mercedes Spall, Kitty and Kieran Whately, Matthew and Louis Healy, Matteus Fairbank, and my own Tom and Fred are the junior cast members I know of; there may well be more. Would our lives have been altogether different without the phenomenal success of that show? I know I wouldn't be in the position I'm in today if it weren't for *Auf Wiedersehen, Pet*. Sooner or later the others would most likely have broken through to national acclaim. As for me, but for that show, and Miriam, I'd have been either running a property empire or languishing in a jail cell. I reckon that's what the fates would have held in store for me – maybe still do, you never know. And, as Gerald Ronson proved, the two can be successfully combined.

Cut to England and a sweltering Saturday night in May. Miriam and I were having dinner at Orsini's in Holland Park with Ian and Doris – they were in town on their way to Prague to see their son, Michael, who was shooting a movie with the lovely Anjelica Huston – Franc and his very pregnant wife Corinna. It was not a good night for me: my sinuses were bad and I couldn't contribute much by way of conversation without sounding like the guy from the Tunes commercial. Eventually Ian said to me, 'So, about *Auf Wiedersehen, Pet*? What are we going to do?' I don't know, I answered. Where are we? Franc told us he had an idea for a storyline, and that Alan Yentob was keen to make it happen as a BBC project. Ian also seemed keen.

Dinner over, we wandered towards Ian's digs at the Halcyon, then a funky little Holland Park boutique hotel, now sadly closed. I asked him if he and Dick would be up for writing a new *Auf Wiedersehen, Pet* screenplay. 'Yes, as long as we have a good storyline,' he answered. His interest surprised me: apart from being very busy, he's a hard man to get aboard a project. But in writing those new scenes for Ronnie's charity bash, in breathing new life into those old characters, it seemed he, too, had been reminded of how uniquely special the experience we'd all shared had been. If this project ever happened, the irony of how it had come alive again wouldn't be lost on me. Ronnie would have loved it.

On the way home from the restaurant Corinna went into labour and a few hours later gave birth to her and Franc's fourth daughter, Zazou.

The following week I spent a couple of fun days at Franc's place spitballing, kicking ideas around (including doing three hundred-minute films rather than the mooted one: my shout, that one, and cost-effective because you can shoot them all back-to-back, but tricky story-wise. Also, it would have been three times the pay-packet). Franc had two main ideas he wished to incorporate in the tale: the historic Middlesbrough Transporter Bridge and the plight of the Native American community – two pretty disparate elements, on paper at least.

However, there was no point in doing too much work until we'd spoken to the other actors to see how they felt about it. This was a crucial and delicate moment. If it appeared to them that I was somehow involved in the production side of the project, they might have been put off. And understandably so. But I was where I was: Franc had asked me to work on the storyline with him, that was legitimate, and I'd not be producing, so it should be OK. All the same, gently does it.

I put in calls to the other five players. Turned out they were all up for it, which I really hadn't expected. Spall in particular had good reason to pass: movie work was plentiful and who wouldn't rather shoot a feature instead of a film for television? But he was up for it, as long as the script was right. Kevin had so enjoyed the Ronnie benefit concert that he felt the same: as long as the script was right. That might seem a given, bearing in mind who was doing the writing, but one thing you learn quickly in this game is that nothing can guarantee your screenplay will actually play, that the cake will rise. For this project, though, there was no alternative: if Dick and Ian couldn't get *Auf Wiedersehen, Pet* to play, it couldn't be done.

Alan Yentob was now calling to Franc over the garden wall: what's happening with *Auf Wiedersehen, Pet*? It was time for a meeting with my ICM agents, Duncan Heath and Paul Lyon-Maris, to clarify what was on offer and what was wished for. The plan was then to meet somewhere in the middle.

Come July, and Franc, who believes in starting negotiations firmly on the front foot, had told the BBC what he planned to do: a series of three hundred-minute films, with a single storyline running through them, to be written by Franc Roddam and yours truly, scripts to be written by Dick Clement and Ian La Frenais, cast to include Tim Healy, Kevin Whately, Tim Spall, Chris Fairbank, Pat Roach and yours truly. Storylines to be delivered to Dick and Ian by the end of October, first drafts to be in by the end of April 2001, to shoot June 2001 for six months. Actors and writers to be contracted ASAP before they got signed up to do something else. It was an ambitious schedule. I told Franc that, in my experience, things tended to move at less than a snail's pace within the BBC, and a project you should be able to do in a year might well take two, three or four. Everyone is so terrified of making a wrong decision that nobody makes any. Franc wanted to push ahead: he was concerned that Alan might not be there in eighteen months' time. Perhaps he knew something I didn't, or he might just have wanted to get on. Whatever: the real deciding factor on this one would be when, or whether, Dick and Ian could get started on the writing, and how long it would take them to deliver the first drafts.

The BBC wanted to do the films in-house, and initially that worried me: it's widely accepted that the best of the production staff left the corporation long ago, only to come back and work as independents, doing exactly what they'd done previously but usually for higher rates of pay. So much for the cost-effectiveness of deregulation in broadcasting. But it had its up-sides: the BBC would negotiate directly with Franc, and that was fine by me – I wouldn't be involved with that side of things. Hopefully I'd avoid being tagged as a mercenary. I guessed Franc would probably kick off a production entity specifically for the venture and then do what's known as an 'above-the-line' deal where he'd take in the actors, writers, directors and producers – all referred to in budgeting terms as 'above-the-line' – and the BBC would provide all below-the-line items, i.e. everything else. It's a sensible deal unless you want to get involved in the day-to-day nuts-and-bolts of television production. I've been there and I don't wish to if I don't have to. There is one more, major, plus to this set-up from a programme-maker's point of view: because the BBC costs its projects internally and, more to the point, inter-departmentally, not only is the worry about the overall project cost their worry, but because of the aforementioned costing methods, true and accurate budgets are seldom if ever known. That could only be a good thing from Franc's point of view. Once they'd agreed to his story-line, any spiralling costs would be their problem.

While I was at Sotheby's auction house *en famille* for a *Spitting Image* sale, I bumped into Alan Yentob. He said hello just as I was leaving: I'd got my troops marshalled and moving together through the sip-and-snap bun-fight towards the exit and was loath to break the momentum although I knew I'd have to. As I watched Miriam and the boys being swept along by the crowd, Alan introduced me to a programme-controller colleague of his who couldn't muster more than a disinterested hello, then asked me how I was. I like Alan: he was never less than straight and fair when we had dealings with him at the BBC throughout the early nineties. He and I made small-talk and I knew he was waiting for me to mention *Auf Wiedersehen, Pet*, but it was not the place for such a conversation, sur-rounded as we were by photographers and those desperate to be photographed. There was a bit more small-talk, then a pregnant pause. I told him I had to get off to feed the kids. Just as I was heading back into the scrum, he mentioned it, had to: 'I was talking to Franc. Great news, isn't it?'

'What's that?' I somewhat disingenuously inquired.

'The project.'

The project?

'*Auf Wiedersehen, Pet.*'

Ah, now I've got you. Yes, great, I replied half-heartedly. I'm not sure why I was being so casual about it – never appear too keen, I suppose. I told Alan that I had been surprised all the cast members were up for it, and he nodded enthusiastically. So, there it was – from the horse's mouth, so to speak: confirmation from a broadcaster. And not just any old broadcaster: the BBC, my preferred and favourite home. My mam, God rest her, was so proud of seeing that three-initial logo on my programmes, and so was I. Now, for the first time since all this had started up again, I felt a new *Auf Wiedersehen, Pet* might really happen.

There was something more to this for me, though, something even more important than all the fees, costs and the budget: ever since the idea had surfaced I'd been asking myself one question: could we make television that would be as good as, if not better than, what was being screened at that moment? I'd seen nothing to make me doubt that we could.

In late July, a distraction: I received a script from the casting director Sheila Tresize. It turned out to be a major Hollywood movie called *Behind Enemy Lines* and one of my favourite screen actors, Gene Hackman, was playing the lead. For years I'd dreamed of working with him – just one scene, please! Shooting would be for three months in Slovakia, starting 1 October. The family was making preparations for a camping holiday so I didn't have time to deal with the script when it landed on the mat and took it away with the intention of reading it under canvas.

Behind Enemy Lines turned out to be a major disappointment. The character I'd been asked to read was Arkan, an indicted Serbian war criminal, right-hand man-cum-enforcer to Slobodan Milosevic and Radovan Karadzic, gangster, leader of the Tigers, his own paramilitary force, allegedly one of the Balkans' biggest butchers and recently shot dead in the lobby of the Intercontinental Hotel, Belgrade. Any decent-minded, right-thinking human being would want less than nothing to do with such a scoundrel. I'd cross a continent to avoid him, but as an actor considering a part, that would have counted for nothing if the character had been well written and the story factually correct. The opportunity to try to get inside the head of such a beast would have been a great temptation and a huge challenge. But the part had been underwritten: it was one-dimensional and factually incorrect. As scripted, this Arkan was to be captured by four heroic Interpol agents while trying to board a train to make good his escape. To put the tin hat on it, there were no scenes featuring him and Gene, so had I landed the gig I probably wouldn't even have met the great man. That was it. I'd not be going to the Balkans.

Among the dozen messages waiting on the answerphone for my return from the wilderness was one from Ian La Frenais and one from Mark Boomla of Prager & Fenton, my accountants. Ian was just calling to say hello, which was unusual, if not unprecedented. Mark had taken a call from a journalist at *Marketing Week*, a media trade magazine, who had it on good authority that we were about to do some more *Auf Wiedersehen, Pet* with the BBC: did I have any comment to make? My comment was, and always is, 'No comment,' but the cat was out of the bag. That was bad news, bearing in mind that not everyone was under contract. Franc had taken the same call, which he said he'd also blanked, and had spoken to Alan Yentob. The BBC were keen to lock the deal and get the actors signed up. Franc told

ICM he wanted it all put to bed before he left for Australia that week, where he was to begin preparatory work on a movie based around the Waltzing Matilda story. The BBC was waiting for confirmation and specific detail of the Canadian tax-refund situation. There was a possibility we might shoot in Canada instead of Arizona where the new series was to be set. I told Franc that if this was all sorted out within a week I would eat not only my hat, but every other item of headgear in the capital, including crash-helmets!

It's worth recounting the following, I think, just to make the point that not all of my ideas and projects get made as a matter of course. Around this time I met with Jane Tranter, the BBC's head of drama, to try to move things forward on *The Road To Somewhere*, a project telling the true story of the 1936 Jarrow marchers. I'd written a pilot episode for what I hoped would be a six-part serial and I had high hopes. According to Duncan, my agent, the BBC liked the idea, but not the script. My script! After I'd worked on it for two years! How dare they? Didn't they know who I used to be? A few years ago that kind of response would have crushed me. But it's different now. *I'm* different. My priority was to get that project made whatever it took because I consider the true story of what happened in Jarrow back in 1936 to be of great historical importance and social significance. If they wanted another writer, I could live with that.

Duncan and I went to the BBC. I almost had a punch-up at the gate-house, before I'd even got on to the premises. A van driver was shouting and screaming at me. What is it with some people? The weather? Guys driving convertible sports cars? It's no wonder they get smacked. In the car park, Duncan stripped off down to his knickers, in full view of anyone who might have been interested, threw on some Ralph Lauren agenting casuals, and we were in the building.

He got straight to it with Jane. Did the BBC want to make my Jarrow serial or not? The answer was, no, they didn't, but they'd be up for a single film, or a two-parter. That was fine by me – with a book to accompany the film, plus the possibility of an educational DVD, details to be thrashed out. To lull me into a false sense of optimism I was given my own project executive. I should have been doing hand-springs, especially after all the time and energy I'd put into the project.

But it's odd, but with the successful securing of a com-mission – which, in my experience, usually means a commit-ment by a broadcaster to spend millions of pounds on your idea – I've found that when the moment comes, and they say the *yes*-word, I'm never as euphoric as I thought I would be. There's more of a sense of relief than anything else. It's back to that feeling of anti-climax on achieving your dreams, I guess.

While all this power-broking was going on, right next door to Jane Tranter's offices, Miriam, Fred and a boot full of discarded playthings were at the sprawling White City car-boot sale. Good idea: the house was so bunged up with old clothes, toys, bits and bobs it felt as though it needed a good shit. Not my idea of fun, though, with scores of people out to kill an afternoon, looking through your stuff, pulling faces, haggling for pennies over things that originally cost a bundle.

It was a resounding success, and Miriam and Fred raked in an impressive hundred pounds (never mind that the stuff they flogged had originally cost ten times that amount: it had lain around in boxes for years and simply had to go). As soon as they arrived people were thieving from them, so when they went back for a second bash they took along Tom as their minder and managed to make another fifty pounds, with nothing swiped this time. Good for you, big boy. I got much more pleasure from their result than I ever did from deals of my own. Feeling like winners, we had lunch in a tiny Chelsea bistro, Italian food served by Czechs. Pizza inedible. Hey-ho.

I returned Ian's call of earlier in the week and spoke to him and Doris. A project with Liam Neeson, which they'd been working on, had taken a bit of a body-swerve, as had Liam himself, by all accounts: his Harley Davidson had collided with a red deer on a road in upstate New York and, according to Doris, he had been sent tumbling down a fifteen-foot slope. He managed to crawl up again and flag down a passing motorist, who got him to a hospital where it was discovered he'd sustained, among other injuries, a broken pelvis, a broken heel and internal bleeding. He wouldn't be doing anything for a while. It sounded as if he was lucky to be alive. Would this alter Dick and Ian's thinking on *Auf Wiedersehen, Pet*? We'd have to wait and see. Although the contrary would probably have suited me better, I wished Liam a speedy recovery. It was bound to take a while, though: as you get older the body takes longer to get over knocks.

Franc and I took a trip to Canada to look at possible locations in and around Toronto, but it was soon obvious they weren't what we were after. We'd have to go for the real thing. If you think getting into New York or LA from London is a draggy chore then you really should try entering the US via Toronto. It makes those New York/LA immigration experiences seem positively pleasant. Carry-on bags at our feet, we became part of a slow-moving queue that snaked twenty yards each way, about ten coils deep. After about two hours of this bag-shuffling misery we arrived at the security X-ray machines. Make that 'machine'. There was only one to cope with the three hundred or so tired, sweaty, smelly people who made up the undulating snake queue. It was a little after six a.m. Babies screamed, crotchety nicotine-addicts grumbled, and tempers frayed. I have to say that getting on and off aeroplanes is one of my least favourite things.

Arizona. As soon as we got there we knew. November sunshine, cacti and big hats. Really big hats. And we weren't even outside the airport. This was the place we had to come to make our series. We spent a night at the fabulous Biltmore Four Seasons Hotel, then picked up our rental car and headed north towards Lake Havasu. That was where they'd rebuilt London Bridge. We smartass Brits like to think we sold some dumb American guy the wrong bridge, sold him a pup, but it was bought by a Mr McCulloch, the man whose company brought the world, for better or worse, the chainsaw, and who was, even back then, worth millions of dollars. He had the bridge painstakingly dismantled and shipped, lock, stock and barrel, to Lake Havasu where it was carefully reassembled and now makes the holding company millions of dollars a year as a tourist attraction. There's dumb for you.

We walked the short distance over the bridge on to a small man-made island on the lake. The only places you can go when you get across there are a few coffee and gift shops. And guess who owns the shops and the island? That's right, daft old Mr McCulloch. We enjoyed a funny breakfast experience out there early one morning. I asked for eggs. You always get served two in America, God bless 'em. The waitress asked me how I'd like 'em cooked. Fried, I replied, with a smile. She asked me how I'd like them fried. Not being able to decide between over-easy or sunny-side-up and getting bored as well as hungry, I asked for one of each. The commotion that simple request caused! Our waitress took a step back, rocked on one heel and looked at me as if I'd asked for boiled bull's balls. She asked me if I was shittin' her. I assured her I wasn't. She brought out the short-order chef, who scratched his head and frowned. In the end the entire diner staff, half a dozen people, came and had a look at the weird English guy who wanted 'one of each' for his breakfast. There is a salient point to all this: in America you're usually all right as long as you don't divert from the norm. So be warned: one little detour can result in a short-circuit.

20

It should have been an exciting time for me, but the run-up to the principal photography on *Auf Wiedersehen, Pet* was overshadowed by the terminal illness of my ex-boss and close friend John Watson. A man tougher than old boots, who'd never suffered a day's illness in his life, he'd become unwell at the turn of the year and colon cancer had been diagnosed. Sadly, the disease was already at an advanced stage and palliative care was considered the best option.

My pal Ray Black had called me in January to tell me of John's illness. When I visited him in the Freeman Hospital, Newcastle, I was dismayed to find he couldn't hear and had to be shouted at by the doctors and nurses. John's hearing was severely impaired and without his hearing-aid he could understand little. It was frightening for him because, on top of being gravely ill, he couldn't hear the questions he was being asked by the medical staff and he was worried that he might give a reply that could prove fatal.

I asked about his hearing-aid: it needed fixing. The menders were situated in a shopping precinct in the city centre no more than a mile from the hospital but no one was available to sort it out. Social services were busy right now, we were told. Here was a man who'd never been out of work for a day in his entire adult life, never cost the country a penny. He'd diligently paid his taxes and his stamp for fifty years, and in his hour of greatest need the nation's much-vaunted health service couldn't manage to get his hearing-aid repaired. We took it to the menders. Turned out it would take three days to put it right. When we explained John's predicament, the head man fixed us up with a temporary hearing-aid. We took it back to John in hospital and, hey presto!, he could hear again. It wasn't too difficult.

Some weeks later, Miriam and I travelled up to Newcastle to see him again. He was now in the Newcastle General Hospital and in a pitiful state. Propped up on pillows in a bed in the corner, he looked like a wounded animal, the fight knocked out of him. Ray had been looking after things and helping out as best he could, but John was so depressed he just wanted it over, wanted to get away. Miriam went straight out to M&S and bought him new pyjamas, sponge-bag, everything he needed. It perked him up no end. The sad thing about John's lot was that, although by most people's standards he was a wealthy man, he never spent anything on himself. He had come from a life of poverty, so money in the bank was a security blanket for him, a comfort to be looked at on paper statements rather than used. I'm exactly the same, although I try to fight it. I know it's not logical, but in matters like this logic doesn't apply. John could have lived in opulent splendour; but chose instead to live in near-squalor. It was heartbreaking to see.

We managed to get him moved to the Marie Curie hospice in the west end of the city and he couldn't get over what he considered to be the luxurious conditions. Ironically, it was the first decent place he'd ever lived in. When we went to visit him a week or so later the turn-around in his spirits was nothing short of incredible. If I wasn't such a sceptic I'd have called it miraculous. After just a week in that brightly coloured, sweet-smelling, warm, peaceful and, above all, caring environment where a dedicated, friendly group of staff and volunteers offered nothing but kindness, compassion, respect and encouragement, John had gone from wanting to die to wanting to live again. He talked about going home, and although we knew, and I think John did, too, that his days were numbered, it was lovely to hear him being so positive and optimistic. He had even regained his unique sense of humour. He was well looked after, and eventually he went home, but sadly he was not so comfortable there. By this time he was beyond taking care of himself but if it hadn't been for Ray calling in every day with food he would have gone without.

We took him to Tynemouth, his last day out, and a bit of a pantomime it turned out to be. He was wearing a pair of trousers that had previously belonged to his brother. Joe was slightly bigger round the waist than John and, with him being so ill, the weight had dropped off him. He had no belt, so when we got him out of the car and on to the busy pavement by Tynemouth Priory his trousers fell down to his ankles. He couldn't move so Ray and I got on our knees to pull them up.

At that moment a group of children came out of the priory with their teachers. They just stood and stared at the sight in front of them: two middle-aged men on their knees, their faces level with an elderly man's crotch, their hands on his crusty kecks. I half smiled and said to one of the teachers, 'He's not well.' She recognized me and looked confused. Then the kids were led away at a brisk pace, while being told it was rude to stare.

John passed away at the end of July, a week before filming on *Auf Wiedersehen, Pet* was due to start. It was a major downer. I feared a sparse turn-out at his cremation but his pals from the Heaton Buffs club arrived on a coach and did him proud. He would have liked that. I read the eulogy, kept it brief but acknowledged the great debt I owed him and his elder brother, Joe, now also gone. It made me feel a lot better to say it publicly like that. Most people would have dismissed

John as a scruffy old bugger, and he certainly was, but he was so much more besides. What you saw wasn't all there was. John and Joe Watson, two proper Geordies: their like will not be seen again. It's our loss.

I'd asked the production office not to contact me during the week of John's cremation, but of course they did. Although I'd asked to read with actors up for the parts of Oz's son and lover (different parts!) they had gone ahead and cast them. This made me angry. As I saw it, there could only be benefits to having a leading member of the cast in attendance at casting readings. The producer and the director considered otherwise. They had thought I might insist on the actors of my choice no matter how they felt. That was not only wide of the mark but deeply offensive. I felt it questioned my professional integrity. If I'd wanted any more clout I would have made sure I got it. Franc had already offered me a co-executive producing credit, which would have given me a veto over any and all casting decisions, but I neither needed nor wanted it. As a matter of fact I wanted nothing to do with any behind-the-camera stuff. It would be challenge enough to get the character properly pegged and the ensemble work right. I'd have my hands and my head full with all that brought with it, and I wanted to concentrate on the acting. It was always the most difficult area for me, and so it would prove once again.

Only days before we were due to begin rehearsals a mini-crisis developed. I was unhappy about the way Wyman Norris, Gary Holton's character's hitherto-unknown son, appeared on the scene and no one passed any comment on the fact that he was of mixed race. The production staff were thinking, no doubt, in terms of political correctness. They didn't want to go near the subject with a barge-pole, and the writers, on holiday in the South of France, weren't thrilled at the prospect of a major rewrite at this late stage. From an acting point of view, this was one of the pitfalls of signing up to a job before the scripts were in – but the subject had to be acknowledged. Something had to be said. I informed the BBC that unless a rewrite was forthcoming I might not turn up for work. Of course, the guys at ICM had a fit, warning me I'd never work again and all that stuff, but where getting it right's concerned, that's never bothered me. Thankfully it didn't come to that, and the rewrites were carried through. Inevitably, Oz was the one to deal with the difficult issue of race and skin colour. It's not pleasant to say stuff like that even as a character, but it had to be addressed. If the situation had existed in Newcastle, it would have been mentioned and commented on. That's always my personal benchmark for *Auf Wiedersehen, Pet*.

The rehearsal period was strange: the old hands mingled a little awkwardly with the new boys and girls, fumbling around as we tried to feel our way back into character. The production staff gave us plenty of respectful room. Fletcher Rodley, the second assistant director, and Scott Bates, the third, looked after us well that week, and that was how it was for the duration of the shoot. Along with Dominic Fysh, the first AD, the assistant directors' department played a blinder. It helped that they all professed to liking the show. Lots of respect came our way. Maybe a bit too much at times. You could feel it in the air. It was a bit intimidating.

One rather unsettling situation occurred during rehearsal week. I had been pulled by Kevin Whately, who felt I'd given Noel Clarke, the young lad cast to play Wyman Norris, a hard time. I certainly hadn't intended to. The director, Paul Seed, came to me at one point, his lip literally trembling, to have a word in my ear about it. I was aware he'd had a heart-bypass operation so I explained to him there was no need for him to be nervous with me – there's no place for that stuff at work, or anywhere else. Maybe I'd been less gentle or diplomatic than I might have been. I have no problem giving anyone a hard time if I reckon it's merited, but I had no reason to do so with Noel as I didn't know him. I'd met him once at the read-through the week before and worked with him for all of one day so the jury was still out, but he seemed a pleasant young man. I was well aware it was difficult for him, coming into such a top-heavy show. I spoke to him and made my position clear: my beef was with Wyman, and it went back to the beginning of this third series.

After our initial story recce across most of Arizona Franc Roddam and I enjoyed a break back at the Biltmore Four Seasons Hotel. It was a beautiful place, designed by the renowned American architect Frank Lloyd-Wright. Dick and Ian flew down from LA and joined us there for storyline discussions. Over dinner and a couple of expensive bottles of red wine we wrestled with the one problem we'd not satisfactorily nailed down. How were we to deal with Gary Holton's absence? Although Gary had died, Wayne Norris, his screen character, had finished the second series very much alive and had last been seen sailing off into the sunset with the rest of the lads, bound for North Africa and uncertainty. Dick mentioned the possibility of a son, hitherto unknown to the rest of the lads, who would turn up to tie up the Wayne loose ends. We all liked that one, but what to do with the son once he'd served his purpose in the story? My suggestion was for Wyman to appear at Oz's fake wake – a plot device to bring the guys together again – and explain to the chaps that his dad had passed away. Then the wake breaks up, he's given a bed for the night by the ever-accommodating Neville – but, like father, like son, he shags one of Neville's daughters. Neville rumbles the pair and sends him packing the next day with a flea in his ear. I felt it was a clean way of dealing with the problem and would get the whole thing out of the way in the first episode. Dick and Ian didn't fancy it, and they won the day, in part, I believe, because it would allow BBC executives to point to the fact that they had a young, mixed-race character in the cast. Hooray for PC. I still feel the same about it. From the story point of view the Wyman character was woefully under-employed. Once he'd served his purpose as a plot device he was all but surplus to requirements, and everything he said or did was something the established cast could and should have been saying or doing. In the end, Noel's acting ability and his genuine on-camera warmth made it work.

Another problem surfaced in rehearsal week. Paul Seed was messing around on his hands and knees trying to get a beatbox to work. When I asked him what he was up to he said he wanted to play a piece of music. I said he needn't scrabble around on the floor like that: it was my job. I'd been contracted to supervise the show's music. Paul continued with the same routine for a few days until I pulled him about it. We sat outside the rehearsal rooms in Ealing and I explained the situation again, as I understood it. It was very simple: I was contracted to look after the music side of the production and, whether he liked it or not, that was how it was. He said that that was not what he'd been led to understand. I called Joy Spink, the producer. She came over and took Paul for a walk. On their return, he sloped off into the rehearsal room and she came over to where I was still sitting. Had the situation been made clear to Paul? I asked. It had, said Joy. I'm sure it had, but that was far from the end of the matter.

After the week of rehearsals it was time to get down to business and start doing it for the camera. The schedule read thus: first up, a couple of weeks filming in and around

London and the south-east; Middlesbrough for the whole of September; October in London; Arizona in November; three weeks at Bray Studios, Berkshire, in December. I felt a fair bit of anxiety but my first scene was to be with the mighty Bill Nighy – who would be so memorable as dodgepot Geoffrey Grainger. I'd worked with Bill on *Still Crazy*, where he'd turned in a bravura performance as the over-the-top, over-the-hill lead singer with Strange Fruit. We'd got on well so that made day one a little easier. All the same I felt terribly rusty and the weight of expectation seemed almost palpable. The best thing to do on day one is just get stuck in and get it out of the way. On a shoot of ninety filming days you can guarantee it won't ever be your best day but the fact that it's all shot out of story order usually sees to it that your first fumbling efforts are buried somewhere in the middle of the series.

The other thing I remember about that day is getting to the unit base, a pot-holed car park in Maidenhead, finding my trailer with my name on the door, going in, coming straight back out again and saying to Fletcher Rodley, 'That can't be my trailer, son. It only goes half-way down the length of the vehicle. Must be some mistake.' He reminded me of the contract agreement whereby we'd all have split trailers – i.e., semi-detached ones. Months ago I'd suggested this arrangement to save on costs and transport logistics, then forgotten about it.

Once we'd shot those first fraught couple of weeks and got ourselves off the mark it was time to move the circus to Middlesbrough. I'd forgotten how bleak it is. Dominated by the chemical plants of Zeneca ICI and all the other multinational conglomerates based up there, the sky has a permanent grey-brown colour, the result of round-the-clock discharges that seep into everything and everybody unlucky enough to come into contact with them. If you're up there you have no choice but to breathe the filthy rubbish into your lungs. I'm sure the local councils will insist the factories are all operating within EU emissions limits, but don't take my word for it or theirs. Have a trip up there and decide for yourself. Fill your lungs, rub your eyes and then make up your mind. The Geordie football fans refer to the locals as smog-monsters, due to their mutated forms, which is a bit harsh but that's football-terrace humour.

We had been put in a brand-new hotel, the Seaham Hall, and it couldn't have been more of a contrast with our grim, grimy locations twenty miles down the road. It was an amazing place, with every mod con you could imagine and quite a few you couldn't. The suites were voluminous sets of rooms with en-suite facilities as good as any I've ever come across. The lighting and music system, worked via a touch-sensitive panel on the wall, took a bit of mastering, but once you were on top of it you had total mood and modal control of your environment. The restaurant was tip-top, with great food and service to match. The hotel staff couldn't do enough for us. We had some rare old nights there and I'd recommend a visit to anyone thinking of spending time in that neck of the woods.

We were about a week into filming when the schedule blessed me with a day off. As Oz was pretty much integral to the series I was working most days so it was an unexpected treat. I decided to ask my pal Geoff Knox to drive me home to see the family and get Sue Dalgetty, my hairdresser for some twenty years, to give me a short-back-and-sides. Next morning we drove to London, arrived around midday, and made straight for the salon. When I came out it was around one o'clock. I climbed into the back of the car. Geoff told me I'd better take a look at the dash-mounted television. It was showing what I initially took to be scenes from an action movie: a commercial jet was smashing into the side of a New York skyscraper, followed by a fierce ball of flame. I remember thinking, That's pretty impressive, it looks almost real. But it couldn't have been real: it was beyond anyone's reality. Then the stunned tones of the reporters made me realize it wasn't fiction.

I got home as soon as I could – in time to see it wasn't over: a second jet ploughed into the other of the Twin Towers. We all stood together in the peace and quiet of the living room, and it was very frightening. I wondered if we were witnessing the beginning of the end. Fred was thirteen at the time, and pretty shaken by what he saw. We looked for words of comfort, but it was impossible to explain away.

The events of 11 September 2001 cast a pall over every-thing. Our piddling everyday production problems paled into comparative insignificance. No, that's wrong: there was no comparison. I was born in the 1950s and had grown up accustomed to horrific global happenings being beamed straight into the living room by the in-your-face sixties gener-ation of television news-gatherers and broadcasters. They gave it to us raw and often uncut, whether we liked it or not. International scandals like Vietnam, where kids ran burning through the streets, their skin on fire with napalm, vied for the viewers' attention with domestic tragedies, such as the Aberfan disaster, in which over a hundred Welsh children lost their lives when a slagheap engulfed their primary school. But nothing in my lifetime came even close to the dreadful sequence of events that went down on the morning of 11 September in those clear skies above New York and Washington. Like most right-thinking people the world over, the entire *Auf Wiedersehen, Pet* unit was knocked sideways, stunned, unable to take on board what had happened. After the initial shock had subsided, we realized we'd be directly affected by what had happened: we were all scheduled to fly to Arizona in a few weeks' time. We worked on in limbo, no one knowing what would transpire. I spent a lot of time in front of the telly and reading the papers, trying like everyone else to get a handle on it all, but it was impossible. How do you rationalize the actions of a group of people who want the entire population of the western world dead?

In the short-term the US government put a block on all but essential travel in and out of the USA. Everything was now in doubt. Usually when there's a problem on a shoot there's a way out of it, even if it costs a fortune; in any other circumstances I think we could have completed the shoot somewhere else, but these circumstances were unique. We couldn't relocate at that late stage: it was just not possible. If it turned out that we couldn't go to the USA, we didn't have a series. We carried on and waited to hear whether or not we had a show.

Every member of the crew had been looking forward to the US leg of the shoot. I dare say that was why some had signed on in the first place. Now it was all up in the air. No one knew what was happening and you couldn't get a firm answer out of anyone. Despondency began to creep into our chirpy team. Then we had some news. We were told to submit the names of all the crew to the US Embassy in Grosvenor Square, London. Everyone was encouraged by this until it was announced that only heads of department would be allowed to go to Arizona. More despondency. All the while we continued shooting.

Time was fast running out as we waited for a decision. Near the deadline we were told that, against all the odds and contrary to our expectations, we would be allowed to take the entire UK crew to Arizona. This was fantastic news and buoyed up the whole unit. Gary, our props man, was ecstatic, beaming, bouncing. He was already two bundles of upbeat energy, but it meant so much to him to see the job through to completion. That was how the whole unit seemed to feel.

Because of the show's history this was a prestige gig, and a lot of people had wanted to be on it. Joy Spink had done a top-notch job in selecting and putting the crew together. You're looking at and talking to the same faces for twelve hours-plus a day, six days a week. And then there are all the egos that have to be accommodated, lots of highly strung people working under the constant pressures of time, cost and quality. We're not in the business of shelling peas. At the end it has to be great: a little bit of magic has to be conjured up, so it's an art *and* a skill to get the crew balance right. Over the weeks we'd all been together, though, in the trenches, so to speak, it had become more than that: a bond develops, especially when you're away on location. You work hard and you tend to play hard. Those days are behind me, but I'll tag along once in a while, just for the crack.

It was unusual, maybe even unprecedented, for a UK production to be allowed to take its entire crew into the USA, so we all heaved a big sigh of relief, then started buying maps and planning road-trips. We spent our last UK location day before departing inside a Russian-built Ilyushin aircraft on a runway at Lydd airport in Kent. It was a horrible day. The whole thing was a compromise, from the way the scenes were shot to the time we actors were given to pull something out of the bag, which was no time at all. Some of the continuity props and costumes had already been packed and sent to the USA. Some people seemed more concerned with getting away to pack a posh bag than completing the shots we needed. Their heads were already across the Atlantic. It was like a Christmas party with no booze, one of those days when performances came a poor second to just getting the scenes shot and in the can. That was all that mattered – but I guess, ultimately, that's all that does matter. But I felt I'd been screwed and couldn't wait to get away.

I'm sure anyone who had to get on an aeroplane around that time felt at least a little uneasy, and I was no exception. I liked to have the family accompany me when I worked abroad – at least, I did until the boys grew too old to be enamoured with all the schlepping around and put their collective foot down – but not this time. I'd go alone. I flew out a week before everyone else to get settled in and sorted, but my back had been playing up. An accident in 1998, when I pinged something while carrying a pinball machine up the stairs at home, a Christmas present for the boys, had resulted in many a morning's crawling across the carpet to the bathroom. Painful spasms came and went without warning and it had been giving me gyp for months. I needed to make sure the bed, the car and the chair in my hotel room were all OK. So off I went, with bag, cards and lumbar support.

The journey on BA from London to Phoenix was an anxious ten-hour plod that seemed to last ten days. After enjoying the super-security and resultant delays you'd expect a month after 9/11, it was over to a small runway and on to a nineteen-seater prop plane for the two-hour hop to the town of Page, way up on Arizona's northern border. Before that, though, more security checks. Everyone was very nervous and you'd better not be cracking one of your lame-ass Limey jokes, because whatever national sense of humour there was had temporarily disappeared. I was made to empty out all my belongings so that the security lady, along with all my fellow travellers, could have a good squint at my kit.

'And what would you be doing going up to Page where there's nothing much except the big hydro-electric dam? An actor, huh? Making a drama series for the British Broadcasting Corporation?' Yes, madam, and there's the visa, proof, it tells you on the top. Long pause. 'Sure don't look like an actor.' Thanks for that, pet. You should see my fellow cast members!

The town of Page, Arizona, is a small place, situated on the southern shore of Lake Powell. It boasts a main street half a mile long with a few shops, a few bars and a half-dozen hotels. There's a lovely little primary school where the majority of pupils are Native American, reflecting the area's demographics. We were in the Marriott, the best place available, and it was fine. It was the low season so we had the place pretty much to ourselves and made it our own. About an hour or so down the road was Marble Canyon, one of our main locations, and beyond that, the majestic deep red ranges of the Grand Canyon. It was an incredible landscape to be in the midst of. Best of all for me was the journey to and from work each day. Because I'd had lumbar trouble getting into and out of the low-sprung and soft-seated Lincolns the production had hired for the actors' transport, I was supplied with a big, fat-wheeled Ford SUV. They may lag a long way behind the Europeans in terms of planet-friendly engines et cetera, but in terms of what Americans want and need a tool to do, they have their SUV design down to a fine art.

Long before sun-up I'd climb into the cavernous cab and fire up the big V8. Ooh, just feel that baby throb – a petrolhead's dream. I'd select Dylan's just-released *Love & Theft* album on the CD player and Bob would kick off into 'Tweedledum And Tweedledee', just as he had every other morning. You can rely on Bob: he's the man. Then it would be on to the highway for the spectacularly scenic hour's drive into Marble Canyon. I'd arrive at the unit base just as the big red sun was coming up. Same in reverse on the way home. The sun's long shadows turned the landscape into something resembling another planet. Indeed, the dirt and cactus scrub looks so convincingly alien that film-makers regularly make the trek from LA to use the area for just this purpose. The *Planet of the Apes* production had been there not long before us, shooting their exteriors. I found listening to Bob's songs in those surroundings a much more potent, relevant, affecting experience. Makes sense, I suppose: America and Americans are what the songs are all about.

The wondrous settings had an equally wondrous effect on the cast and crew but, sadly, not on the filming process. Our director and the director of production didn't seem to communicate with each other a great deal, and the end-result was that the camera was almost never allowed any movement. We shot everything on tripods – or legs, as they're known. This old-fashioned style of shooting is highly unusual nowadays, if not obsolete, and with an ensemble piece such as ours, top-heavy with cast, moving the camera would have made the thing not only much more dynamic and enjoyable from an acting point of view, but infinitely more achievable from a scheduling standpoint.

This thing of not moving the camera really bugged me. I had asked Paul Seed about it many times and he would always say it just wasn't his style. Fair enough, I suppose. The problem was, the piece cried out for camera moves, for dynamics, for a bit of visual ambition. Having witnessed the sumptuous reality of our surroundings I was hoping we'd have some breathtaking shots, but when I saw the end-result it was such a letdown. It looked at times as if we'd locked off the camera and shot a postcard. I suppose it might be argued that, as this show is first and foremost a character-driven piece, and ultimately the series was a great success, it didn't much matter how it looked. Another case of what might have been.

Life for a teetotal actor on location can be boring. Thrills are few. Next to bumping into Gary the props man in a Flagstaff tattoo parlour and almost getting a tattoo, one of the most exciting things I came across while I was stationed in Page was the local Ralph Lauren retailer. I'm a big fan and I didn't expect to find lots of it out there in the wilds, but I was pleasantly surprised at the wide choice on offer, and thrilled by the prices. Everything was reduced! Jeans were twenty-five dollars! Jackets were forty! This was no out-of-date swag, either: all the garments were for the current season. Never able to resist a bargain, I bought a load of kit, including a fantastic pair of dark blue all-weather trousers for the give-away price of twenty-five dollars. That's fifteen quid, almost too cheap. When I asked the lady who owned the place how come the prices were so ridiculously low, she told me with a shrug that, around those parts, at that time of the year, the autumn, people simply weren't willing to pay any more, so that was that: you either marked it down or watched it gather dust. Strike one for consumer power. I bet it doesn't catch on over here. I still have most of that stuff and I wear it all the time. The all-weather strides I particularly love. Can't wait for some awful weather so's I can pull 'em on and get out there.

Because a state of national emergency was in place, I was arrested on suspicion of being a terrorist while walking near the Lake Powell dam one balmy evening. The locals were jittery: they constantly feared yet more terrorist attacks, and wild rumours were fanned by the nightly TV news broadcasts, some of them downright irresponsible. The whole country was on a knife-edge; the police and the armed forces were super-sensitive. Patrol cars and military vehicles cruised the highways day and night. For me, coming from the UK, it was oppressive. I was half-way across the dam when a loud-hailer ordered the person on the footpath, which had to be me as there was no one else around at the time, to step over the low guardrail that separated the path from the road, then remain still. I did exactly as I had been ordered. No time to be playing smart-Alecs. A young cop got out of a patrol car, his gun already drawn. Over he came, gingerly. What was my business on the bridge at that time of night, he wanted to know. I said I was out for a walk. He asked to see some ID. I explained I wasn't carrying any as I was staying at the Marriott just up the road and had decided to take a walk under the stars after dinner to breathe the fresh clean air and give my food, Mexican and very heavy, an opportunity to go down. He radioed my name, along with that of the Marriott, to his control and a long moment later they cleared me. He offered his best wishes and bade me goodbye.

We were made aware of an impending meteor shower, the like of which wouldn't be seen again for at least another sixty years, so I decided to check it out and took the SUV to the dam in the late evening. I parked up, switched off the lights and clambered up on to the roof, there to await the evening's entertainment. I waited. And waited. And waited. Nothing at all for at least an hour. Now, if this had been the UK I would have given up and buggered off back to my digs, doubting the accuracy of our Met Office. But in my experience the Yanks tend to get their predictions right in matters like this, so I decided to stick it out a little longer, and thank goodness I did. The show began with a single lateral streak high across the sky, so quick I wondered if I'd imagined it. A moment later, there was another, and then two together, then a couple more, slightly lower this time, then more, and more, and more until the black Arizona sky seemed filled with rocket-sized fireworks. Act of God or natural phenomenon, whatever it was I take my hat off to its magical wonder. Walt Disney might have put together a night sky such as that. The only downer was that I was watching it all on my own. I really felt I should have been with Miriam so we could have enjoyed it together.

Lack of camera movement apart, those five weeks spent filming in the wilds of Arizona were really enjoyable. The scenic splendour played its part, of course, but for me it was mostly to do with working with the *Auf Wiedersehen, Pet* regulars, a cast-iron cast who'd become my close friends over the years. Tim Spall was my closest buddy, but we all had a lot of fun together, shooting the breeze, catching up with each other and, of course, acting together. People often talk about there being a special bond between the actors on long-running series or shows, but I've never known anything like the thing we share. It's hard to define or even describe but it's to do with respect and love. Real love. I'd bet it's a similar thing between the England football team of 1966. We don't all see eye to eye politically or philosophically. We don't hang out together when we're not shooting. But something ties us together: it's strong and it runs deep. Spall reckons there's an *esprit de corps* about the *Auf Wiedersehen, Pet* cast like no other. It's the show I've most enjoyed working on as an actor. Usually making television drama is either a pain, plain hard graft, or grief.

There was a general feeling of magic among the cast and crew about our time over in Arizona where we felt we were part of something special. One incident stands out. We were shooting a sequence of scenes in Marble Canyon late one afternoon with a big crowd of Native Americans all kitted out in their ceremonial feathers, paint and beads. There were about sixty people in all, and as we stood in a wide circle our characters were given a traditional welcome by the Chocinaw tribe's medicine man, Saginaw. With a wizened face that made him look older than God, Saginaw was a real medicine man, a friend of Franc and godfather to his daughter, Ithaka. He was an amazing guy, mystical and special. As the sun disappeared behind the western edges of the canyon he slowly made his way around the inside of the circle, nodding, shuffling his feet to the beat of the talking drum, incanting, high-pitched, in his own language and wafting smoke from a smouldering sage plant. The effect was mesmeric. Dominic, our first AD, called quietly for the camera to be cut. The filming stopped. We had our scene in the can but no one moved away for fear of breaking the spell. We were in the midst of something that had transcended scripted words and actors' reactions and we all wanted to be a continuing part of it and savour every moment. So on it went, with us standing stock-still and Saginaw making his way around the inside of the circle. Then it was over, the sun had gone and the fires we'd stood in front of were little more than embers.

I remember shivering, but not because I was cold. A few other people did the same. It was an elemental thing. A spontaneous round of applause rippled around the circle. Nothing remotely like that had ever happened to me before. As I was preparing to make my way back to the hotel, Saginaw came over and gave me the sage plant. He told me I should use it only if there was a big life problem and I needed the power of good medicine. I have it at home, haven't needed it yet, but I wouldn't rule it out.

Saginaw gave me another gift, a baseball cap he'd designed for the Navajo tribe with an unusual and distinctive feather-motif woven on the front just above the peak. I'm not one for baseball caps as a rule but I loved that one and wore it all the time until it went walkies from my trailer up at

Luton Hoo while we were filming the fourth series of *Auf Wiedersehen, Pet*.

It was while we were in Page that the prospect of a fourth series was mooted. The BBC had already let it be known that they were thrilled with what was already in the can and wanted to know how I felt about making some more. I was up to the eyes with acting and music supervision duties but it was exciting to know that, back in W12, someone wanted to carry on with the project. Where in the world should we next send our intrepid team of international grafter-garglers? It would have to be somewhere pretty special to beat the Grand Canyon.

Franc had told me the BBC would like us to go to Australia, as they had a co-production deal with a TV channel down there and would be able to offset the potentially massive budget. Australia did nothing for me as a shooting location, left me flat, didn't excite or inspire me one bit. Viewers have become used to seeing series go down there on the flimsiest excuse. It looks like nothing more than a jolly for the actors and execs and makes for pretty flat television. No offence, cobbers, I'd loved the place as a holiday destination, but for *Auf Wiedersehen, Pet*, our boys and our audience, I was sure we could do better. So where did I think we should go to? the BBC asked politely, if a little impatiently.

My fancy was the Caribbean: there was drama aplenty out there, what with the South American drug cartels using whole islands as their staging posts, the Yardies, poverty, pirating and the rest – the other side of the coin to those Bounty commercials. It also had one more important advantage over Australia: if someone was taken ill they could be back in London, courtesy of Concorde, in just over four hours. More than one person on the team had been seriously ill so this mattered.

We set our minds to finding a good reason for our chaps to be in the Caribbean. I suggested they could be out there initially rebuilding after a hurricane. Not bad. Then Ian called from LA. How about Cuba? As soon as he said it I knew it was the right place. It had everything we needed and more: it had Spanish colonial mansions falling to bits, it had a people's revolution *in situ*. Best of all, it had Fidel! I got very excited at the prospect. Cuba! Could we be the first people since 1959 to be allowed in to make a television drama series? And we hadn't even finished the Arizona one!

But it was almost December, almost Christmas. We'd nearly done. Just another three weeks at Bray and that would be it. Where had the time gone? All too soon the Arizona shoot came to an end. We packed, said goodbye to the locals and headed to the airport for the short hop down to Phoenix. On the way, I stopped off at the school and gave the head-mistress a Sony beatbox I'd bought on arrival – I couldn't be bothered to cart it home. It wasn't much, but they were knocked out and made an awful fuss.

Later, sitting slumped in a deep armchair in the darkened, cavernous Phoenix International business lounge, I drank tonic water as the television news blared out its endless noise. Then, at the top of the hour, came some news that shook me. The newscaster said the world was in mourning following the death of Beatle George Harrison.

Ian had told me George was close to death when he'd called to suggest going to Cuba, but that news bulletin was still a shock, and I feel the same today. It wasn't just that I'd been lucky enough to know George as a pal for a while – although that was fab – but I'd got to meet, know and hang out with one of my heroes, one of the world's heroes, a Beatle, the Quiet One. He'd been everything you could have hoped for in a hero and much more. He was truly a beautiful human being. All things must pass, as George sang, but if there's a beyond, and he firmly believed there was, it will be the better for having his loving soul within it. 'Isn't it a pity? Isn't it a shame?' Yes, it is. It's our loss, but we have his musical legacy.

The first three weeks of December were taken up with shooting on that same sound stage at Bray studios where, almost a decade earlier, Geoff Knox and I had sat on the fire-escape stairs as guests of George. I'm a sentimental person at the best of times and it was tough finishing up there.

By the end of the shoot, everyone was on their knees, but there was still the feeling that we had turned in something special. It kept us all going. On the penultimate day, I found Joy Spink collapsed in a heap on the floor of her office. I put her into my dressing-room bed then I ran off to find help. Battle fatigue. On the final day Tim Healy and I came near to blows, but it passed. We were just frazzled. Then it was over.

The word in the press was mostly positive, though one or two were predictably sniffy about our return. Everyone involved with the show was fairly confident, but we'd been away for a long time – a lifetime in viewing terms. Tastes had changed in the twenty years since those first bricks and insults. Nothing could be taken for granted. We wondered if we would get an audience at all. The BBC programme schedulers had decided to screen *Auf Wiedersehen, Pet* at nine p.m. on a Sunday evening, which I thought was a big mistake. I thought mid-week would be its best home, and that Sunday was the God-slot. Just shows how much I know. *The Forsyte Saga*, ITV's glossy flagship drama, was airing at exactly the same time: it was a period drama with lots of lust and intrigue, low-cut dresses and moody glances, chalk to our cheese.

You'd be hard-pushed to think of a better example of two polar opposites in drama. They'd had a two-week jump on us, time to establish themselves in the viewers' consciousness. So we all held our breath and waited for the ratings figures to come in.

We needn't have worried. The overnight ratings for episode one were thirteen million, similar to what we were getting in the good old days before the advent of Sky and cable, and almost unheard-of in present terms. We weren't just thrilled, we were shocked. It seemed too good to be true. However, it was only week one. The test would be whether we could hold those figures through the run. A popular Sunday broadsheet wondered, rather sarcastically, what the viewing figures would be by week four, when all the media hullabaloo had died down. They turned out to be twelve million. I had to smile.

I sat and watched the show on television like everyone else. No matter how many times you may have seen a piece of work before, there's something different about seeing it on the telly for the first time, hearing the tones of the anonymous announcer as he or she tells the nation this is it, here it is, you're on. It also enables you to see the thing in context, surrounded by other programmes, and get an idea of how good or bad it really is. Despite my concerns about its visual shortcomings and last-minute score, I thought our series stacked up just fine. But what were we in terms of categorization? Predictable headlines were trotted out – 'National Treasure' and 'Britain's Favourite Brickies'. These were twenty-year-old phrases that hadn't even been original the first time round. I've concluded we inhabit a place all our own somewhere between *Last of the Summer Wine* and *The Wild Bunch*. That'll do me. Not a bad place to be.

2 2

After the runaway success of the series I was looking to spend an idyllic few months at home resting, relaxing, basking in all the glory, and hoping to land a lucrative commercial. The old days when the entertainment industry regarded doing a television commercial as selling out, the domain of the desperate and certain career death, were long gone. Commercial realities, along with stars like Rowan Atkinson and his wonderful turns in the Barclays Bank commercials, had seen to that. No joy there, though. Instead I spent the entire summer bringing libel actions against thirteen different newspapers, magazines and individuals, some of them powerful corporations, stemming from the show's re-emergence and new-found popularity. I won them all, but it's taken two long years and a lot of grief.

The trip I'd made to Havana in January, to meet up with Franc, then Dick and Ian, to look for a suitable storyline, had been of the usual order, sometimes incredible, sometimes unbearable. I hadn't wanted to go as I'd arranged to spend a week or so hanging out with Brian Johnson, an old mate from Newcastle and the singer with AC/DC, who lives in sun-kissed Sarasota, Florida, but Franc felt it essential that I was along for the ride to add the required grit. I went to Florida for about ten days, the beautiful Keys, which my dad had visited sixty years previously during the Second World War, while he was serving temporarily with the US Navy, then flew to Havana from Miami via Mexico. You can't do it direct – even with journalistic clearance, which I had. As far as Uncle Sam's concerned Cuba is still the bad guy, Fidel the bandit. An entire day was devoted to and wasted on unnecessary air travel. I was met at the airport by Irene Prado Capo, the Cuban government's cultural representative charged with chaperoning us for the duration of our trip. Anything we wanted to know, we were just to ask Irene. Anywhere we wanted to go, we had just to ask Irene. *No problema.* Just ask. Which in effect meant we couldn't go anywhere or do anything without first asking Irene, couldn't make a move without Irene's knowledge, consent and accompaniment. Unintentionally I caused Irene to burst into floods of tears in the mini-bus one day when I asked her if she was a spy. Turned out she was. Bit of a giveaway. The hotel phones sometimes clicked before you'd put them down.

When I met up with Franc at the hotel he informed me of Dick and Ian's intention to stay for only four days instead of the pencilled eight or nine. Apparently they had other commitments they couldn't move. We'd not even started work and the plan was already under pressure. Four days. Time would be tight, so we got stuck in. We kicked some stuff around but it wasn't going anywhere special, and we were flapping a bit. We needed a spark, something that would fire us all up.

We did the cigar factory and the nightclub, the sugar cane plantation and the ballet, accompanied at all times by the lovely if occasionally tearful Irene. The ballet was incredible. We were allowed to sit in on a dress rehearsal, with full orchestra, of *Don Quixote*. The dancers were sublime and the musicians magnificent, but what made it all the more moving was that their costumes were threadbare, as were the auditorium's sad old seats. Yet there was no self-pity, only dignity and pride. It brought tears to my eyes.

As we left the auditorium I had an idea about Oz and a prima ballerina. Could there be a romance between the two? Beauty and the Beast? We travelled across town in the local transport, bright orange two-seater scooter taxis with Outspan-shaped outer cowlings for protection. Franc and I were in one, Dick and Ian in another. I told our young female driver that if she got us to our destination before Dick and Ian we'd give her twenty dollars. That was a mistake. There followed a hair-raisingly fast journey across town, which we won. It was a blast.

In no time at all (four days!) it was time to head home, and we had little to go with. We had one last jaunt scheduled, a visit to the British Embassy, where we were to be welcomed by the ambassador, and then it was off to pack a bag and argue about the hotel bill with the receptionists. The visit was a scream, dafter and more clichéd than anything you see in sitcoms. On our arrival we were led into a huge room containing a big table and a dozen flunkeys and spooks. Over to one side there was another, much smaller table, on which sat cans of beer and Coke. A sugar bowl contained Twiglets. I asked if I could have a cup of tea. Once they'd stopped laughing and twigged I actually did want a cuppa it caused no end of consternation. Someone, no doubt of lowly rank, was despatched to sort it out. Some fifteen minutes later I got my cuppa, all milky and tepid. During that time I'd learned a lot more than I'd ever wanted to know about the assembled bunch.

Eventually it was time to go, thank goodness. After we'd thanked the gang of Brits, which had included Richard Bebbington, an ex-ICI employee who is now working part-time as the British consul in Finland, we made our way to the foyer and out into the sunshine and fresh air. I happened to comment on the immaculate stucco exterior of the embassy to the head of Security and asked him who they entrusted with such work. He told me the outside of the building was done by CubaCon, a local company, but for security reasons all internal works were the responsibility of the OED. Then the driver was calling: we had to go. Dick, Ian and Franc drifted towards the big main gates. But this was the first potentially interesting thing I'd come across all day. What was the OED? I asked. Our mini-bus driver was tooting his horn now. Head of Security told me OED stood for Overseas Estates Department. A young lady, Susannah Payne, from Hexham, asked if she could be of help in her capacity as second secretary. I asked her whom we could talk to about the workings of the OED. She told me they were based in Croydon. The driver was calling me now. I was in danger of capsizing our travel plans. Susannah gave me her card and promised to e-mail me the details.

The Overseas Estates Department is charged with the maintenance of government buildings all over the world, and sends top-notch tradesmen and -women to all corners of the globe. These workers are in a sort of grey area whereby they aren't fully protected by diplomatic immunity but they are representing the government abroad, and have to sign the Official Secrets Act. Susannah helped arrange for us to visit their offices in Croydon and it was a revelation. After the rigmarole of signing in we were escorted to the twentieth floor where we were introduced to three of the men whose job it was to run this mysterious department. In a past life they'd all been civil engineers. Now, dressed in regulation dark suits, they made an odd trio behind their big conference table. Crucially, they were all fans of the show. There was immediate goodwill, common ground, and we soon relaxed.

After tea and small-talk we got down to it. I explained I had an idea for a storyline I'd like to tell them about and we'd appreciate their reaction to it. It was probably nuts, I said, unworkable, but if they'd pay us the courtesy of listening to it they could shoot it full of holes once we'd done. It wouldn't take long. I started off on my idea, with Franc filling in bits and pieces as we went. Ten minutes later we'd finished. The three suits sat there for a moment, then they laughed. One said, 'It's as if you'd worked in the department for twenty years!' Our little idea was right on the money. In fact, the stuff we thought might be too preposterous turned out to be anything but. They gave us the low-down on the way it all worked, with incidents, anecdotes, stories and scandals. I couldn't believe what we were being told.

Outside, I looked at Franc. We were like a couple of kids. We both knew this was paydirt, absolute gold. We'd just been given a template for as many *Auf Wiedersehen, Pet*s as we ever wanted to make. No need to worry about dreaming up a plausible dramatic reason to get the brickies out to wherever we wanted them to go. Via the OED we could legitimately send them anywhere in the world. I did a little dance on the Croydon pavement.

Next job was to put it all down on paper. This was no problem as the guys over at Croydon had given us so much wonderful source material. A week later, after clearing it with Franc and making sure he was happy, I sent e-mails to Laura Mackie at the BBC and Dick Clement in LA. Along with my cover note was a five-page beat-sheet containing an outline of the Croydon info. A week or two later Dick sent back a draft storyline for me to have a look at. It was strong and read well, but there were one or two points I wasn't happy with. My concerns were to do with plot credibility. I often steer too close to the naturalistic side of things but that was what Franc had asked me to bring to this particular party – a dose of reality. I went through it with Franc then e-mailed

Dick and Ian with my suggestions. Soon we were all happy and the thing was moving at a pace.

For a long time it had been touch and go as to whether we'd be able to film in Cuba. Nothing like that had been allowed since Castro seized power in 1959. In terms of achievement it would be a real coup. The BBC were given permission for us to go on a recce, then to proceed with our plans for production. Everything was looking rosy and we were buzzing at the prospect of pulling it off. Then, two weeks before we were due to set off and without any consideration for the hard work we'd put in, George W. Bush and Tony Blair declared war on Saddam Hussein's Iraq. As far as making the show went, it wasn't the greatest thing that could have happened.

Post-9/11, Cuba was high on the Bush administration's list of states and regimes that sponsored terrorism. Washington made no secret of its burning desire to do something about this perennial thorn in its side and was threatening to deploy US forces down there. This was at exactly the same time as orange-suited and manacled terrorist suspects were being held in cages by the Americans at their military base in Guantanamo Bay – situated on the south-eastern coast of Cuba. If anyone can figure that one out I'd like to know how it works. Havana told the BBC that any friend of George W. was an enemy of Cuba and that was that.

I was given the news at ICM by Chrissy Skinns, our newly appointed producer, and went away to mull it over. There were two alternatives and not much time: we could move over to the nearest available Caribbean island, which was the Dominican Republic, or we could cancel. For a while I favoured the latter option. Never mind the Dominican Republic, there was nowhere on earth that resembled Havana with its wonderfully faded, multi-coloured Spanish colonial villas and architecture, its wacky 1960s eastern-bloc buildings, its massive Che Guevara murals, its people, its history and the unique sense that time had stood still for five decades. It was such a let-down. On the other hand, an awful lot of work had gone into the project, and the design team felt they could convincingly re-create Havana in Santo Domingo. I had my doubts but I thought, Let's give it a try. Hopefully the worst we'd end up with would be a well-made show that didn't look 100 per cent authentic. We'd be in for one or two letters and sniffy reviews. A compromise, for sure, and by no means perfect, but in these days of grey, drab telly I could live with that.

Me and my lumbar cushions arrived in the Dominican Republic after a ten-hour BA flight from London to Miami, a four-hour stop-off and then a four-hour hop down to Santo Domingo. By then my back was giving me terrible gyp. It had started up a few weeks earlier and I could hardly get in and out of bed. More worryingly, it was going to impact on my ability to perform. I wondered if I'd be able to do anything at all, so bad was the pain. After an MRI scan had shown up no sign of bone or disc damage I'd been to see the top chap in Harley Street. He'd administered steroid injections: local anaesthetic followed by a great big needle into the end of my spine. It was all of ten minutes before the syringe was empty. The procedure was painful and unpleasant.

Worse: a week later I was still in great pain. I was getting desperate. I'd requested the Santo Domingo production office to organize an osteopath for me and was relieved to learn, on arrival at the hotel, that the island's best practitioner was coming out to see me. A lady turned up and introduced herself as Isis Martinez, manual therapist. Little did I know she would be my saviour.

Isis explained to me, in her sweet broken English, that she had never before made a trip like this to treat anyone, especially a man. People might get the wrong idea, you understand, as to what she was offering. I explained to her that even if I got the wrong idea I was in so much pain I'd be incapable of doing much about it. She didn't laugh. With her dark look and gruff manner, I thought maybe she was a dyke. She examined me, asking me to bend forward slowly. When I told her about my Harley Street jabs, she shuddered. After a while she pronounced her diagnosis. I was suffering neither from disc nor bone trouble. The problem was ligament damage. And, wait for it, she was going to fix me. Somewhat sceptical, I explained she was flying in the face of the best Harley Street doctoring that money could buy. She tut-tutted and shook her head disdainfully.

It turned out Isis was no dyke. She was a warm, lovely woman with a sixteen-year-old son. And just over two weeks later she had indeed fixed my back. It was not far short of miraculous and, although I was not quite 100 per cent, I was able to complete the location work and the rest of the shoot in the UK. I'm still pain-free, touch wood. Anyone who's suffered a back problem understands how thoroughly it affects your life. It's debilitating, sickening, the absolute pits, and you'd pay any amount to get yourself sorted. I am eternally grateful to Isis for blessing me with her healing gifts. Although I'm not a believer in specific destiny things, I did wonder about the sequence of events that led me to Isis. Had there been no conflict in Iraq, I would have been in Cuba and she and I would never have met. I might still be hobbling around. Life's a miracle indeed.

By any standards the Dominican Republic is very poor. I always feel a twinge of guilt on seeing the plight of those around me when I'm away on location somewhere, taking visual advantage of their lot; I usually assuage it by reminding myself that I'm spreading around a bit of moolah, which is true. Outside the capital, which itself was dirt-poor in many places, things got really rough. Most families had no more than a flimsy one-room wooden shack with a corrugated-tin roof. No doors. No floor other than the earth. Yet the pride the local people took in their humble belongings and surroundings was humbling. Most impressive of all, the kids were always immaculately turned out for school, their hair neatly combed or braided. Just how and where they ironed shirts and blouses was a mystery.

As desperate as it was, the locals didn't seem to resent their lot. They looked upon the jungle, with its plentiful supply of bananas, coconuts, exotic fruits and vegetables, as their back garden. Mind you, they were much better off than their neighbours, the Haitians. The Dominican Republic's inhabitants were predominantly of Mediterranean stock, and the Haitians were of African descent. Their difference in appearance set the many Haitian immigrants apart and the indigenous people tended to look down on them as second-class citizens. According to my driver, Ariel, there was no love lost between the two peoples.

The only thing I knew about Haiti was that it was off-limits to foreigners. The beautiful, lush island of Hispaniola had first been discovered and settled by Christopher Columbus, whose son became its first governor. Now it was home to two different nations, separated by a border running roughly from north to south. The French-speaking Republic of Haiti occupies about a third of the island to the west of the border and the Spanish-speaking Dominican Republic accounts for the rest. According to the CIA website Haiti has a population of around eight million to the Dominican Republic's sixteen million. There is no economic infrastructure, no national export, no tourism industry. How does the place survive? As a staging post for drugs, it would seem. As a result of the Colombian drug cartels' all-pervading influence the place is all but lawless, and extremely dangerous: unrecognized visitors are often being dragged from their cars and shot. Nobody went there other than those up to no good. We were under strict instruction not to visit. This normally acts for me like a red rag to a bull but Ariel did a good job convincing me of the folly of any such adventure. He and others told me something else about the place. There were zombies there. Real zombies. Not like the ones depicted since the 1920s in Hollywood movies that are fond of bursting out of the earth to go looking for new bandages. These are people kept under the spell of witch doctors. Apparently a certain species of fish, found only in the coastal waters of Haiti, is caught, dried and ground into powder by the local witch doctors. When given to unfortunates in drink or sprinkled over food, it renders them semi-comatose. Repeated doses keep them in a trance-like state. True? Maybe. Or maybe they were all just stoned. I'm inclined to believe Ariel.

It was very hot, usually in the nineties throughout the day and the high eighties at night. Then there was the humidity. Within a minute of stepping outside an air-con zone you and your clothing were soaked. I'd visited the Caribbean on holiday many times but not to work. I didn't mind the conditions, but the sun-block was another matter: to prevent continuity problems, we were issued with factor 1000. Duck fat. It was quite a sight, all those greasy actors reclining by the hotel pool.

Because it was all a little last-minute, the shoot kicked off without the usual thorough preparation necessary for the success of an ambitious venture such as ours, and it soon showed. Organizationally it was a shambles, and partly because there was no real film infrastructure on the island: other than the odd commercial nothing much happened there. So we muddled along from day one. Location food was a good example. Four times in the first week of filming, over a period of six days, I arrived on location after a forty-five-minute drive to be informed there was no food left. The location caterers, a lovely bunch of people, were restaurateurs and had no experience in film-industry catering. On one memorable morning the boss pulled the lid off one of the big metal serving trays with a flourish and a smile, rather as a magician might reveal a rabbit, only there was no rabbit, or anything else, for that matter. All gone, he said, with a satisfied smile. I ended up sending Ariel for some sandwiches. It happened all too often.

There was real cause for concern with the action vehicles. The production needed to fill the streets with the type of colourful 1950s American gas-guzzlers you still see in Cuba. It wasn't easy as there weren't many on the island – in fact, there weren't many decent cars of any kind, vintage or modern. The Dominican Republic is a very poor country, rotten with corruption. It ran from top to bottom. I witnessed an example one day in the business lounge bar of the hotel. An official from the Department of Tourism and a Russian businessman, who had the deepest voice I've ever heard other than Paul Robeson's, sat two metres away from me discussing deals, developments and kickbacks over omelettes and vodka. The amounts being bandied about were in the millions of dollars. Maybe I should have asked them if they could sort us out some decent vintage cars. As it was we were lumbered with tired-out old dogs, which looked all right as set dressing but were good for not much else. We must have lost hours while they were pushed and pulled into place. On one occasion a continuity vehicle, one of two identical trucks, didn't turn up for an all-night shoot. Cue pacing up and down, pulling of hair and expletives. When the owner was eventually tracked down he said he didn't know which of the two vehicles we wanted so he'd thought it best not to bring either.

A BBC insurance assessor came out from London. I was glad to see him. He immediately condemned one of the action vehicles, a pick-up truck, declaring it unsafe and highly dangerous. No brakes to speak of. This after Tim Healy had been driving it up and down the set for the best part of a day with us perched on the back. Not that this would have deterred the locals. I've never been anywhere like it in terms of both how and what they drove. For the likes of us, used to new cars, the state of the motors over there was hard to believe. Forget safety, MOTs and emissions controls and think instead total corrosion, sticky tape and choking filthy fumes.

The filming was a bit off-kilter for the first three weeks because Tim Spall was tied up in New Zealand with Tom Cruise on *The Last Samurai*. Big-budget with locations world-wide, it was overrunning and Tim was delayed. He ended up joining us direct from finishing down there. He'd not been home for something like eight months. Not healthy, that. Once he'd joined us it felt like the beast had all its limbs again and we began slowly to resemble the well-oiled ensemble of old. I'm not the biggest fan of the filming process from the actor's point of view: I find the waiting around unbearable. Reading a book doesn't work for me as I need to be tuned into what I'm about to do, not detached from it. The same goes for a snooze. For me it becomes one long waiting game and if I'm not occupied I end up getting involved with all the mini-dramas and distractions that tend to bedevil a shoot.

Or I used to. Now I'm better at ignoring stuff that doesn't really concern me.

We had some fun out in the jungle, but most days it was just plain hard slog. I'd be up around four forty-five a.m. to leave the hotel an hour later. After an always-eventful drive I'd arrive at the unit base around seven, to get changed, made up and, if my luck was in, fed. Ready to rehearse on set for either seven thirty or eight. Shoot till one p.m. Lunch till two. Back to the set, rehearse and shoot till seven. Get changed and head back to the hotel, arriving around nine. By the time I'd taken a pummelling from Isis, it would be gone ten o'clock. Order a snack, go over tomorrow's lines while waiting for it to arrive. In bed by eleven. Book an alarm call, set the alarm on the bedside clock as a back-up. Lights out. The next day, run the whole routine again. Six days a week for six weeks.

And on the seventh day you rest, right? Maybe in biblical times, but they weren't making television series in those days, so you do your washing, make your calls home, always a pain with connections and the time differences, and that's about all you have time for. As usual, I missed the family terribly. The boys, being teenagers, aren't nearly as interested in shooting the breeze with their dad as they used to be.

'But you're paid a bloody fortune!' I hear you cry, and there's no denying we're lucky in that respect. I'm just pointing up the mundane, draggy nature of the daily routine that is filming. Glamorous? Yeah, right.

It was lovely to see Spall at long last. His arrival brought joy to the set and the business lounge bar. He's such a funny man, and since his illness he's become even more irreverent. Having known him before, I wouldn't have thought this possible. He's not a bad actor, either. It's always fun to be in scenes with Tim, and sometimes it's nothing short of thrilling. It's a treat just to watch him at close quarters as he does his thing. Once or twice I've made the mistake of thinking, Nah, that's not going to work, only to see it later on, in the context of the piece as a whole, and realize I was well wrong. He's a man at the top of his game. The show is lucky to have him at its heart. For me he is the jewel in the *Auf Wiedersehen, Pet* crown, but for a long time it looked as if we'd have to do that series without him. He didn't fancy another five months reprising boring Barry the Brummie and knocking out six hours of UK television, no matter how good the scripts. Who can blame him? If your choices happen to include working with some of the world's top movie actors and directors, which would you plump for? In the end, Tim chose to do another *Auf Wiedersehen, Pet* and we were all glad to have him back on board. We couldn't have done without him. But his other commitments made our job a scheduling struggle.

I was incredibly lucky with the bugs and the mozzies. The once-a-week anti-malarial pills were no fun, resulting in double vision and dizziness among other things, and the daily dousing in what smelt and tasted like kerosene was a real stomach-churner, but I wasn't bitten once in the entire six weeks I was out there. I must have been the only member of the production to get away with it. Poor Justine Luxton, our lovely, gifted costume designer, was poorly almost before we'd started. It turned out she'd contracted dengue, a thoroughly unpleasant mosquito-borne virus. Justine has a fair complexion and the mark left around the spot where the insect had bitten her was awful. It looked as though it would be there for good, but things could have been worse: dengue fever, a more aggressive strain of the same virus, can be fatal.

As a result of the heavy schedule I had only one opportunity to flee the capital and enjoy the island's beautiful beaches and clear blue seas. Rather surprisingly, the best beaches were to be found on the island's north coast, facing the Atlantic. Smack in the middle of the shoot I had three whole days free, so Kevin, Chris, the two Tims and I were driven to the resort of Punta Cana on the easternmost tip of the island. Not only was it a Bounty-bar paradise with palm trees and white sand, the complex was all but deserted so we had the place to ourselves. From our beachside cabanas it was a few paces across the sand to the ocean's edge. After a golf-buggy ride through tropical grounds we were dropped off at our digs and we all immediately stripped off, donned our swimmies and got into that glimmering water. Kevin and I were a little further from the shore than the others, standing chest-deep in beautiful warm gentle waves when a shoal of glistening gold flying fish, scores of them, appeared from nowhere and swam, leaped, sparkled and splashed their way past us, around us, straight through us, it seemed to me. In an instant they were gone. The others missed it completely.

After a shambles of a journey from Santo Domingo via New York to London, we began the latter stages of the shoot at the beginning of June. We spent six weeks on location in and around London and the South East, and five weeks on the sound stages at Pinewood Studios in Buckinghamshire. It was a long, arduous shoot and by the end, in mid-August, I was wiped out, mentally and physically exhausted, and felt I never wanted to do another day's filming in my life. Unlike a lot of people who tend to react to the end of a long filming stint as they would a bereavement, I'm always ecstatic that it's over, that we've managed it without murder or mishap and that it's in the can. I guess it's proof, if proof were needed, that I don't like the filming aspect of what I do. I don't like being in the middle of all those people and their knowing my day-to-day business. I don't know if I'd feel the same had I not fallen into this line of work all those years ago, but it's my guess I would. I'm basically a private person who likes to keep himself to himself. I prefer pottering about at home with a newspaper and a cup of tea. However, Miriam's always reckoned I'm good for about a month and then I go stir-crazy. In the past I would have agreed with that, but I'm not so sure these days. Making programmes matters less and less to me.

The up-side of this adventure was working with the show's directors, Maurice Phillips and David Innes Edwards. Maurice was new to me and it's always a worry as to how people you don't know will be. Will their thoughts, ideas, aims and ambitions for the project correspond with your own? On a more basic level, will you get on with them over a five-month filming period? Maurice turned out to be gifted, laid-back and, most important of all, very likeable. I'd known Dave from when he'd worked as a first assistant director on the *Spender* series a decade earlier. A big fellow, he tends to suffer from people assuming wrongly that size is somehow linked with subtlety. Not so. They were both great men to work with, had a sense of humour similar to mine, and time spent with either or both of them on the floor was always enjoyable, never a chore. Though we occasionally disagreed on points of interpretation, I trusted their judgement implicitly. They were ambitious for the series, wanted to take it on to the next level. Best of all, they moved the bloody camera!

When I got back to London, it wasn't long before we were bereaved. Jack, Miriam's dad, had been terminally ill for some time and wasn't expected to live as long as he did. He'd had a severe stroke twenty years earlier and had been all but incapacitated. Having started off as a scene painter, he'd ended up running the entire BBC Light Entertainment Department in Wales and was responsible for a lot of successful programming, including the first Welsh-language soap, *Pobl y Cwm*, which is still going strong today. It was heartbreaking to watch a man who'd been so articulate struggle to say a single syllable, but it meant I could say goodbye to him, which was important for me, and let him know everything would be all right with the rest of the family. I reassured him I'd always look after Miriam. He nodded, then said, 'Nice to hear, though.' Jack was a wonderful man and is greatly missed by us all.

It was time to get stuck into organizing the house renovations and the *Sunday Night For Sammy* concerts we now stage every other year. I'm not sure which was the more traumatic, but I do know which was the more expensive, by a long way. We had a ball: Brian Johnson did a guest spot, and this year alone we raised over £100,000. Not bad for a daft Geordie, eh?

23

'Thank fuck that's finished!' That was my overriding reaction to the nice people at Penguin finally telling me, 'No more. That's enough.' Other, more complicated feelings have since kicked in, but after fifteen months of almost daily slog I still feel an overwhelming relief at having got the thing down and done. In taking on the writing myself, I had had no idea of just how hard it would be and what I was letting myself in for. I now understand why most folk choose a ghost-writer. In retrospect I would've preferred that route but it wasn't an option: the Penguin people insisted I wrote every word. In a way I'm glad they did. There's a satisfaction in getting to the end, I guess, as there would be in finishing any kind of marathon, but in terms of what I've managed it's a hollow victory. Reading over it all just makes me aware of how woefully ill-read I am. If I'd read more, instead of propping up bar counters and lying in gutters, I'd know more and have a much better turn of phrase than I do. How I envy those writers who can draw on their accumulated knowledge and conjure up literary magic.

A pal of mine who must remain nameless (Sting) was writing a similar book and he finished before me. Well, he would, wouldn't he? I asked him how he felt on getting to the end. 'Depressed,' he said, and I understood exactly what he meant because I was going through the same downer. All the life-shit you've buried, either deliberately or subconsciously, has to be dredged up, raked over and dealt with as you struggle to bring some kind of hindsight perspective to it all. For better or worse, my life can neither be relived nor undone. All those moments are now memories. It's also impossible to avoid a sense of the best things being over and gone. Certainly my fitness has peaked. Although I feel great, the natural way of things means it'll be a downhill run from here on in. I reluctantly accept I'll never play football for Newcastle United, although there's always the charity matches.

It's been an enlightening, sometimes sobering experience in as much as I now realize my memory of incidents and occasions is no more than that. I wish I'd kept a diary, but that wasn't on the menu back then. Photographs, too. Without filmed or recorded evidence there can be no definitive version of events. Even so, my own research has shown my recall of times past has often been wide of the mark. I've tried to temper that with this new-found reality. I hope the balance struck is near to the actual. Miriam's recollections have sometimes been sobering and difficult for me to accept, but have mostly been deadly accurate, bless her.

There have been one or two big surprises. Somewhat oddly, I couldn't remember which year I was in jail. I knew it was either 1976 or 1977 but had no record (ha!) of events. When I asked my sister, Val, about it I discovered she'd kept all the letters I'd written to her from my cell in Strangeways. This blast from the past came as a complete shock, and I confess I've still to read them. I'll have to be in the right frame of mind, sit on my own on the seat under the tree in the garden one day and just look through them. I did read a little of one, at my sister's prompting, and was pleasantly surprised by how articulate it was. I'd remembered those letters as messy, ink-stained, clumsy and mistake-ridden, but they weren't at all bad. I'd signed off by asking Val if she would send me some books, music-related, as I was down to my last two from the prison library: biographies of Hughie Greene and General Franco!

I wish I could report that I had answers to life's big questions, at least ones that made more uplifting reading than 'We're born, we live, we die, we're dust', but I don't. I wish I had my mother's unwavering faith, but I don't. I don't trust organized religion: it usually means that the poor are encouraged to give what pennies they have to folk offering them entrance into one or other of the various kingdoms on offer. It could be argued, though, that even if it's all a load of con-man's cock and bull, it gets some through the night. Maybe, but shouldn't we be trying to make the 'here' better instead of worrying about the hereafter?

The nature of religious belief means there's no indisputable proof of anything after this life. But that's not to say there's nothing. And there's the rub. It's an attractive proposition, and I can testify to its value and importance, having watched my mam get through terrible times with nothing more than her faith and a hot-water bottle. And yet . . . and yet I'm not convinced. In the end there are just too many contradictions. It's tempting, though, the whole God thing, and I do envy those with enough pure faith to transcend the logical anomalies within most religions. As a set of rules to live by, the basic Christian values are as good as any I'm aware of. We try to adhere to them and have our kids do likewise. Like most professed non-believers, I hedge my bets and harbour the quiet hope that, come the time and I'm proved wrong, the Great One will take pity on me and allow me to eat grapes while I'm reclining on a cloud.

I've never had what could be considered a game-plan, or a career plan, or any plan, really, other than making enough to get by, keeping the bairns in shoes, and after that having a good time. I've managed to do those things, but too much forward planning is asking for trouble. I'm not a believer in luck, as it implies some sort of predestination, but I know I've been extremely fortunate. I have no ambitions as such. I don't know what the future holds in terms of what I'll be doing, but I do know it'll not involve acting. The politics are plain horrible. I became an actor by accident and have no great passion for it. I'm working with Franc Roddam on a script for a new BBC drama series that, if it works out, will keep me busy for a year or two. Eventually it'll peter out, but that's fine by me. I'm more than happy reading the papers, buying and selling the odd house and indulging in my two real passions outside the family: motor cars and music. I'd like to do a stage musical at some point, but that's about it.

Would I change anything, were I to have my fifty years over again? You bet! Margaret Thatcher apart, I'd like to see more women in charge of the world. There'd certainly be a lot less bother, and they're much easier on the eye. I'd keep a civil tongue and I wouldn't drink alcohol – I'd never fall for that one again. All those wasted hours, days and years, spent either lolling around aimlessly or propping up bars and causing a disturbance, would instead be spent sober and focused. I'd fill my head with as much learning as I could take on board. That said, I did meet the love of my life (and, no, we're still not married) in a pub, so I guess some good came of it.

As time passes, I'm thankful that most of the close friends I had in my earlier years are close friends still. In the flaky, here-today, gone-tomorrow world of entertainment, there's real reassurance in that. I wonder about pals who've gone from my life, and in some cases gone from this life altogether. One of my closest friends, Tommy McCulloch, was almost certainly murdered and I wonder sometimes what he must have suffered in those last moments. I think about my parents, and particularly my mam, more and more. She really was goodness personified, refusing to think badly of anyone, even those who set out to do her family harm, instead insisting gently that there'd be some reason for their actions. How I wish I'd appreciated her wisdom more fully while she was alive.

Most of all, I marvel at the act of creation that gave us our two sons. Every single day I watch them, just living and breathing and laughing, and I give thanks to the heavens. Every single day I've reason to count my blessings. Surely this is the blessing. They are beyond wonderful and, because of them and others like them, I have real confidence in the future of this planet. I'll sign off with a couple of lines by my favourite wordsmith, Mr Paddy McAloon, which say it all much more succinctly than I ever could:

Life's a miracle,
we've got to make the most of the passing moment
got to do our best, before it's time to rest.

Jimmy Nail

Film

Still Crazy (1998) Columbia Tri-Star. Dir. Brian Gibson. Played LES
WICKES
Golden Globe nominations 1999: Best Picture, Best Original Song
('The Flame Still Burns', performed by Jimmy Nail). Winner: Ivor
Novello Award. Best Original Song In A Movie: 'The Flame Still
Burns'.

Evita (1996) Cinergi/Buena Vista. Dir. Alan Parker. Played AGUSTÍN
MAGALDI
Academy Award 1997: Best Original Song ('You Must Love Me',
performed by Madonna). Golden Globe Awards 1997, Best
Picture, Best Actress (Madonna), Best Original Song (Rice/
Lloyd-Webber)

Danny, the Champion of the World (1990) Portobello/Disney. Dir. Gavin
Millar. Played RABBETTS

Just Ask for Diamond (1988) Goldwyn Co./Warner Bros. Dir. Stephen
Bayley. Played BOYLE

Dream Demon (1987) Palace Pictures. Dir. Harley Kokliss. Played PAUL

Crusoe (1986) Walt Disney. Dir. Caleb Deschanel. Played TARIK

Morons From Outer Space (1985) EMI Films. Dir. Mike Hodges. Played
DESMOND

Television

Auf Wiedersehen, Pet (2004) BBC. Dir. Sandy Johnson. Played lead role:
OZ
2 × 1-hour episodes scripted by Dick Clement/Ian La Frenais.

Auf Wiedersehen, Pet (2004) BBC. Dir. Maurice Phillips, David Innes
Edwards. Played lead role: OZ

6 × 1-hour episodes scripted by Dick Clement/Ian La Frenais. Co-writer storyline.

Auf Wiedersehen, Pet (2002) BBC. Dir. Paul Seed. Played lead role: OZ
6 × 1-hour episodes scripted by Dick Clement/Ian La Frenais. Co-writer storyline.

Crocodile Shoes (1994–6) Big Boy Productions/BBC. Dir. David Richards, Roger Bamford, Baz Taylor. Played lead role: JED SHEPPERD
13 × 1-hour episodes on film. Creator/writer, producer, lead actor. BAFTA nominations: Best Original Music, Best Song ('Crocodile Shoes', performed by Jimmy Nail). Soundtrack album sales quadruple platinum.

Spender (1989–93) Big Boy Productions/BBC. Dir. Mary McMurray, Roger Bamford, Richard Standeven, Matt Forrest. Played lead role: FREDDIE SPENDER
20 × 1-hour episodes on film plus 1 × 90-minutes single film. Co-creator (with Ian La Frenais)/writer, producer, lead actor. BAFTA nomination: Best Drama Series. Television and Radio Industries Award: Best Drama Series.

Shoot for the Sun (1986) BBC. Dir. Ian Knox. Scr. Peter McDougal. Prod. Andre Molyneaux. Played lead role: GEORDIE
BAFTA nomination: Best Single Film.

Wallenberg (1986) Paramount Pictures. Tel. Dir. LaMont Johnson. Played: VILMOS LANGFELDER
4 × 1-hour mini-series.

Master of the Game (1985) NBC Tel. Dir. Kevin Connor. Played: SCHMIDT
4 × 1-hour mini-series.

Auf Wiedersehen, Pet (1982–6) Central Tel. Dir. Roger Bamford, Baz Taylor. Played lead role: OZ
26 × 1-hour episodes written by Dick Clement/Ian La Frenais. BAFTA nomination: Best Drama Series. Broadcasting Press Guild Award: Best Drama Series. Television and Radio Industries Award: Best Series. Series voted (by the public) Most Popular British Drama of the Decade.

Index